SPECIAL NEEDS IN ORDINARY SCHOOLS
General editor: Peter Mittler
Associate editors: Mel Ainscow, Brahm Norwich, Peter Pumfrey,
Rosemary Webb, Sheila Wolfendale

Further Opportunities

Titles in the Special Needs in Ordinary Schools series

Further Opportunities

Learning Difficulties and Disabilities in Further Education

David Johnstone

CASSELL

Cassell
Wellington House
125 Strand
London WC2R 0BB

215 Park Avenue South
New York
NY 10003

British Library Cataloguing-in-Publication Data
A catalogue record for this book is available from the British Library.

ISBN 0–304–33105–8 (hardback)
      0–304–33107–4 (paperback)

Typeset by Falcon Oast Graphic Art
Printed and bound in Great Britain by
Biddles Ltd, Guildford and Kings Lynn

Contents

Editorial foreword

Students with learning difficulties and disabilities have full rights of equal access to further and continuing education, but provision for meeting their needs has always varied greatly from one part of the country to another. Some FE colleges have been light-years ahead of others in providing full and equal access to their courses; others have paid lip service to such access but adopted highly selective admission policies or provided only segregated learning opportunities. The majority are struggling to provide better access but lack guidance and funding on how to turn the vision into a reality. This book will provide the foundations and the context for such guidance.

Now that colleges of further education are undergoing radical change, it is essential that the needs of students with learning difficulties and disabilities are fully integrated into planning and provision from the outset. In the past, their needs have all too often been overlooked. For this reason, the report of the Tomlinson Committee set up by the Further Education Funding Council is eagerly awaited as this book goes to press. The report should mark a turning-point in the history of provision and guarantee a framework for study and accreditation within a fully inclusive environment. To achieve such a goal, however, there will need to be a change of attitudes and assumptions at all levels. The task is nothing less than adopting a 'whole-college' approach which will provide full and equal funded access and support to all students in the community, regardless of disability or learning difficulty.

The publication of this book could therefore hardly be more timely.

Professor Peter Mittler
University of Manchester
April 1995

Preface

Further education and training has undergone massive change in recent years. From being considered the uncomfortable rump of the education process, the Cinderella left in the shadows of an essentially elitist system, it has come centre stage. Further education and training is also perceived politically as the favoured vehicle for changing national fortune in the international league of vocational training. Economically, the structure of further education has the ultimate attraction of appearing both efficient and cost-effective.

For many people further education has been interpreted as a means of developing opportunities for and access to employment. Certainly for all those who work in the area of post-compulsory education and training the concentration has been on trying to ensure that access to employment is not made more difficult. This element of equal opportunities has tended to highlight discriminatory factors relating to gender, age or ethnic background.

In comparison to these groups, issues relating to students with learning difficulties and disabilities have often seemed neglected. This might be attributed to a number of reasons. First, it is apparent that the number of people with disabilities is much smaller than is the population of the other groups. Secondly, if discrimination is encountered in relation to the issues of gender, sexuality and ethnic origin, there is the opportunity to turn to legislation to clarify the position. Despite supportive rhetoric around the Civil Rights (Disabled Persons) Bill, people with disabilities still do not seem to attract the same support as do other minorities as a result of the Sex Discrimination Act and the Race Relations Act. The recent Disability Discrimination Bill reflects concern about employment, but does little to promote civil rights. There is law that applies to the rights of disabled people in the form of the Chronically Sick and Disabled Persons Act 1970 and the quota scheme enshrined in the Disabled Persons (Employment) Act of 1944. However, these laws are also couched in a paternalism that has little to do with proper choice or real opportunity. As an illustration, the quota scheme – which requires employers with twenty or more employees to employ at least 3 per cent registered disabled people – is increasingly recognized as unworkable. The Employment Department argues that there are not enough registered disabled people to allow all employers to employ their full quota and only a third of those eligible to register (about 1 per cent) do so (Enable, 1994).

The third explanation for the lack of attention given to development of further opportunities for disabled people might, in fact, lie within the further education system itself (Oliver, 1992; Hurst, 1992; Dee and Corbett, 1994). It could be that colleges and employers have colluded in perpetuating discrimination by their failure to face the issues inherent in their patterns of recruitment and enrolment of disabled people. There is certainly the suggestion that resourcing the cost of provision is a consideration (*Disability Now*, 1994). It is also evident that the recent advances in further education offered to students and young people with disabilities are in danger of being sacrificed in pursuit of the wider political vision of market forces. The development of educational entitlement in mainstream education is also accompanied by heightened anxiety in specialist residential colleges and amongst staff who have seen 'special' education wax and wane. Recent changes in the funding and governance of further education suggest that the needs of students with learning difficulties and disabilities will continue to be recognized. However, low expectations have long been associated with the education of students emerging from or associated with special education and there are suspicions that the rhetoric of opportunty will be stronger than the reality. This will serve to disadvantage students with learning difficulties and disabilities even further (Warnock, 1978, 1993; Dee and Corbett, 1994). Nevertheless, with the recent changes in the legislation, management and funding of further and higher education there are new expectations, demands and requirements. The further education system is now required to confront, rather than ignore, the inequalities that face students with disabilities as a condition of funding.

The book attempts to provide a comprehensive, contemporary view of further education as it is developing in the 1990s. I have tried to make the text as useful as possible to students in education, the behavioural sciences and to interested parents, teachers and young people, as well as students on advanced courses and established professionals in the social services. I have also attempted to combine thorough, current coverage of the research literature with detailed bibliographic references. If desired, most chapters can be read or assigned separately as a coherent, self-contained presentation of the topic under consideration. For this reason, there are some places where points may appear to be reintroduced. This is intentional and is meant to make chapters more self-contained.

The book contains eleven chapters. Chapter 1 sets out to establish the historical context of the forces for change from which further education for students with learning difficulties and disabilities has emerged. The defining characteristics of disability within the medical model are traced to the physically and psychologically determined perceptions of disability and disadvantage within the needs model. The third model, formed around the developments of rights, forms the focus of the socio-political examination that is taken up in subsequent chapters.

Chapter 2 explores the establishment and shaping of the present further education system, the emergence of the Further Education Funding Council (FEFC) and the development of specialist programmes for students with learning difficulties and disabilities. A critique of the forces of efficiency and effectiveness arising from the political attacks on outdated and irrelevant practices in further education management and teaching (influenced by the decline in the industrial base of the United Kingdom) form the foundation of discussion in Chapter 4. The extension of vocational training, competence and National Vocational Qualifications (NVQs) for students with disabilities and learning difficulties is examined.

Chapter 5 undertakes an appraisal of the ways teachers teach in further education, with an outline of behavioural and humanistic approaches. The exploration of ways in which the curriculum can be negotiated with students is addressed. Chapter 6 focuses on the continuum between the extremes of inclusive education and segregated provision in specialist colleges. Staff development issues are investigated in Chapter 7, an increasingly problematic area for further education with incorporation and cuts in staff development budgets. Chapter 8 considers the impact of further education on the relationships of young people with learning difficulties growing towards adulthood and their parents/carers. The management of learning and the specific rise of learning support in relation to all learners in further education is investigated and described in Chapter 9. Chapter 10 takes a wider perspective on cross-cultural comparisons of provision with other countries in the European Union.

The final chapter poses some considerations on the link between further and higher education for students with disabilities and returns to some questions about the real meaning of entitlement and rights for a student group. This continues to be defined and redefined as a problem to be dealt with rather than a group of individuals in control of their own educational destinies.

I am indebted to the assistance and advice of a number of people in the preparation of this text. I would particularly like to thank Janet and our children Ben and Rebecca, for their patience and understanding. Peter Mittler has offered his encouragement throughout. Mary Bamborough, Jenny Clift, Jenny Corbett, Derri Coultard, Sally Faraday, Richard Harris, Alan Hurst, Rod Pye and John Smith have commented and provided their expertise as have Deborah Cooper and the staff and members of Skill. My thanks go to all of them.

David Johnstone
October 1994

Introduction: The structure and function of post-school opportunities for students with learning difficulties and disabilities

Further education is not a straightforward affair. It is better defined by types of institution than by the types of instruction given and it is also marked by the different times and patterns of attendance. It involves students of all ages over the age of 16, although some young people are involved in further education from the age of 14. It is not the same thing as a university, although some colleges offer degree courses; but neither is it like school.

The structure of the further education system is overwhelmingly influenced by employment patterns. By far the majority of students in colleges are there as a consequence, or as a condition of employment, or as a means of obtaining a qualification for a specific employment:

> English further education cannot be understood without realising that virtually everything that exists in it has come into existence as the conscious answer to a demand arising from industry or from individual workers. Where something does not exist, it is because no effective demand for it has been expressed.
>
> (Ministry of Education, 1959, p. 333, para. 488)

The dependence of further education upon employment is very clearly linked to the variety of attendance patterns and qualifications that have emerged. Part-time day release in college is clearly associated with employment, as perhaps are evening classes – the original form of further education. This association indicates another characteristic of provision: it is essentially local and regional in its make-up. By far the largest number of colleges respond to the needs of students who see further education as an alternative to school for the final years of study towards GCSE, A levels, or GNVQs (General National Vocational Qualifications). Students on such courses tend to be aged 16 to 19 and to be studying full-time.

Today all young people are growing to maturity in a rapidly changing, complex society. The existing structures of education and training are expected to prepare students and young people to meet this increasing complexity of social and vocational demands. Traditionally education has functioned on the basis of a rudimentary form of social justice; sameness of treatment has been equated with equality. All students within the state system attend schools and colleges in similar circumstances, in the form of management structures, standard curricula and instructional provision.

The education system has continued to claim that it is essentially neutral in the distribution of educational opportunities. The school system has provided everyone with a fair and notionally equal opportunity for channelling educational attainment and access to resources. It has thus ensured that students have to compete openly for their allocation of educational benefit and academic success. At the same time the examination system and other educational rituals such as prize days have encouraged the distribution of outcomes on the basis of personal effort and the distribution of reward based on merit. Educational success is thereby perceived as the most appropriate reward for the most deserving students and educational failure is, logically, the student's own failure.

For colleges to be seen to be concerned with issues of social justice, in terms of fairness and educational entitlement, they, too, have to retain the legitimacy of the competitive process by accounting for persistent educational failure as a result of deficiencies in the student, environment or society. To sustain the meritocratic assumptions of college education, colleges must explain failure through factors outside their control. In this context the concept of disability and learning difficulty constitutes one legitimizing mechanism for ascribing student failure to an individual defect or pathology, rather than inequable competitive practices (Christensen and Dorn, 1994; Christensen *et al.*, 1986).

Any study of the further opportunities for students with learning difficulties and disabilities is the study of differences within a system that cannot accommodate student diversity beyond very narrowly prescribed limits. The student with learning difficulties and disabilities is different in some way from the hypothetically 'average' student. Spoken of in very simple terms, he or she will be perceived to have some differences or special talents in thinking, seeing, hearing, speaking, socializing or moving. More often than not, the student will be considered to manifest a combination of special abilities or disabilities. It was estimated that in the mid-1980s there were close to 100,000 students with learning difficulties and disabilities in England and Wales (Stowell, 1987). This estimate, extrapolated from survey data, is more convenient than precise. It is still, unfortunately, safer to assume that neither the number of students nor the definition of what constitutes learning difficulties and disabilities is properly understood. At the time of writing this is awaiting proper consideration from the specialist committee chaired by John Tomlinson.

What is beyond question is that the provision made for all students in further education has undergone major changes in both policy and practice. During the course of the last twenty years the nature and structure of further education in the United Kingdom has altered beyond all recognition. What had served once principally as a work-oriented training system for part-time and day-release students and apprentices has moved to the centre of the educational stage and become a market-oriented, consumer-led industry that is required to compete with rival providers of training. In such a system, where educational ideals are coming to be equated with cost-effectiveness rather than personal-effectiveness, the lot of students with learning difficulties and/or disabilities does not appear to be necessarily best served.

This book sets out to examine some of the reasons why further education has come to be a major ideological battleground for the recognition of educational rights and entitlements. Another intention is to document the shifts in approaches to teaching and learning that have developed for disadvantaged young people as they transfer from the culture of school to a less certain post-school environment. My third aim is to capture some of the flavour of working with students with learning difficulties and disabilities in further education. The concept of learning difficulties and disabilities itself has emerged from the legislative terms of the 1988 Education Reform Act and the Further and Higher Education Act 1992. The definition draws heavily upon, but is distinguished from, the concept of 'special educational needs', which tends to be associated with children who are still at school. As a result of legislation, the colleges of further education are instructed to have 'regard to the requirements of persons over compulsory school age who have learning difficulties' (Further and Higher Education Act 1992).

What constitutes the concept of further education is not easily defined. It is a somewhat organic construct that expands and contracts with the demands made upon it. The system therefore encompasses all aspects of education more readily associated with upper secondary schools as well as the leisure-oriented atmosphere of adult non-vocational evening class education.

It meets the needs of people aged from 14 to retirement and beyond. It is an amoeba-like organism that pushes out tentacles to suck in courses and mould its shape to meet the demands of its market-place. As a system it has prided itself on being infinitely flexible, covering educational provision from the womb to the tomb. It could be more accurately defined, for the purposes of attracting younger students, as that form of education which occurs between the time that a person officially leaves school after their sixteenth birthday and the time that they are 25.

The length of time that a young person is expected to stay within education is expanding. This has placed colleges of further education at the centre of the education stage. They have moved out of their more traditional place in the shadows of the elitist university system and brought with them a far greater variety of educational and training choice for all school-leavers, including those with learning difficulties and disabilities. The centrally driven initiative to provide more further education and training has arisen in response to a concern both about the high numbers of young people leaving education and training at 16 and about future employment needs at both national and local level. This increasing emphasis on choice means that at the age of 16 young people are now more likely to continue their education or training than enter employment. 'The number of enrolments on further education courses at colleges in the further and higher education sectors at 1 November in 1993/94 was 2,185 thousand students, an increase of 4 per cent compared with the previous year and an increase of 33 per cent compared with 1983/84' (*DfE News*, 1994b). The most recent statistical calculations of the enrolment of students with learning difficulties and disabilities into colleges of further education are at present available up to 1992. They too show an increased enrolment pattern. (It is interesting to note, in passing, that for the purposes of statistical returns students in colleges of further education with learning difficulties and disabilities are still being referred to as having special educational needs: SEN.)

It is immediately noticeable that the increased numbers of students enrolled on special needs programmes have consistently risen, but that this development is offset by a marked decline in the popularity of link programmes or in specialist programmes for students with learning difficulties and/or disabilities on YTS (Youth Training Scheme) programmes. Other interesting indicators suggest that the age-range of students has expanded in the four years between 1988 and 1992. The proportion of students classed as having special needs outside YTS and link, in the age range 25–60+, rose from under 50 per cent of the total SEN student population in 1988, to close to 57 per cent of the population in 1992.

Table 1 *Further education students over three years (1988, 1990, 1992): age by type of student in England*

Type of student	16	17	18	19	20	21–24	25–29	60+	Unknown	Total
1988										
SEN link	9,256	802	469	92	1	–	1	–	488	11,109
SEN YTS	2,789	2,492	590	229	109	5	–	–	147	6,362
Other SEN	1,586	1,240	677	631	553	1,738	7,169	945	2,695	17,234
1990										
SEN link	1,231	660	563	126	4	29	120	4	398	3,135
SEN YTS	2,258	2,013	835	348	184	73	9	1	92	5,813
Other SEN	2,287	1,714	1,305	1,160	1,092	3,118	14,059	3,058	4,113	31,906
1992										
SEN link	1,162	859	572	83	7	34	109	2	364	3,192
SEN YTS	1,384	1,449	691	305	149	96	8	–	50	4,132
Other SEN	3,174	2,279	1,491	1,349	1,344	3,933	19,563	4,146	3,665	40,944

Source: DfE Analytical Services Further Education Statistical Review data (1994)

Whereas universities and institutions of higher education tend to be exclusive and operate on a national basis, colleges of further education are spread more locally in their influence and range of teaching. They provide educational and vocational training that ranges from A levels, access to higher education and professional organizations to basic skills. They can provide advanced courses in business studies and part-time courses in motor mechanics. Because they are also essentially local, they reflect regional differences in cultural outlooks to employment and training. Colleges of further education are above all responsive to a changing social and political scene and are mirrors of the market forces hitting our economy. Whilst some colleges still include leisure programmes others are reducing this provision, considering it to be more the preserve of a separate adult education network, an area of remarkable student growth. Since the 1992 Education Act all colleges are expected to be planning the development of successful courses, building student numbers and at the same time to be financially and academically accountable to their governing body and the FEFC.

This shift in accountability marks part of the essential difference between colleges and schools. Schools have a statutory responsibility to provide education in accordance with the guidelines of the National Curriculum; there is a requirement that parents co-operate in ensuring that their children attend school. Attendance at colleges of further education is voluntary, so to attract students courses have to be marketed and attractively packaged. If they are too expensive to mount, do not recruit, or if local conditions change, the courses will be discarded. It is in this climate that courses for students with learning difficulties and disabilities have to be measured and held accountable.

In the last fifteen years the number of college courses which cater for such students has grown dramatically. The choices that have developed reflect not only the impact of ever-rising youth unemployment patterns but also a shift in policy towards the development of vocational education and training which is required to include and recognize a formerly disregarded population. This apparent expansion of opportunity nevertheless also marks a shift in the employment pattern of college lecturers. As the more traditional, craft-driven areas of vocational training became redundant in the colleges, they were faced with spare accommodation and reduced teacher timetables. This enabled colleges to develop basic skills courses and to offer provision to the special school sector. For example, Wigan and Leigh College and North Nottinghamshire College began to build their considerable reputations for work in the area of learning difficulties and disabilities at the same time as the decline in the coal-mining industry in these regions. The emergence of these new specialist courses gradually became formalized into a loose federation of programmes that included staff training and resource development in this new area of further education. The *ad hoc* and sporadic outcrops of provision for students with a variety of 'special educational needs' have been well summarized elsewhere (Bradley and Hegarty, 1981); they indicate that the enthusiasm for both the emergence and the quality of provision was dictated by the enthusiasms of committed individuals and the whims of local college principals rather than by any national policy.

MAIN OPPORTUNITIES FOR STUDENTS WITH LEARNING DIFFICULTIES AND DISABILITIES AT THE POINT OF LEAVING SCHOOL

- special school or mainstream
- home

- day centre
- long-stay institutions
- employment (open employment, sheltered, supported)
- training
- school (sixth-form college, 16–19 unit, special school)
- FE college
- workshop-based training
- employer-based training
- social education centre
- specialist college
- Training and Enterprise Council (TEC) courses

There is no doubt that, in comparison with the early 1980s, there are now more educational and training choices available to school-leavers who have experienced difficulties with learning. The contraction of employment opportunities for all 16-year-olds has seen to this and has led to an expansion of alternatives to employment. Young people who have been the recipients of support teaching in mainstream schools, or who have spent all their schooling in some form of special education, now have a range of further education opportunities at the point of leaving.

Whether or not these opportunities amount to anything more than incidental change in the education system is more open to question. For too long special education has been concerned with 'fairness' and 'sameness' as the basis for equity, underpinned by personal effort and merit. It needs to move more towards the exploration of educational practice shaped by the values of equity as social justice, founded on the recognition of diverse student needs. The world of further education provides an opportunity to develop this perspective, but it may also be in danger of perpetuating old mistakes through a confused and contradictory understanding of its purpose in relation to students with learning difficulties and disabilities.

—1———————————————————————
The background to furthering opportunities in FE

Whilst it is true that the rapid development of further education for students with learning difficulties and disabilities is a comparatively recent phenomenon it would be incorrect to ignore the pioneering work that had been gradually emerging since the end of the Second World War and in some cases even earlier. Bradley and Hegarty (1981) have asserted that 'until the mid-1970s there was little or no provision in the normal further education colleges for disabled young people'. This is not strictly true. There have always been some opportunities for students to attend courses in basic literacy, leisure courses or the like where the emphasis is upon self-motivation and personal improvement. Nevertheless, much of this early work took place in night schools and is more allied to adult education (Sutcliffe, 1992). It is also not easy to discover how many of the students on such courses came into the category of 'special education'.

As with so many other educational initiatives involving a group of people who have been marginalized, the beginnings of specialist provision for students with learning difficulties and disabilities are uncertain. It would inevitably have been sporadic and the numbers of students involved are unknown. However, there are sufficient examples of practice to suggest that concern for the development of vocational education and training is not new. It certainly does not mean that there had been no opportunities for the continuing education and training of people with learning difficulties and disabilities before the development of a recognized system of further education.

The emergence of further education for people with learning difficulties and disabilities can be traced using three broad and overlapping models. All three are associated with phases of political, historical and economic development. These phases are not really distinct, and there are traces of all of them still to be seen in current educational organization, practices and discourses about the expansion of educational entitlement. They can, however, be traced in an historical linear progression as follows:

medical care → needs and segregation → rights and entitlements

MEDICAL CARE MODEL

The beginnings of education for people with disabilities, like the history of provision for disabled people in general, is shrouded in some mystery. It is hidden in official records, religious super- stition and the accounts of charitable organizations. Nevertheless, from the outset it has involved the relationship between the demands of the labour market and the social costs of providing services for disabled people. It is, above all else, the history of political groups working to further their economic interests under the guise of philanthropy:

> for too long education in all sectors has colluded with the demands of the labour market to keep disabled people out of the workforce. Most disabled children leave school thinking they are unemployable and immediately have this reinforced by social education centres and colleges of further education with their offers of 'further on' courses and 'independence training'.
>
> (Oliver, 1992, p. 6)

The relationship between education and the economy is seen in the original 'philanthropic' ideals that lay behind the development of a structured system of further education and training in the institutions and 'colonies' that were built in both Europe and the United States in the nineteenth century. In some areas they continued to form the basis for residential care until the present shift in policy towards 'care in the community'. Some semi-formal education and vocational training for people with disabilities and learning difficulties had been an established feature of the asylums of the nineteenth century. The *Edinburgh Review* of 1865 gives an interesting and – from an equal opportunities perspective – somewhat voyeuristic and patronizing insight into the activities in the Earlswood Asylum, situated just outside London. There, young men and women with learning difficulties and psychiatric disorders were given training in carpentry, needlework and horticulture as well as basic literacy and numeracy instruc- tion.

> It was in furthering the many schemes for the improvement of idiots, a most important object to enable those capable of reaping the highest advantages, to become adept in some useful branch of

industry, and to make their work remunerative, exchanging their solitary and idle habits for social, industrious and productive occupation.

(*Edinburgh Review*, 1865, p. 56)

This enlightened if paternalistic approach was soon to be replaced by the harsher, more custodial activities associated with asylums as arenas for the protection of society, rather than as places of refuge for disabled people. In the 'moral panic' that arose around eugenics, the populist demand grew for asylums to become places of custody. This meant a shift in emphasis from training individuals in order to protect them from the threats and exploitation of the rest of society, to the protection of society from the supposed debilitating effects of physically, intellectually (and by association morally) inadequate people. The guiding model of care imposed was fundamentally akin to the age-old model of medical treatment where a powerful professional, in the guise of a doctor, conducts a diagnosis of the 'problem', prescribes a treatment and as a result of this expertise the patient is cured. In the case of diagnosing or assessing disability, such ultimate judgements were still firmly in the hands of the medical profession.

Disability in these circumstances was considered to be a personal affair and a tragedy for the person concerned. This had a profound effect on the kinds of education and training provision made and also on the manner in which it was implemented. Even today, if a person has a disability the medical model of causation implies that to all intents and purposes 'It's your own fault!' As Oliver (1990) has pointed out, this pervasive influence of medicine is a major factor in the individualization of 'care' issues. Brisenden, writing as a disabled person, has put the medical model even more dramatically in perspective:

the problem from our point of view, is that medical people tend to see all difficulties solely from the perspective of proposed treatments for a 'patient', without recognising that the individual has to weigh up whether this treatment fits into the overall economy of their lives. In the past especially, doctors have been too willing to suggest medical treatment and hospitalisation, even when this would not necessarily improve the quality of life for the person concerned. Indeed, questions about the quality of life have sometimes been portrayed as something of an intrusion upon the purely medical equation. This has occurred due to a failure of imagination, the result of the medical profession's participation in the construction of a definition of disability which is partial and limited. This definition has portrayed disability as almost entirely a medical problem and it has led to a situation where doctors and others are trapped in their responses by a definition of their own making.

(Brisenden, 1986, p. 8)

It is not difficult to see how, from the beginnings, special education has borrowed from and tended to be dominated by this medically defined construct. For students with learning difficulties and disabilities in further education, who have come through a school system that continues to pay great heed to the interpretations and wishes of the medical services, there is a tacit acceptance that medical interventions and interpretations of difference are part of their way of life. As Oliver (1986) has suggested, their education may have been disrupted by the inputs of a variety of para-medical professions: physiotherapy, speech therapy and the like. If children have left school and become adults believing, as a result of a range of such interventions, that they are ill, then it is no real surprise if they accept the passive role of being sick and dependent: receivers of care and expected to be grateful for it.

The evidence that disabled people are denied the full rights to citizenship as a result of the demands of the labour market is overwhelming. It would be unfair to suggest that, in such circumstances, colleges are deliberately colluding with the 'medical model'. However, it seems evident that despite political rhetoric to the contrary 'social disadvantage' has become associated with disability and learning difficulties and that young people with disabilities are cases to be treated rather than individuals with rights.

NEEDS AND SEGREGATION

Just as we cannot really be surprised that students with disabilities take on the sick role, we should also not be surprised when we see students emerging from discrete special education courses considering themselves to be 'in need' and often as entitled to the benefits of charitable and statutory services. However, if students and people with disabilities see themselves as having 'needs' it is often because they have been socialized into accepting the definition of disability as a personal tragedy. Images of disabled people and child-care, together with the range of resource materials in both children's literature and adult horror magazines and videos, all of which are available to schools and colleges, have tended to continue to portray disabled people in a contradictory fashion. They are either pathetic victims, arch-villains or heroes. The stereotype of the disabled child is either that of the brave little lost boy/girl overcoming personal tragedy, or of the scheming malcontent determined to have revenge on society for the misfortune that has befallen him/her (e.g. Captain Hook, Quasimodo, Dr No, Freddy from *Nightmare on Elm Street*). The other alternative is the hero overcoming personal loss but conquering all, for example Long John Silver or Douglas Bader.

The concept of 'need' had first emerged in education in 1946, in regulations that indicated how to implement the 1944 Education Act. These regulations led to the establishment of services and schools that acted on behalf of, rather than in consultation with, disabled people. This in turn has led, until recently, to a kind of passive citizenship on the part of disabled people within a fundamentally needs-based provision determined by professionals. The legal framework of the UK has consistently portrayed disabled people as a cost to the Exchequer rather than as individuals entitled to participate in the exercise of citizenship. Far from becoming involved in legislation that establishes the rights of disabled people, enabling them to determine their own needs, we have created a system that continues to exclude.

A feature of the 1944 Act was the creation of categories of handicap reflecting society's needs rather than individual considerations. Regulations in *Pamphlet 5*, following the Act, actually stated that some pupils may require special educational 'treatment', borrowing heavily from the medical model already referred to. For young people with handicaps and disabilities, leaving school meant a probable future in sheltered or closed employment. Even in 1968 it was estimated that there were approximately 70,000 severely mentally handicapped adults in England and Wales, approximately 24,500 of whom attended adult training centres (Whelan and Speake, 1977). The need to re-establish employment for returning members of the armed forces following the Second World War had the effect of excluding disabled individuals from open employment, even though some of them had fulfilled important work during the war years.

The much more specific definition of learning difficulties within the concept 'special educational needs' formed part of the legal framework of the 1981 Education Act and followed from the recommendations put forward by the Warnock Committee of Inquiry (1978). The suggestions it laid down in relation to students with special needs in further education are embedded in the notion of progression and 'transition to adulthood' in Chapter 10 of the Report. Very little was included in the way of guidelines either for differentiating the college from the school curriculum or for distinguishing in law the status of a student, a young person, or a child with special needs. For the purposes of definition, a child was described as somebody who remained in school until their nineteenth birthday, but no indications were given for the status of an individual who might leave at 16 and go to college or on to a training scheme. In terms of developing the rights and entitlements to adult status implied in the phrase 'transition to adulthood', the Warnock principles left a good deal to be desired. Other confusions have still not been fully resolved: these relate to the very definitions of special educational need and learning difficulty which were at the heart of the committee's report and which have formed the basis for legislation in the 1981 and 1993 Education Acts.

As Booth (1992) has argued, the implications of the definitions are that children and students are to be measured using both 'within the individual' measures e.g. standard tests of intelligence or ability (which in themselves suggest that measuring the incompetence or failure of a person is the basis of learning difficulties) and 'environmental judgements' of the adequacy or otherwise of the resources available to facilitate and support teaching and learning. The whole concept of 'need' is problematic and confusing. For children in schools, it has led to an increase in services established for the purpose of meeting individual need and providing support. It is only recently that some commentators have begun to question whether the very services set up to help establish better learning may not instead be helping to create the problems they were designed to resolve (Booth, 1992; Corbett and Barton, 1992).

The fundamentally child-centred Warnock Report (1978) attempted to establish a concept of citizenship by building on the notion of need, determined by the collaboration of 'experts', and tried to achieve wider integration of children from segregated educational provision into the mainstream. It has in fact failed to alter many of the old prejudices. Had the recommendations made been adequately resourced in the first place, the demands for change might not have become so strident now. The move towards inclusive education (described more fully in Chapter 5) is itself a recognition that full integration is an ideal that may not ultimately be achievable or even desired by everyone. More than anything else, however, the concept of special educational needs failed to face up to the fundamental issue of ensuring that basic educational rights are part of every child's entitlement. As Booth points out, 'special educational needs' has become such an abused and misunderstood term that it has diminished two perfectly honourable and worthwhile concepts: 'care' and 'need', which fundamentally influenced the use of the term in the first place. The system of meeting a child or student's 'needs' has continued to perpetuate some of the worst abuses of the old models of medical care through the imposition of bureaucratic assessment procedures on young people and their families and the perpetuation of segregated educational and residential facilities which deny the right for some people to live where they choose. This in turn has denied them any feelings of 'normality'. In short, the concept of 'special educational needs' has continued to label young people who experience learning difficulties or disabilities as a problem, in the same fashion as the old categories of handicap which the construct had been intended to replace (Fulcher, 1989).

FROM NEEDS TO RIGHTS AND ENTITLEMENTS

The examination of rights and entitlements moves the discourse of further opportunities for students with learning difficulties and disabilities into an exploration of the tensions between the private and public arenas of equal opportunities. It moves the debate from the narrowly private world of personal circumstances to the wider political examination of the publicly accountable provision made for and received by disabled people. This demand for civil rights, coming from various groups at the margins of an increasingly consumer-driven society, began to emerge as a phenomenon of the late 1950s and early 1960s in Western Europe and the United States. The battles for legislation to outlaw discrimination against various groups – women, gays and lesbians, blacks and disabled people – have been, and are being, fought separately; but the underlying issues are the same.

The major civil rights campaigns developed in the United States around the struggles of black people seeking to achieve their basic rights to vote, to hold elective office and to be tried by a jury of people representing the whole community, rather than a rigged selection of individuals. As these rights gradually came to be achieved, the movement became more concerned with broader social rights in vocational and educational arenas. The landmark case of Brown *v.* the Board of Education of Topeka, Kansas (1954), ensured that 7-year-old Linda Brown would attend an integrated school. This was the case that changed everything, tearing down legal segregation and demonstrating the power of the civil liberties movement throughout the south. The cause of black rights in turn acted as a catalyst for other groups, including disabled people (Bynoe *et al.*, 1991). The black civil rights movement was fundamental in its influence on disabled people for a number of reasons:

- It reconceptualized unequal treatments of marginalized groups into a more appropriate political context of equal opportunities and human rights. Rather than a human tragedy and therefore an individual 'problem', the cause was seen as a public and political concern.
- It demonstrated the possibility of achieving social change within a society. It also galvanized all people, who until then had overlooked their own role in the construction and perception of disability and special needs as a 'problem'.

Forty years on, in 1994, the original enthusiasms are looking somewhat hollow. Topeka schools are still segregated, and in terms of educational equality schools in the USA are more than ever segregated by poverty as well as race. Judge Robert Carter, who worked on the Brown case in 1954, has noted that 'the very powerful link between racial and poverty segregation is a central element in perpetuating the educational inequality of minority students' (*The Nation*, 1994, p. 688). Whilst it may be easy to attribute the maintenance of segregation and inequality to broad economic trends, it still posts a warning to those groups that fail to remain vigilant. It also reinforces the political dimension of any examination of further education as a means of building social justice as an integral feature of resource allocation in special educational provision.

Other major influences on the development of rights for disabled people are still currently emerging from the United States. The campaigns have all tended to come to successful fruition as a consequence of direct action and political activism. The Americans with Disabilities Act 1990 (ADA) (Morrissey, 1991) is an example of legislation that has come to be a powerful testimony to the campaigning zeal of disabled people. It is also a symbol of the potential strength of political activity in the development of civil rights for people with disabilities in other parts of the world.

In the United Kingdom legislation has been used to outlaw discrimination on the grounds of race and gender. These successful outcomes have encouraged disabled people to demand similar legislation with its major focus on 'rights' rather than 'needs'. By so doing, disabled people are arguing for legislation that challenges and stops the unfair discrimination that exists in society's attitudes and practices in both direct and indirect forms.

This shift towards addressing disability and learning difficulties within a political framework of rights and entitlements has been part of a process that has been given its lead in the world of further education. As Corbett and Barton (1992) have pointed out, special education is in danger of being perceived as apolitical, focused on shallow judgements of individual needs as selected needs, and the business of access to buildings and the curriculum. Rather than this, it should be considered as an issue to be studied within the curriculum, with a proper examination of both the institutional and structural inequalities inherent in society. If by so doing we place the exploration of disability and special education in its proper context of equal opportunities, it then becomes part of a more fundamental discourse related to the wider distribution of opportunities and privileges in society.

Further education and training in the United Kingdom is now effectively a player in a larger political poker game or, perhaps more aptly, in attempts to pin the tail on the donkey. On the one hand it is being played by those seeking to recreate old certainties and 'family values'; on the other by those who consider that the requirement for wholesale change in education and employment is now irreversible. This has taken the form of an economic and class debate around poverty, 'family values' and 'back to basics'. It does not bode well for students with learning difficulties and disabilities. The structure of the National Curriculum and opting-out is acting as the driving force for curricular and managerial change in schools. This in turn is promoting initiatives that are being followed up in colleges and vocational training programmes. Whilst these circumstances include 're-gard' for students with learning difficulties and disabilities, it is difficult to set the debate for educational change in terms of 'rights', 'entitlements' and 'citizenship'. To many teachers and lecturers, such terms appear to carry little weight and may even be considered rather vague and naïve. Any attempts to influence change in the funding of provision for students and young people with learning difficulties and disabilities now needs to recognize the additional responsibilities of engaging in political challenge, not simply seeking to affect legislation. The challenge is inherent in the language of debate, as well as participation in forming the agenda for action. In order to influence the structures of power and control in the education services the debates and judgements will have to be in terms of 'rights' rather than 'needs'. As Corbett and Barton (1992) have pointed out, this can be alien to staff accustomed to working within the narrow focus of individual needs, isolated from wider political involvement. Nevertheless, if services for students and young people with learning difficulties and disabilities are to emerge as a rights issue there is a need for all staff concerned to recognize their shared responsibility for the development of a new kind of political activism campaigning for civil rights. This may well involve the uncomfortable acknow-ledgement that there is still injustice towards disabled students in the education system. This sense of inequity and injustice needs to touch the lives of the vast majority of British families if real changes are to occur, and if the consistent sources of funding to sustain them are to be secured. If this does not happen the responsibility for making provision and bringing about change will remain with a small group of people. As a result, the quality of the educational experience for students with learning difficulties and disabilities will be in danger of being reduced to little more than the charitable rump activity from which it emerged.

SUMMARY

The background to the development of further education incorporates considerations of individual and institutional pre-judice and suspicions, rather than toleration of individual difference. It also demands that we question our understanding of the tension between the role of education and the role of employment as the arena for equal opportunities. In the next chapter we see how the rhetoric of equality of opportunity for students with learning difficulties and disabilities is emerging with the increasing influence of the Further Education Funding Council. It may, however, serve as a relatively hollow concept: to pay lip-service to the equality of people with severe and multiple disabilities may do little to meet their real needs.

2

The development of further education for students with learning difficulties and disabilities

It has already been suggested that many of the educational services we have developed to meet the needs of people with disabilities tend to perpetuate their own forms of bureaucracy and paternalism. Schools have a statutory responsibility to provide education, and all children are by law expected to attend until at least the age of 16. Part of the tension inherent in schools is that they insist on doing things to people, for which they are then expected to be grateful. The further education system of England and Wales, despite a general move towards equality, is in danger of becoming a victim of the same malaise. In the 1970s HMI were reporting that some further education courses were tending to repeat the content of special education at a junior level. 'Ladybird reading books and plastic money are still used' (HMI, 1977). Browne, writing about the introduction of further education for the 'educationally handicapped', also painted a somewhat gloomy picture:

> Obviously courses vary from college to college but what usually happens is that lecturers who have had no professional training in dealing with backward and troublesome students are timetabled into doing so for a morning or afternoon per week. Since status and career prospects within a college are often related to the grade of work, lecturers may not regard the teaching of retarded students as likely to enhance their status.
>
> (Browne, 1978, p. 8)

Today colleges are not only more varied in type but are by general acceptance ranked as of greater or lesser prestige. In further education there are yet more differences, not only in status, but also in such things as the degree of management autonomy, the amount of research conducted, staff conditions of work, average levels of pay. We have, however, moved nowhere near the concept of the comprehensive university or college. It might indeed be argued that we have merely replaced selection at the age of 11 by selection at 18.

The division of the education system has tended to follow the socially prescribed visions of the future labour force it was established to create. Ainley (1988, 1990b) has pointed out how the tripartite division of the 1944 Education Act into three types of state school echoed social divisions of labour between non-manual, skilled and unskilled manual work. The school system established immediately after the war was intended to produce a workforce to meet the needs of the reconstructed economy. This it was imagined would correspond to that which had served the nation so well in the past. The new technologies and shifts in social attitudes have broken down many of the more strident markers of the class symbolism on which these divisions were made, but there are still some vestiges of this elitist thinking in the selective worlds of further and higher education.

The concept of further education colleges as a form of tertiary education in England and Wales for students with disabilities is comparatively recent. Further education colleges were primarily designed to be local resources, open to the flexibility of provision required by a local community. Such ambitions echoed the recommendations of the Ince Report of 1945, which had urged that all school-leavers beginning work should be treated as 'trainees' with opportunities to acquire vocational skills and prospects for career progression (Ministry of Labour and National Service, 1945). It is also interesting to note that the Report suggested general day release for everybody wishing to undertake general education together with part-time release for vocational studies. Nevertheless, these ideas were not new: part-time education until the age of 18 had been a cornerstone of the 1918 Education Act, although it had never been implemented (Roberts, 1984).

Technical schools established after the war to produce the skilled workers of the future continued to remain under-funded and very much second best (along with secondary modern schools). Even in 1958 these schools contained only 4 per cent of the secondary school population and did not exist in more than 40 per cent of LEAs (Shilling, 1989). They were subsequently absorbed into the comprehensive schools that developed during the 1960s. The abandonment of these technical schools was recognized as 'one of the greatest tragedies of British education after the second world war' (Halsey *et al.*, 1980). The mixed enthusiasm for City Technology Colleges is without doubt linked to these memories. The desire to link vocational training to part-time further education was also a feature of the Crowther Report

(Ministry of Education, 1959) and formed part of the deliberations of numerous other working parties. However, even as late as 1977 the Manpower Services Commission (MSC) was lamenting that two-thirds of all school-leavers still received no further education.

The thrust towards the industrial modernization of Britain had begun in Harold Wilson's Labour administration of the mid-1960s. Projections of the future envisaged new technology demanding higher skills from suitably trained and flexible technicians. Education and curriculum innovation in both schools and training was considered to be the key to these developments. However, as Ainley (1990a, 1990b) has indicated, these brave aspirations were almost immediately hampered by the onset of recession, an oil crisis and the dismantling of Britain's manufacturing base. The foundations for structural unemployment were being laid in Britain's industrial heartlands. The planned expansions in education in the 1960s tended only to increase access to higher education. More, mainly middle-class, youth entered universities and polytechnics, preferring the prospects of non-manual employment in the ever-growing service industries.

What remained of formal technical education tended to take place in night schools and further education colleges. The curriculum was shaped around part-time education for students who were predominantly at work in factories and offices. The procedures of the apprenticeship system still operated for the development of craft skills and these often informal and varied training routes involved, in the main, male manual workers. The numbers of apprentices peaked in 1966, with the majority of places being taken up by young men. As Ainley (1990a, p. 2) has indicated, 'especially for young working class men, apprenticeships still sorted the skilled, regularly employed breadwinner from the insecure and unskilled labourer. Distinct labour markets thus remained based upon divisions of class, sex, age and race.' Interestingly, Ainley does not mention the populaton of disabled people, who remained invisible and effectively excluded from further education and training.

The impetus to the post-war development of further education for students with any form of disability came with the creation of the Manpower Services Commission in 1974 and the inexorable rise in unemployment during the 1970s. As unemployment rose the Labour government used the MSC to run a series of temporary employment schemes like the Youth Opportunities Programme. However, the uncontrolled rise in youth unemployment brought with it an expansion in special education (Tomlinson, 1985) as social disadvantage was translated into educational blame. It also gave the MSC an opportunity for unbridled growth as the

Department of Employment, which was responsible for training, challenged the efficiency and effectiveness of the Department of Education, which was responsible for education in schools and colleges. The crisis in confidence in formal school and college education emerged with the realization that teachers could no longer hold out the guarantee that hard work in school led to certain employment. The last Labour Prime Minister, James Callaghan, attempted to begin the redefinition of the purposes of education in his 1976 Ruskin College speech (Callaghan, 1976). He rounded on the education system for causing unemployment by being out of touch with the world of work and not teaching the appropriate social attitudes which would help leavers to get jobs. The intervention of the Prime Minister marked a clear shift on the part of the Labour party towards policies that would mean greater government control of the education system (Finn, 1987). In relation to socialist aspirations, such ideas seemed to turn equal opportunities on their head. More damagingly, the argument ran counter to the earlier, equally unrealistic socialist ideals that education alone could solve the malaise in British society. The then Opposition spokesman, Sir Keith Joseph, is reported to have said of this speech 'James Callaghan can claim to have started to build on the work of the Black Papers' (Ainley, 1990a, p. 3). Callaghan had also, and perhaps inadvertently, given the opportunity for expansion of 'the new FE' and had begun to include students with special educational needs in basic education courses for the first time.

Until the mid-1970s there were few alternatives to the expectation that students accepted on to courses in further education would both be able-bodied and have reached a minimum educational standard of achievement. Courses providing some form of work experience did exist but they were largely experimental and offered little evidence of an overall policy incorporating the education of the less able (Browne, 1981). The study conducted by Tuckey *et al.* (1973) and the first enquiry of its sort, sampled the views of special school-leavers and their future destinations. This interest in school-leavers with special needs was continued by others (Brindley, 1977; Jerrold and Fox, 1979). The sample by Tuckey *et al.* did not include students considered to be severely learning disabled as they were then outside the education system. Taking the sample as a whole, 1 per cent went into higher education, 10 per cent to colleges of further education, 9 per cent to special residential courses, 7 per cent to employment rehabilitation centres, 5 per cent to training centres and a further 5 per cent to other varied provisions. Fifty-one per cent of those considered 'suitable' found themselves with no provision at all. The low further education take-up was attributed in part to inadequate co-ordination and collaboration between LEAs, schools and colleges. Generally it was considered that the provision of post-school education and training was less than adequate.

The only other comprehensive survey in England of the student population with learning difficulties and disabilities in further education was published as *Catching Up?* (Stowell, 1987). This Skill/NBHS survey found there to be some 6,250 young people with special educational needs attending English colleges of further education full-time. Students with special needs, in this context, were defined as those receiving some special or extra support in order for them to gain access to education. The support could be human or financial or in the form of special equipment. An additional 3,200 young people under the age of 19 were attending colleges as part of a youth training scheme. For some this might be for one day a week only, as part of an employer-based scheme. However, for most the college served as the manager of the scheme and attendance at college was full-time, except on occasions when periods of work experience were arranged with employers.

In 1985 the 6,250 students with special educational needs attending college-designed and run courses were mainly from special schools for young people with moderate learning difficulties. The courses had titles that implied the need for transitional arrangements between childhood and adulthood, such as 'Transition to adulthood' or 'Preparation for work', and were intended as a bridge to other college courses or, more commonly at that time, the Youth Training Scheme.

Stowell (1987) identified some 250 courses of this type in approximately half the colleges of further education in England. In addition there were almost 80 full-time or near full-time courses for students with severe learning difficulties; as he commented in a later article: 'in these instances work might be a more distant goal, and greater emphasis given to the development of daily living skills and independence training' (Stowell, 1988). An astonishing number of students – Stowell estimated 13,400 in 1985 – never attended college at all, but were taught on an outreach basis in day centres or adult training centres by college staff. In 1985 more than 25 per cent of all further education colleges had arrangements such as this in place, with a curricular emphasis 'again largely confined to improving general life skills or else leisure pursuits such as art, pottery and dressmaking' (Stowell, 1988).

Whatever the nature of the courses, their distinguishing feature was the recognition that, as in school, students with learning difficulties and disabilities required additional support. At the same time special courses were not perceived as an end in themselves, but as part of a general progression to mainstream classes. However, at the time of the survey in 1985, considerably fewer than 2,000 students with special educational needs were to be found in mainstream classes working and studying alongside their non-disabled peers. Mainstreaming by 'in-filling' or providing integration for some of the time in mainstream classes was nevertheless beginning to occur.

Stowell's survey confirmed that young people between the ages of 16 and 19 represented the largest group of full-time students with learning difficulties and disabilities (then special educational needs) in further education colleges. They were, however, a minority of the disabled student population. Over the age of 19 the majority of students were and continue to be part-time, including some 3,000 day course and 1,500 evening students in 1985, who attended for perhaps a maximum of only two or three hours a week. More than half of the part-time courses on offer tended to promote general life skills, adult literacy and basic skills, often with a mixed range of students with learning difficulties and/or physical and sensory disabilities. A quarter of all part-time courses covered leisure pursuits such as 'dressmaking for the handicapped', or 'crafts for the blind'. In 1985 there were also some forty colleges that specialized in running specialist disability courses in, for example, lip-reading or Braille, while a few also ran specialist sports fitness or computer classes.

Since the survey there have been developments in the involvement of students with learning difficulties and disabilities across the full range of college courses. This has coincided with an increase in both the awareness of lecturing staff and the sophistication of support mechanisms that may be needed for students to participate effectively. New posts as co-ordinators for learning support have been established and there has been an increase in the numbers of personal care staff. Volunteer helpers and items of specialist equipment have increased the potential for access and course completion. The development of these services has come about rapidly; meeting the needs of a new student population has brought new challenges for teaching staff, in both curriculum design and methods of delivery.

THE LEGISLATIVE BACKGROUND TO FURTHER EDUCATION FOR STUDENTS WITH LEARNING DIFFICULTIES AND DISABILITIES

There is a considerable amount of newly established legislation relating to the education and training of young disabled people as they move from school to adult services. Cooper (1994b) usefully summarizes some complicated issues and highlights some of the confused language of definition employed by different services and government departments. Much of the legislation is accompanied by Circulars or guidance for the purposes of interpretation or implementation. This section outlines some of the key legislation in relation to further education and training for students with learning difficulties and disabilities.

THE FURTHER AND HIGHER EDUCATION ACT 1992 AND THE DEVELOPMENT OF QUALITY PROVISION

The Further and Higher Education Act 1992 for England and Wales was passed in early 1992 and fully implemented in April 1993, having been preceded by the White Paper, *Education and Training for the 21st Century* (DES, 1991a). A similar Act of Parliament was introduced with specific reference to further and higher education in Scotland. Both pieces of legislation brought into focus a number of specific duties with regard to the needs of students with learning difficulties and/or disabilities. The responsibility for implementing and driving forward the legislation has increasingly become the job of the Further Education Funding Councils for England, Wales and Scotland.

The establishment of these Councils created an opportunity for introducing educational targets and a new funding methodology to the competitive business culture of an already entrepreneurial sector of the education system. It is unlikely that the cost-effectiveness and demands for quality control that are now being insisted upon would have been introduced if colleges had remained under LEA control. The White Paper published in May 1991 had clearly signalled the new competitive climate within which the government intended colleges to operate. The Further and Higher Education Act 1992 transferred to the Councils some of the statutory duties formerly in the hands of local education authorites. These included the duty to secure the provision of further education in some 500 colleges that had formerly been the responsibility of LEAs.

While the Act does not, by and large, alter the statutory

duties that had previously been the responsibilities of LEAs, it does reiterate the responsibilities of the Funding Councils for the allocation of funds to these colleges in order to fulfil two important statutory duties imposed by sections 2 and 3 of the Act.

Section 2 of the Act requires the Councils to secure the provision of sufficient facilities for full-time education suitable for the requirements of 16- to 18-year-olds. Section 3 requires the Councils to ensure the provision of 'adequate' facilities for part-time education suitable for the requirements of persons over compulsory school age. It also requires the provision of suitable full-time education for those aged 19 and over, where such education falls within the scope of Schedule 2 of the Act. As has been indicated, Schedule 2 includes courses that:

- lead to academic and vocational qualifications;
- lead to entry to higher education;
- prepare students for the kinds of course listed above;
- teach basic skills in mathematics;
- teach basic literacy in English;
- develop proficiency in English as a foreign language (Welsh in Wales);
- teach aspects of independent living and communication skills to students with learning difficulties in order to prepare them for entry to any of the courses listed above.

It remains the statutory responsibility of local education authorities to secure an 'adequate' range of all other kinds of further education, that is, part-time provision such as non-vocational leisure courses, and provision for people over the age of 18, which is not the statutory responsibility of the Funding Councils. LEAs also continue to have a duty to provide for young people with statements who remain in school in accordance with their statement. LEAs are therefore obliged to fund a place for an individual in an independent special school if his or her statement specifies that such a form of provision is required. This has implications for the status of students with statements who wish to continue their education in colleges on courses funded by the FEFC, as we shall see.

Other powers that continue to reside with LEAs concern the duty to provide transport to all students on full-time courses and the awarding of discretionary grants. For students with learning difficulties and disabilities, the Act anticipates that the existing statutory duties to provide for and to have regard to their requirements will be carried forward. In discharging their duty, the Funding Councils are required to take account of the provision that is available for this age-range in institutions which it does not fund, for example in schools. LEAs are equally under a statutory obligation to secure further education for people with learning difficulties wherever the Councils have no such duty. This is increasingly becoming the case with students with statements, who are unlikely to meet some of the interpretations of progression that are implicit in the expectations of Schedule 2.

Cooper (1994b), in summarizing the implications of the legislation, has indicated the division of basic duties between the FEFC and the rump LEAs, for the provision of education:

LEA	FEFC
full-time secondary education for all 11- to 16-year-olds	
provision for individual statemented pupils up to age 19	sufficient full-time education for 16- to 18-year-olds
adequate further education for 16+ year-olds not covered by FEFC duties	adequate part-time education for 16+ year-olds if covered by Schedule 2
	adequate full-time education for 18+ year-olds if in Schedule 2
	education in independent specialist colleges if no provision is available locally up to the age of 25

Where suitable or 'adequate' provision is not available in the FEFC maintained sector for any student with learning difficulties between the ages of 16 and 25, the Councils must consider provision for them in an independent institution, including the possibility of residential education.

The interpretation of the meanings of 'sufficient' and 'adequate' has been the subject of much debate and some suspicion. It is clearly related to the duties of the newly established further education inspectorate with their responsibilities for the monitoring of quality and achievement in the sector. Furthermore, although the Act does not prescribe arrangements for the assessment of students with learning difficulties, this responsibility is clearly part of both adequate provision and any measurement of quality. The Secretary of State, in his letter of guidance to the Funding Councils and subsequent DfE Circulars (FEFC,

1992c) emphasizes the importance of ensuring that adequate arrangements exist for the measurement and assessment of needs in students with learning difficulties and identifying appropriate provision for meeting these needs within further education. The FEFC Circular 94/03 (FEFC, 1994a) gives details of arrangements for assessing students, placing a particular emphasis on those going into the independent sector.

Evidence is now beginning to emerge that there has been some general improvement in college systems for the assessment and resourcing of students with disabilities since the passing of the Act. However, this is less satisfactory in the case of students with more complex needs. The results of college inspections have suggested that there is concern about the resourcing of students with multiple and complex disabilities who have expressed a preference for attending their local college rather than an independent specialist college.

The Further and Higher Education Act 1992 gave the FEFC for England the duty to ensure that satisfactory arrangements exist to assess the quality of education provided in colleges within the sector. According to Huxley (1994), the fundamental criterion for the development of a distinctive approach to quality issues in relation to provision for students with learning difficulties and disabilities must not simply be fitness for purpose. The approach should also

> aim for high standards and excellence, assuring the government that the large sums of money devoted to this sector of education are well spent. Such an approach requires the recognition that quality in further education is dependent upon many inter-related factors. It is to do with the standards set and achieved, choice and diversity, the pursuit of rigour and competence in student achievement and all that supports teaching and learning.
>
> (Huxley, 1994, p. 2)

The quality of further education in the sector will be assessed through a system of inspections employing a flexible process of:

- direct observation of teaching and 'curriculum delivery';
- monitoring and inspection of a college's performance against the Charter for Further Education;
- evaluation of the college's own quality assurance strategies.

According to Huxley (1994, p. 1), 'the framework for inspection is sufficiently flexible to encompass the full range of students in further education. However, an aide memoire focusing specifically on students with learning difficulties and disabilities has been developed to enhance the framework.' This is a welcome nudge to college senior management in recognizing the contribution that students with learning difficulties and disabilities can make as part of the college community. It is also a reminder that, despite the rhetoric of equal opportunity, some colleges still have a long way to travel in developing courses that promote access and progression: 'Sometimes there is inflexibility in the way course programmes are designed, organised and delivered. Many lecturers still lack skills in differentiated teaching strategies. Too many classes are taught as a whole group and there are too many unfinished worksheets' (Huxley, 1994, p. 4).

ESTABLISHING THE FEFC IN ENGLAND AND WALES

Throughout the last fifteen years educational and social provisions for people with disabilities have increasingly been threatened by the tension between expectations and expenditure. Social provisions have gradually become under-resourced, as central government has attempted to control expenditure in the public sector. During the same period higher expectations have been placed upon the education services from both government ministers and the community at large. The funding of further education has not escaped this search for more cost-effective provision. The expectation that educational standards can be raised and cost-effectiveness achieved simultaneously is central to the creation of the Further Education Funding Councils. The whole of the further education system has, in effect, finally become a victim of its own remarkable ability to make successful and flexible responses to the demands placed upon it.

Just as the entitlement to special education has increased within the school system, so the demand for services has increased from the further education and adult sector. The benefit of education to young people with learning difficulties and disabilities is unchallenged by parents and teachers alike within the school system. However, it has become more apparent that just at the time when people with disabilities are beginning to acquire skills and abilities in the school years, it is time for them to leave compulsory education. As a result of this belief, and also on the grounds of equal opportunities, there has developed a demand for the continuation of educational entitlement and the services that go with it in the post-school years. The challenge then, in this new climate of further opportunity for education and training, is to maintain and preferably increase the quality of this educational and training provision while at the same time reducing costs. This essentially is the task imposed upon the Funding Councils.

Nonetheless, the apparently new-found autonomy of the further education colleges and the establishment of the Funding Councils did not guarantee the necessary enlightened understanding of special education or the needs of students with learning difficulties and disabilities. It certainly has not guaranteed the necessary funds to ensure a student's educational entitlement to an appropriate further education experience. Prior to 1 April 1993 LEAs had been responsible for the provision of funding for the majority of students with learning difficulties and disabilities. This fundamental responsibility has now passed into the hands of the FEFC. The Further and Higher Education Act 1992 placed the duty on this newly established body to secure sufficient and adequate facilities for further education and 'to have regard for the needs of persons with learning difficulties and disabilities'. This shift away from a concentration on special educational needs has been welcomed by those who feel that the term tends to reflect child- rather than adult-oriented services and curricular considerations. However, the duty to 'have a regard' is not the same as providing a guarantee to entitlement. There is a danger that provision for students with learning difficulties and disabilities will be marked out by the emphasis solely on skills for independence and basic skills – those elements that are funded by the FEFC. Thus, not only will choice become more limited but the 'deficiency' model of learning from which the colleges had been trying to escape will be reinforced.

The changes in terminology and definitions have, in fact, done little to shift the focus of student 'need', which remains firmly rooted in the language of the 1981 Education Act. Within the 1993 legislation persons with a learning difficulty are still considered to be experiencing:

> a significantly greater difficulty in learning than the majority of persons of their age.
>
> *or*
>
> [to have] a disability which either prevents or hinders them making use of facilities generally provided by institutions within the further education sector for persons of their age.
>
> (Education Act 1993, s. 156)

The Act also states that a person must not be regarded as having a learning difficulty solely because the language, or form of language, of the home is different from the language in which he or she is, or will be, taught.

So students with learning difficulties and/or disabilities are still categorized in relation to their social position within a continuum of resource-dictated need. These socially created categories are employed to exclude rather than to include and have been used to oppress rather than to enable. As Fulcher (1989) has argued, any disputed categories like 'disability' and 'special educational need' continue to be disputed precisely because they are socially created entities. The term 'learning difficulties and disability' is still ultimately defined in terms of measured disability. Thus, although no impairment may be visible, the presumption is made that it is and that the cause resides within the individual concerned.

This creation of a disabled or special needs identity draws heavily on the medical model, within which disability is viewed as a deficit, as individualized loss or impairment. This suggests that it is the individual who has the impairment, disease or incapacity. The legislation concerning the definitions in further education for students with learning difficulties and disabilities has done little to shift this view. The medical model of disablement continues to encourage a discourse of 'person-blame' and insinuations of personal irresponsibility. This suggests that an individual with a disability who does not abide by decisions made by others on his or her behalf thereby contributes to many of the negative reactions to disabled people. As Fulcher (1989) asserts, the concept of disability is far from a neutral technical or scientific status. It is essentially a political act that continues to perpetuate distinctions and grows in importance as people with learning difficulties and disabilities move from child to adult status.

The establishment of the FEFC has brought about the imposition of some centrally controlled guidance on an area of work that has prided itself on the *ad hoc* entrepreneurialism that has been its hallmark. Colleges of further education and sixth-form colleges may now have achieved independence from LEAs, but they are also expected to become more competitive with schools and other training providers. It is an almost certain bet that the long-term funding arrangements provided by central government will increasingly be tied to agreed outcomes and targets set by the FEFC. Yet, whilst the fundamental role of the Councils is financing and quality control, they are at the same time currently trying to learn about and respond to further education colleges and their management systems. As Dee (1993) points out, many of the colleges are themselves learning to face a new world. They are becoming more flexible, accessible and learner-centred for the purposes of teaching and delivery of courses, in the belief that this will be in accord with guidance from the FEFC.

It is clear from the vast numbers of published Circulars that the FEFC, as a newly formed body, is itself on a rapid learning curve. As it gets to grips with understanding the business of further education, it is also evident that the Council is well aware of its responsibilities to the needs of students with learning difficulties and disabilities. There is a requirement that for 1993–94 colleges continue to provide for the same numbers of students with learning difficulties and disabilities as in previous years. This directive, plus the establishment of a specialist committee on the concerns of students with learning difficulties and disabilities, under the chairmanship of Professor John Tomlinson, indicates the intention to continue consulting and gathering information as widely as possible on the issue.

Fifteen years before the establishment of the FEFC, the Warnock Committee of Inquiry (1978) had established the concept of special educational needs as embracing a continuum of need for up to 20 per cent of the school population; from children and young people who need a high level of intervention to those whose needs are relatively short-term. The 1992 Further and Higher Education Act has placed a similarly clear duty on the newly established Funding Councils to continue to make provision for young people with learning difficulties or disabilities in further education. This raises a concern, not about the 2 per cent or so of students with statements of clearly defined needs, but about those other young people with no obvious long-term needs, whose educational and training needs may be overlooked by the new legislation. This esentially involves the 18 per cent of young people, in the Warnock terminology, who exhibited a range of educational needs that had been addressed in ordinary schools, but who will not be assured of receiving the kind of support they require when the time comes to move on to further education (Dee, 1993).

The FEFC is setting about changing the educational climate for all students in post-compulsory education, including those with learning difficulties or disabilities. Throughout the period of rapid expansion in the 1970s and 1980s, the major task in colleges and in society had been to raise awareness to the significant equal opportunities implications of including students with learning difficulties and disabilities in colleges. As Huxley (1993a) has indicated, many colleges have had to develop a new concept for the work, because the opinions of those working in the area 'indicated that embarrassment, sentimentality and sheer ignorance' still tend to combine to thwart the educational and vocational progress of people with learning difficulties and disabilities.

These prejudices and almost atavistic fears still pervade some colleges. Nevertheless, inappropriate labels and stereotypes have been more successfully challenged, using the evidence contained in Warnock (1978), the Fish Report (Fish, 1985) and the Education

Reform Act 1988. These seminal documents guided the development of policies and values that include the principles of entitlement as a key focus of equal opportunity. The requirement that the FEFC develop interest in students with learning difficulties and disabilities has also begun to change attitudes. There has been some concern about the lack of recent statistical and qualitative information on the lives and circumstances of students with learning difficulties and disabilities and the cost of resourcing their provision. The last extensive survey was conducted in 1985 (Stowell, 1987) and more recently there has been the qualitative survey of Wade and Moore (1993), which calculated that some 43,500 disabled students were receiving some form of education in a college of FE. This estimate of numbers is less than half of Stowell's extrapolation and emphasizes the need for better researched evidence on numbers. Lack of recent information has led to the establishment of a national committee of inquiry into provision. The committee has a three-year life (until 1996) and a relatively small membership under the chairmanship of Professor John Tomlinson of Warwick University. One of the committee's first actions has been to establish a call for evidence from students and from all those individuals and organizations directly involved with people with learning difficulties and/or disabilities.

The potential influence of the Committee of Inquiry should not be overlooked. The Warnock Report (1978) had concentrated on becoming a blueprint for special education for the twenty-first century, with its focus on the special educational needs of children of school age. The Tomlinson Committee is specifically directed to target attention on the longer-term needs of students in post-school settings. The impact of the committee in shaping the development of policies and codes of practice together with reconsideration of the language of entitlement is certain to be significant. Making educational provision for students with disabilities and learning difficulties an integral part of college planning has already brought changes in staffing, with most colleges establishing the post of cross-college co-ordinator and appointing learning support staff. The allocation of resources, the monitoring of facilities and physical space within a college in order to meet the requirements of quality control from the FEFC is likely to increase the need for administrative support.

Huxley has played a significant role in the shaping of further education for students with learning difficulties and disabilities in her work as an officer of the FEU (Further Education Unit) and FEFU and an HMI. She has suggested (Huxley, 1993a) that the number of changes in policy and practice to which the FEFC is paying particular attention had begun to emerge from colleges well before the formation of the FEFC. She has pointed out trends that can be traced back over a decade or more as staff began to adapt teaching approaches and management methods.

Changes in legislation

The Further and Higher Education Act 1992 introduced a number of important reforms in the organization and funding of further education. It said very little specifically about curriculum issues, but its recommendations will have a strong impact on the structural and funding provision made in colleges.

The letter of guidance from the Secretary of State (FEFC, 1992c) is particularly relevant to the development of the FEFC's interest in students with learning difficulties and disabilities. It reflects the spirit within which the legislation is to be enacted and the FEFC is expected to operate. Thus, the Council is expected to be consultative rather than prescriptive: 'the Council's role is to act as a framework within which colleges operate as independent corporate bodies' (Maddison, 1993).

The FEFC has been granted significant powers for the allocation of funds provided by the Secretary of State for Education. The needs of students with learning difficulties and disabilities clearly play a significant part in the agenda. Under section 3 of the Further and Higher Education Act 1992, the Council has a duty to secure adequate facilities for certain courses of further education. In other words, courses that come within the interpretation of eligibility will continue to receive funding from the FEFC. These courses are described as Schedule 2 under the 1992 Act. The criteria for assessing eligibility under Schedule 2 are at the heart of whether or not students with learning difficulties and/or disabilities are likely to be able to attract FEFC funding and to continue their further education beyond the age of 19. Without such funding, colleges are unlikely to be able to maintain provision, and disabled students will have to seek out alternative funding arrangements, from social services or other sources.

The interpretation of what constitutes a Schedule 2 course can, in effect, be reduced to a judgement of what is considered to be 'progression' for a student with learning difficulties and disabilities. As things stand, the FEFC appears to be widening opportunities and there is a strong sense in which its interpretation of the Further and Higher Education Act 1992 appears to endorse the spirit of inclusion. By regarding disabled students as being covered by the Council's general duties, the FEFC is treating disabled students the same as all others. Nevertheless, Schedule 2 suggests that the funding of provision extends only to those who are physically and sensorily disadvantaged and to those with only moderate learning difficulties. The FEFC appears to be less inclined to make financial provision for those students with severe emotional difficulties and/or learning difficulties. It is unclear how progression for such students could continue to be justified within the spirit of progression implied by Schedule 2.

Changes in language and terminology

The breadth of language and ideas used in special education makes it impossible to guarantee explanations that are completely accepted or 'accurate'. For example, some of the terminology for services may carry the same title in different colleges but have completely different meanings; for example, does the term 'learning support' mean the same thing in all regions of the country? Language use and terminology is still a fundamental indicator of change (Fulcher, 1989); the term 'handicapped student' has almost completely disappeared from the official language of further education, as has the term 'special needs'. These terms have been replaced by the concept of students with learning difficulties and disabilities. This distinction is an important one for attitudinal differences between the school-focused services and child-oriented practices of the classroom and the more adult, negotiated practices that are anticipated in a college of further education. Most colleges, it seems, are dismantling special needs units and departments and replacing them with systems of integrated learning support and flexible learning. It is, however, worth asking if they are actually capable of providing for individual learning needs throughout the college and whether concepts such as 'flexible learning' convey the same meanings to all those who profess to implement them? Too often the terminology is perceived as unproblematic and goes unchallenged.

Changes in assessment

Huxley (1993a, 1993b) has placed the need for changes in assessment procedures at the heart of the development of quality in further education provision for students with learning difficulties and disabilities. She has commented that it is fundamental to the development of good-quality further education for all students and that if assessment strategies are not designed and used appropriately with forms of learning experience, materials and support specifically designed to meet individual learning needs, 'then we are disabling learning'.

The Further and Higher Education Act 1992 has placed a duty, through the Secretary of State's letter of guidance (FEFC, 1992c), on the FEFC to ensure that adequate arrangements exist for assessing the needs of students with learning difficulties and disabilities and identifying appropriate provision for them, in co-operation with other agencies which have a role in providing for these students. Whilst there is no particular need or legislative requirement for the FEFC to carry out assessments of the specific needs of individuals, there is a requirement that the FEFC ensure the existence of means to meet the needs of students once they have been assessed:

(a) a broad brush assessment in order to determine if a student's needs can be adequately met in an ordinary, local further education college or whether an independent specialist college is required.

In almost every case it is the LEA that will be principally involved in investing significant amounts of time and resources in the support of school children with special educational needs. It is probable that they are in the best position to offer advice on provision beyond the statutory school-leaving age as well. Nevertheless, collaboration between the FEFC and whatever agency carries out assessment is clearly essential in order to provide continuity and co-ordination of both assessment and curriculum planning.

(b) a further level of assessment that may be carried out at the college level, in order to trigger funding from within the college budget. It is increasingly the case that the outcomes of the assessments are being linked to individual learning contracts as well as the identification of the additional support needs to be met arising from the assessment.

The FEFC clearly anticipates that colleges will continue to assess students and relate any demands for additional resources to the clarity of their assessment practices. This has a number of implications for students who are socially disaffected, rather than demonstrating distinct physical and/or sensory disabilities.

THE INFLUENCE OF WIDER LEGISLATION ON STUDENTS WITH LEARNING DIFFICULTIES AND DISABILITIES

The quality of provision made by colleges of further education in their new incorporated, independent status links with other significant pieces of legislation related to disabled people.

Elements of the Disabled Persons (Services, Consultation and Representation) Act 1986 stress the need for liaison between LEAs and local social services departments concerning social services' assessments of disabled pupils/students at the point of leaving full-time education. The governing body of a college, or the FEFC if the student is placed in the independent sector, is responsible for informing the local social services department when a disabled person under the age of 18 leaves full-time education. This consultation remains the responsibility of the LEA when the young person with learning difficulties is over the age of 18 and not attending college. It is more likely to apply to people with severe and complex disabilities.

The link between education and social services is formalized most strongly in the Disabled Persons (Services, Consultation and Representation) Act 1986, which was introduced in order to smooth the transfer from full-time education to adult life. It gives local education authorities and the Further Education Funding Council specific responsibilities to ensure that students with statements of special educational need who fit into the 1948, medically oriented, definition of disability are recorded as such by social security departments. The same Act requires social services to assess the needs of a disabled person if requested so to do by either the disabled individual or their representative. The needs of carers in relation to the development of appropriate care for a disabled person is also covered by legislation within the National Health Service and Community Care Act 1990. The responsibility is to provide information about relevant services in order to meet the needs of a disabled person or their carer.

Other legislation that has some significance for the quality of provision of educational services is related to the expectation of developing links between educational and social services. The National Health Service and Community Care Act 1990 indicates the responsibilities of local authorities for meeting the assessed needs of disabled people under community care plans. This Act draws on services listed under the Chronically Sick and Disabled Persons Act 1970, a long-established, if somewhat toothless, piece of enabling legislation that encouraged local authorities to make provisions for disabled people by developing social and leisure services, including further and continuing education. Section 2 of this legislation indicates the provision that should be made available by a local authority to people with a disability:

> (i) the provision of practical assistance for that person in his home;
> (ii) the provision for that person of, or assistance to that person in obtaining, wireless, television, library or similar recreational facilities;

(iii) the provision for that person of lectures, games, outings to the recreational facilities outside his home or assistance to that person in taking advantage of educational facilities available to him;

(iv) the provision for that person of facilities for, or assistance in, travelling to and from his home for the purposes of participating in any services provided under any arrangements made by the authority under the said section 29, or with the approval of the authority in any services provided otherwise than as aforesaid which are similar to services which could be provided under such arrangements;

(v) the provision of assistance for that person in arranging for the carrying out of any works of adaptation in his home or the provision of any additional facilities designed to secure his greater safety, comfort or convenience;

(vi) facilitating the taking of holidays by that person, whether at holiday homes or otherwise and whether provided under arrangements made by the authority or otherwise;

(vii) the provision of meals for that person whether in his home or otherwise;

(viii) the provision for that person of, or assistance to that person in obtaining a telephone and any special equipment necessary to enable him to use a telephone.

It is clear from this that social services departments can fund educational provision and also transportation to and from other facilities in which education can take place. However, the definition of disability employed by these departments suggests that the interpretation of provision by some departments may restrict the funding to those elements of 'care' which they consider to be their fundamental responsibility. The definition of disabled people used by social services departments focuses on a medically oriented interpretation of disability and comes from the National Assistance Act 1948:

persons who are blind, deaf or dumb, or who suffer from mental disorder of any description and other persons who are substantially and permanently handicapped by illness, injury, or congenital deformity or such other disabilities as may be prescribed by the Minister.

The Chronically Sick and Disabled Persons Act 1970 also makes it clear that there are responsibilities that fall to colleges, schools and universities in relation to the physical access of disabled people into and within buildings, parking arrangements and sanitary conveniences.

The most recent amendments to the Disability Discrimination Bill indicate that the existing powers of the FEFC are to be reinforced. The operational requirements of the Further and

Higher Education Act 1992 will thus become leal requirements when the bill becomes law. Finally, the Education Act 1993 has relevance to students with learning difficulties and disabilities in further education in so far as it contains a Code of Practice that requires transitional arrangements to be made for children with special educational needs. It is anticipated that careful inter-agency assessment and planning will be put into place, for progression to appropriate adult services, at least two years before leaving school. The emphasis of the Act is upon the provision for children and young people with special educational needs in their school years and it is interesting to note the distinctive stress of the legislation on individual deficit as a marker for the provision of additional resources or support. This contrasts with attempts in further education to provide a service to match the learning needs of all learners.

SUMMARY

The chapter has traced the recent development of provision for students with learning difficulties and disabilities in further education. It is a history marked by the persistent association between educational disability and individual deficit. The emergence of further education and training in the 1990s has begun to challenge this stereotype by placing an emphasis on the rights and responsibilities of all learners, including those with learning difficulties and disabilities. Nevertheless, the emergence of a deliberately new and more competitive culture of enterprise in colleges is being steered by the funding mechanisms of the Further Education Funding Council.

The legislation of the Further and Higher Education Act 1992 which has freed colleges from their previous attachment to LEAs has deliberately encouraged the recognition of an entitlement to further education for students with learning difficulties and disabilities, in accordance with the requirements of Schedule 2 of the Further and Higher Education Act. However, this entitlement is linked to the student's ability to show evidence of progression towards ultimate employment. Provision in colleges is still settling down after the massive reorganization brought about by the Further and Higher Education Act 1992. There are bound to be some horror stories as some LEAs and the FEFC wrangle to decide who will pay for what, in relation to the requirements of students with learning difficulties and disabilities, and as the liaison and co-ordination of services for students is renegotiated between service providers and the newly independent college sector.

3

The emerging culture of transition to further education for students with learning difficulties and disabilities

There are some clear differences between the states of childhood and adulthood. In rights, expectations, self-expression and responsibility they are acknowledged to be distinct. However, as Hirst *et al.* (1993) indicate, there is not the same degree of consensus on adolescence, which hovers somewhat uncertainly between dependency on adults and the assertion of personal autonomy and independence. This chapter explores how young people move from childhood to adulthood and particularly identifies some of the contradictions of role and identity faced by young people and students with learning difficulties and disabilities.

Adolescence is a time of growing up physically and sexually and developing the emotional stratagems for coping with the social and psychological adjustments that these changes demand. Some interpretations highlight the distinction between the 'phase' and 'process' of adolescent transition: 'The process aspect refers to the social-psychological development of the individual whereas the phase aspect refers to the pattern of services provided for individuals during transition' (OECD/CERI, 1986, p. 15).

The time of leaving school is also acknowledged to be a period of discontinuity and stress for all concerned. The adolescent is no longer a child who is totally dependent upon adults for direction and guidance, and yet he/she is not fully accepted as someone who can take responsibility for the consequences of their own decisions. It may also be regarded as a separate stage in life, a period when a young person can experiment with a wide variety of roles and identities without the burdensome expectation of full commitment. This period of maturation is normally associated with the years between 14 and 25. However, as Hirst *et al.* (1993) point out, for some people the formation of a coherent value system and the attempt to adopt new ways of behaving may continue throughout adult life.

For all young people, the road to adult life is usually hard; this is particularly so for young people with disabilities. The routes which such students take are largely determined by historical factors (Baginsky and Bradley, 1992). Many of the rites of passage associated with this time, for example the formation of relationships with either sex, under-age drinking, the culture of the peer group or gang, are often either deliberately denied to them or unattainable. For some disabled young people there is no stage of adolescence; the period is truncated into a brief transition from childhood to adult services. The whole of their lives is framed by dependency upon the expectations, attitudes and values of society. Research has indicated that many disabled youngsters lack the confidence, self-esteem and social skills necessary for a smooth transition to adult life (Johnstone, 1986, 1994b; FEU, 1989; Hutchinson and Tennyson, 1986; Hirst and Baldwin, 1994). Some of the stages in the movement towards adulthood involve a whole series of adjustments. Leaving school and becoming an adult means not only qualitative and subjective shifts for the young disabled person, but also a readjustment of the structures of services and resources associated with this new period of experience.

Hirst and Baldwin (1994) have usefully reviewed some of the key elements of transition that need to be successfully negotiated by all on the journey to adult status. Many young people with disabilities encounter a number of additional difficulties and disappointments on the way. In the area of employment (an ultimate marker of adult status), it is markedly more difficult for disabled students to obtain and remain in employment. Young people with severe physical impairments face a particularly uncertain prospect. One survey has revealed that during the 1980s only one-third of severely physically disabled people had obtained any form of sheltered or open employment by the age of 21 – more than three years after the minimum school-leaving age (Hirst, 1987). As a result, a large number of young people never enter employment and instead pass straight from school or further education to long-term placement in a day centre, or they return home to a life of social security and social prejudice.

At the age of 16, all young people leaving school change status within the social security system. Until this age they will have been considered as dependent upon their parents. At the age of 16 the financial situation changes and the financial position of young people with disabilities becomes especially complex. For those continuing with education little changes, save that assessment may entitle certain students to additional funds, through access allowances or additional units of funding determined by the complexity of need arising from a disability. For those who are entering training schemes or seeking employment, a new minefield of adult 'entitlements' has to be negotiated.

For young people with disabilities, the complexity of the eligibility rules and the scales of entitlements often means that information is either incomplete or not fully understood. Anderson and Clarke (1982) noted this over a decade ago and it is disappointing to see that lack of information still means that the take-up of allowances is still very poor, with delayed applications and all too frequently a sheer lack of information (Berrington and Johnstone, 1994; Hirst and Baldwin, 1994).

WHO ARE THE STUDENTS?

The focus of special education has traditionally been on individual needs; however, it is important to be reminded that the provision in further education and training is essentially an economic and political concern. At its least helpful the characteristics of individuals and assessment of need may continue to reflect earlier school perceptions and provision. However, the transition should break away from stereotypes and encourage the creation of new policy, fresh learning agreements and a reallocation of resources. All too often, the stereotypical image of disability as personal tragedy influences rational judgement, and this is emphasized by a concentration on case studies and media imagery.

The excitement of working in further education and training, for students and lecturers alike, rests in identifying the greater 'hidden' potential in every student. This is often masked by some form of disability of either a temporary or permanent nature. A significant number of students with learning difficulties and disabilities will have arrived in colleges and training courses from special schools or units in comprehensive schools. Some may be coming to college in order to make a fresh start after some years of disaffection in the last stages of secondary school. Some, too, may have attended college on a bridging or day-release course while still attending their day school. Often one of the most immediate needs for such students is to build self-confidence. In the larger, more integrated settings of a college there are greater opportunities for this. Developments in learning support also mean there is an emphasis on individual learning programmes linked to the wider range of experiences and curricular activities to which a student is exposed.

Descriptions of the effects of education and training for students with learning difficulties and disabilities pose a considerable challenge to both the language of description and concepts of need in post-16 settings. Post-school students with special educational needs had been excluded from the formal requirements of the 1981 Education Act, which covered only young people up to the point at which school doors finally closed. The 1992 Further and Higher Education Act responded to this omission by deciding in favour of the term 'students with learning difficulties and disabilities' rather than 'special needs' in order to stress the sense of continuum of need and the new breadth of provision available in post-school education. The issue of terminology is further confused by the Disabled Persons Act 1986 and the Children Act 1989, both of which adopt a narrower, medically oriented definition of 'disability'. These are related neither to learning difficulties nor to forms of educational provision. Young people who are the subjects of statements of special needs and those who are considered by social services to be disabled can be very different.

As a result of the 1981 legislation, two different priority groups of children with special needs were created: those who could manage with minimal additional support, mainly educated in ordinary schools, and those who were supported through the legal requirements of a statement of special needs, mainly provided in a special school or unit. LEAs were under a duty to provide and meet the costs of these educational requirements, but only up to the point at which pupils left school. Research conducted by Baginsky and Bradley (1992) suggests that colleges are ambivalent about the fact that this defined entitlement disappears at 16. For some, the statement remains a legal safeguard of provision that would allow colleges to plan carefully and progressively for appropriate levels of support. For others the statement is a characteristic of childhood services and inappropriate for young people embarking on another phase of their lives. Ironically, those school-leavers whom social services considers disabled have a legal right to a planned post-school transition programme.

There are different expectations of young people who have left school, but too many youngsters with learning difficulties and disabilities are depicted in the language of school descriptions and attitudes. Whittaker (1988, 1993) has been a vocal critic of the tendency for 'the system' to dominate at the expense of individual opportunity. If the energies of a college go into the establishment of provision that merely replicates the provision of school, little will have changed: 'once energies go into the establishment of a "Special Needs Unit" or into the "annexisation" of provision away from the mainstream of the college the needs of the students attending such a location can become blurred by the limitations of the annexe and the focus can move away from the potential of the student to the potential of the Unit' (Whittaker, 1988, p. 126).

For any student the transition from one institution to another can be a traumatic experience. For those with learning difficulties, who may have transferred from a small special school, the stress involved may be more marked and the need for a greater degree of pre-planning and empathy more often necessary.

A number of personal accounts of the school and college days of disabled students do exist, although case studies do have obvious limitations in capturing the complexity of individual circumstances. Wade and Moore (1993) have recorded the attitudes and opinions of young people with special educational needs in their final school years, using interviews. Their accounts clearly indicate the self-awareness and untapped potential that is frequently overlooked when listening to the views of these young people. Such accounts and interactions have also become the subject of award-winning novels and films such as *Under the Eye of the Clock* (Nolan, 1987), and *My Left Foot*, which depicts the life of Christy Brown. Other experiences have been identified with photo imagery (Hevey, 1992). These personal experiences carry with them the burning sense of wasted opportunity combined with an element of voyeurism that can both fascinate and repel. Some of the more forthright accounts of educational experiences have begun to come from students themselves. Those who have overcome negative impressions of earlier educational experience have been able to use the fresh chances that further and higher education can provide and their accounts are amongst the most perceptive in relation to the issue of rights and opportunities.

Simone Aspis recalls her experiences of earlier education as a time of frustration:

> after my thirteenth birthday, I attended a computer course which introduced a whole new world of making mathematics fun and more purposeful. . . However, whilst at school I suffered taunts from the child-care staff and teachers about my extensive interest in computing. The child-care staff would pick on me for everything and try to send me to bed early in order to limit my time developing my talent. I used to get up at 5.30 a.m. and write my programs before breakfast.
>
> (Aspis, 1991, p. 17)

Aspis is critical of the low expectations that many teachers have of children with disabilities. She has noted the concern of special schools to prepare young people to be cared for by the community rather than believing that disabled people can contribute to the community. Her overriding concern is shared by many other reports about the lack of opportunity to participate on an equal footing with non-disabled children from outside the segregated special education sector. There are few opportunities to develop sports skills or responsibilities with a community focus, and few real chances to increase self-confidence: 'when our school played football matches against other teams (normally children with no special needs), we looked pathetic. There was no training or proper kit provided. What did the visiting team think of children with special needs?' (Aspis, 1991).

This concern over the repression of individual chances to express oneself within the tight control of a special school environment are shared by others. Simnett (1991) and Hatton (1994) interviewed students who had attended special schools before moving to some form of further education. They identified a number of examples of conflict between the personal perceptions of 'self' and the more socially determined identity developed through roles and relationships in wider society. Simnett captures some of this conflict and self-doubt in the following discussion of 'Martin':

> I felt he had a clear awareness of his own identity as an individual and a social identity which he felt was defined by his school. Through parody Martin acknowledged and humiliated this identity in the same act. He seemed to be hopping from one identity to the next in order to demonstrate the distance between them, and ultimately the separateness of the real 'Martin'. Eventually, however, his act turned to suspicion and his spirit of independence turned to self-doubt; 'You know I'm a bit funny don't you? In your mind ... you don't want to be nasty right, but you're really saying, I'm a bit funny in the head, I'm a spazzy.'
>
> (Simnett, 1991, p. 20)

The majority of students with learning difficulties and disabilities entering colleges come into the general category of experiencing 'learning difficulties'. Some may have progressed directly from a special school for categorical disabilities. Some may have the range of characteristics and backgrounds identified by Faraday and Harris (1989), who have drawn up case study information based on a number of sources. Their study is deliberately not intended to represent any specific category of need – a useful reminder that individual need in young adulthood reflects a complex array of interrelated factors. Based on real students and trainees, they have compiled a range of portraits covering the age-range 16–25, and they convey the levels of emotional complexity that are part of the make-up of all young people during this time of their lives. Their case studies reinforce the belief that the starting-point for meeting any educational need lies in the recognition of the wide range of individual needs, not the simplistic measure of single characteristics such as an IQ score, or a physical deformity.

Hatton (1994) takes this point further in commenting on the development of provision for students with profound and multiple learning difficulties. She has also, perhaps inadvertently, indicated the way in which change tends to emerge as a consequence of the strength of individual zeal and leadership. Her personal belief that students with the most profound and multiple learning difficulties also have an educational entitlement filled her with 'a red mist' of anger in the face of scepticism from some of her colleagues:

> a line cannot be drawn which says some students can and some cannot come to college on the grounds of disability. The question we must surely ask is 'what do these students need in order to take advantage of the educational opportunities on offer?'
>
> (Hatton, 1994, p. 37)

Hatton indicates that although links between schools and colleges for young people with 'severe learning difficulties' have become fairly well established, the development of link courses for people with more profound and multiple learning difficulties has never really been considered. Through personal commitment from key staff, including the co-ordinator for students with disabilities and members of the drama department, she managed to open up her college facilities to just such a possibility:

> The college staff learnt a great deal ... the pupils indicated their enjoyment of the experience in a variety of individual ways, i.e. one young woman rubbed her finger and thumb together when she was enjoying something and ... she did this nearly all the time we were in the drama studio.
>
> (Hatton, 1994, p. 37)

Students on TEC-funded training courses echo many of the concerns identified above by Simnett. Some delegates to a Skill conference for young adults with special training needs indicated that they felt they had been forced to label themselves as lacking in confidence, in order to gain access to the training. On the other hand, one trainee with reading and writing difficulties was unable to read the self-completion assessment paper put before him (Cooper, 1994a). It is clear that not every student/trainee with individual learning needs will want to be labelled as having either special training needs or learning difficulties and disabilities. The key consideration in both further education and training courses is to remember that students and trainees with learning difficulties and disabilities/special training needs are first and foremost students and trainees. They are as interested in acquiring skills and having them recognized as any other student.

It is unfortunate that young adults are forced to decide if they are 'able' to move into employment or work-related training. If they are assessed, or are likely to be assessed, as capable for work this makes a considerable difference to their benefit entitlements. As Hirst *et al.* (1993) amongst others have pointed out, whether a young person is prepared to resign him- or herself to being considered 'unemployable' determines their eligibility for a selection of benefits (including the chance to participate in work leading to 'therapeutic' earnings). This frees them from the routines of regular employment and leaves them to determine how they will spend their time. If, on the other hand, a young adult with disabilities is considered 'employable' they are put in exactly the same position as all other people seeking employment, with no compensation for any disability-related handicap. This benefits trap is a particular dilemma for young people about to set out to establish their role in adult life.

THE SUBCULTURE OF FURTHER EDUCATION

Further education has a long history of responding to needs and adapting to change. The response to the development of equal opportunities and provision for students with learning difficulties and disabilities provides a clear example of the evolution of sets of values and attitudes. The complex readjustment of ideas about the abilities of, and teaching approaches to, a relatively new group of students in further education has challenged what Harris and Clift (1988) have called the 'sub-culture of further education'. This seems an apt term for the range of options and increased choices that become available for students at the point of transition from school to college.

In 1992 the majority of students with special educational needs were still leaving school at the age of 16 (Baginsky and Bradley, 1992). The exceptions were those students with severe, profound or complex difficulties and those with multiple physical and learning difficulties. The availability of options for continuing in full- or part-time further education varied:

> The spectrum ranged from those authorities with no post 16 school based provision for this group (and amongst them were even authorities that had limited FE provision) to authorities which had very actively encouraged these students to stay on in school until they were 18 or 19.
>
> (Baginsky and Bradley, 1992, p. 4)

The majority of school-leavers with more moderate learning difficulties and disabilities progress from school to discrete courses in colleges, youth training or some form of employment. Very occasionally a student with severe learning difficulties will leave school at 16 and progress to a discrete form of provision in a college, but this is unusual. There is, nonetheless, a growing trend for schools to retain their pupils with learning difficulties beyond the age of 16. The research by Baginsky and Bradley (1992) suggests a variety of reasons for this trend:

(1) the feelings of some teachers that the curriculum offered by some college courses offered little that could not be provided in schools that linked with a college and the community;
(2) the introduction of local management of special schools, which placed a premium on the retention of pupil numbers over the age of 16;
(3) a general questioning of the pedagogical wisdom of making a transition from school at the age of 16. Many teachers considered that pupil experiences could be enhanced in schools and that a more successful transition to college would come with increasing maturity which had been developed in a familiar setting.

The variety of provision that has evolved over the last fifteen years includes a number of measures that are designed to ease the period between child and adult status. The growth in provision includes new approaches to vocational preparation, general education and adult and continuing education. 'As each of these has evolved, so it has developed a network of relationships with other agencies (e.g. employers, examining bodies, parents) and sets of working practices underpinned by (often implicit) principles' (Harris and Clift, 1988). In other words the whole of the operational process of further education has had to readjust to the different forms of relationship between staff and students, teaching and training and the very organization of learning with a new client group.

Any new development in the further education system has to have time to adjust and find its place in order to become established. As with all cultural systems, there is a period of assimilation, when the new element or situation is treated with suspicion. The degree to which it ultimately becomes accommodated depends upon the extent to which the new and the existing systems or situations are prepared to adapt towards each other. So the flexibility inherent in the philosophy of equal opportunities within the further education system will only be of benefit to the student with learning difficulties and disabilities if providers are adaptable and innovative in implementing the new systems. These developments are closely allied to staff development and positive policy change for providing appropriately for these young people.

As many writers have commented (e.g. Hutchinson, 1992a; Corbett, 1992b), the systems necessary for providing a good service to students with learning difficulties and disabilities will also benefit large numbers of other, non-disabled students. The special needs arising from a disability are, in effect, a continuum of ordinary needs. Any attention paid to the transition needs of students with learning difficulties and disabilities, therefore, should be seen within the general context of the enhancement of confidence for all students as they move from school-based to more adult-oriented services. The time of leaving school is the opportunity to make a new start. As Fish (1988) has argued, it is also the opportunity to move away from the labelling of learners in categories of disablement and towards a more systematic recognition of their support needs. Thus, any reference to 'special' shifts from the individual to specialist support for certain learners to succeed in their learning.

Fish also provides a warning for all who work in and shape an organization. This relates to an institution's potential ability to become a handicapping factor, rather than a force for emancipation in the transition process. The education/training institution can influence a young person's life by the expectations it has of him or her, the type of provision it offers and the procedures by which it operates. As Fish (1988, p. 43) states: 'A college . . . can either compound society's handicapping effect on the individual learner or help to liberate them from it.'

FURTHER EDUCATION PROVISION

As we have seen, the legislation of the 1980s and 1990s has transformed the face of traditional further education throughout the United Kingdom. The centralization of control over what is to be taught and the assessment and management of learning linked to a new funding methodology have affected every individual and organization engaged in education, not only those involved with students with learning difficulties and disabilities. The emerging culture of competition between colleges in an educational market-place suggests that the spirit of entrepreneurial marketing is re-emerging as the guiding value of the system. As a result any reform of special education as an aspect of social justice is being jeopardized before it has time to be fully explored (Christensen and Dorn, 1994). The brief period of collaboration and co-operation between schools, colleges and employers, which marked the earlier development of provision for students with learning difficulties, may also once again be under threat.

Variety of further educational opportunities is a characteristic of this phase of provision. There are marked differences in style, enthusiasm and levels of progression in the development of courses. However, for school-leavers with special educational needs, the main forms of provision are as follows.

Link courses

This long-established provision in effect links a school with a nearby college of FE, with students attending for a half-day or a day a week. This symbiotic relationship allowed schools and colleges to complement each other in the curriculum offered to learners in their final school years. Schools are able to benefit from the increased access to equipment and resources and colleges can plan for progression from part-time to full-time attendance. Link courses were reported on by HMI in 1991 and were praised for the opportunities they provided in offering an introduction to an adult environment (Baginsky and Bradley, 1992). Link courses also provide chances to extend the curriculum choices of students who have been limited within a small, often special school, environment. The HMI Report identified three varieties of link programme:

(1) students go into college and are taught by tutors who are available, in time that is available;
(2) where students are able to extend and build upon their school curriculum;
(3) where teachers and lecturers jointly plan and deliver a curriculum based on their respective skills and on student need.

Links clearly have the potential for establishing effective school–college continuity. The progression from National Curriculum to National Vocational Qualification provides the opportunity for sharing the assessment and recording of achievements on nationally agreed criteria. However, the emergence of local management of schools and the incorporation of colleges places some uncertainty on the future of effective links. Under the provision of the Education Reform Act 1988 link course students under the age of 16 cannot be included in college numbers for budgetary purposes and schools will have to pay colleges for involvement in links. The delegation of funds may also mean that there will sometimes be insufficient funds for schools to buy into the courses that are worthwhile (Baginsky and Bradley, 1992). As a result some schools will inevitably start attempting to develop suitable facilities similar to those of an FE college. Despite these concerns, it is interesting to note that the Code of Practice (DfE, 1994a) continues to recommend strongly that schools should foster links with local further education colleges: 'this will help in the decision-making process and in the eventual transition itself, easing the move for both young person and staff at the further education college. Link provision with colleges can be of particular benefit to a young person with special educational needs by providing opportunities for integration, extending the curriculum and offering an induction into the adult environment of further education' (DfE, 1994a, para. 6.58).

Discrete special courses

For students who transfer from a special school to a college of further education, the discrete, segregated special course can be part of an unbroken thread of an emerging college culture. The enthusiasts for inclusive education have tended to overlook some of the advantages of the discrete course, which acts as a bridge to the ideal of autonomous learning in mainstream provision. It is unclear from the research conducted by Baginsky and Bradley (1992) if the majority of students with moderate learning difficulties who move between a mixture of discrete and integrated provision are receiving appropriate support for their individual needs or how much such provision actually costs. This evidence provides a strong rationale for the work of the FEFC in their attempts to establish a formula for funding the costs of the needs of students with learning difficulties and disabilities.

Students with more severe learning difficulties are almost exclusively attending college part-time, if at all. Such students pose a number of challenges to staff and the FEFC's demands for progression. They may need intensive physical care, one-to-one support and a curriculum that emphasizes individual need rather than one with a vocational emphasis. Staff who work with students with severe difficulties consider such students ill-served (Corbett, 1991). They may be in college, but they work alongside other students with severe learning difficulties and not with mainstream students. However, if colleges are developing modular courses which are perceived as beneficial for some students, they should be of benefit to all students.

Integrated 'mainstream' courses

There is increasing enthusiasm for integrating all students into modular mainstream courses in a wide range of areas in further education. This accords with the philosophy that students with learning difficulties and disabilities should not be on discrete general studies courses; instead there should be a continuum of choice and progression. The development of 'learning support', provided where and when it is required, is part of the more flexible response of colleges to the needs of all students at this stage in their lives. The notion of student 'rights and entitlements' fits more easily within these well-managed and sustainable programmes that incorporate students with disabilities into all areas of college life. In this context it is important to remember the distinction between disability and 'special need'. For example, the student with a hearing loss may be considered as having a disability; however, with an effective hearing aid he or she does not, necessarily, have a special need. Or the wheelchair user who is fully independent may experience fewer difficulties than the student with literacy and numeracy problems. Certainly neither student should be excluded from the opportunity to participate in an integrated college programme.

SUMMARY

Both the range of courses and the profile of students with learning difficulties and disabilities is altering in colleges of further education. Courses vary enormously, some being no more than half-day attachments for discrete groups of students, others being full-time integrated modular programmes of study. Most discrete courses are tied to the development of independence training as part of the general 'transition to adulthood'. However, the increasing recognition that students are entitled to choice has brought a wider variety of programmes. The culture of further education, along with its management style and increasingly adult expectations, makes the college experience markedly different from that of school. The wider opportunities to participate in a variety of subject choices and to be included in integrated groups are also usually a distinguishing feature.

4

Disability, disadvantage and vocational education

The development of further education has always been associated with vocational training. The present concentration on work preparation and the promotion of National Vocational Qualifications is, nevertheless, taking place when fewer school leavers are finding available work. Relevance to 'the world of work' has, somehow, become a mantra of curriculum planning in schools, as well as in colleges for all students. So as youth underemployment for a whole generation of young people has moved to the centre of the political agenda it has brought a renewed focus on the issue of equity in shared disadvantage for young people with learning difficulties and disabilities.

Equity, associated with a concern for access to employment opportunities, has gradually assumed a key status in the policy documents of many nations beyond the United Kingdom. Equality of opportunity has become a policy priority within education and training for a range of disadvantaged and under-represented groups, in the context of the Organisation for Economic Co-operation and Development (OECD).

> the economic costs to the community of the continuing existence of failure are certainly high; insufficient use by a country of its potential talents and skills, particularly at a time of emerging shortage in labour markets, is likely to prove to be an expensive waste. . . As important today are the cultural and democratic arguments for ensuring that all individuals, young and old, and all social groups, are given the opportunity to engage in the participation that education and training allows.
>
> (OECD, 1992, p. 89)

This realignment behind the social and moral rather than solely economic arguments for developing and extending the concept of 'quality' education and training echoes Skilbeck:

> There has been a tendency in the 1980s to submerge long-term

concerns for access, opportunity, equity and fairness in education to economic imperatives. It would be dangerous and unprincipled to continue along this track, given the realities of our societies. Significant educational disadvantage continues to occur. For curriculum and pedagogy, a next step is to seek a new synthesis which directly and concurrently addresses:

(i) the policy drive towards economic re-structuring;
(ii) the technological revolution;
(iii) the universalist principle embedded in the claim that every person has educational rights and freedom.

(Skilbeck, 1990, p. 79)

Skilbeck reminds us of the changing nature of Britain. The diminishing manufacturing base of the country has arisen as a result of the competition in labour costs with countries in the emerging Pacific basin and former Eastern Europe. The technological revolution has reduced the need for an unskilled workforce or even low levels of skill in the labour market. Training and education initiatives have been deliberately developed in the UK and have been given an ideological steer as vehicles for the political and economic restructuring of the country's economic fortunes. In this context it is interesting to note that the Department of Education and Science (DES) has been retitled the Department for Education (DfE) and that there are clear divisions of emphasis between the philosophies of the two key funding ministries involved in education and training (the Department of Employment and the Department for Education).

As Skilbeck has noted, these dilemmas of economic restructuring have confronted all governments and education services in late twentieth-century technological societies. As training has delayed and in some cases replaced entry to paid employment an increasing number of young people have become alienated from what is perceived to be an elitist hierarchy of education and training outcomes. Achievement in school has become even more important as the first indication of the transition to adult entitlement, to college and ultimately to the workplace. Education and training have become fundamental prerequisites for any sort of employment or income above the merest subsistence level or for the exertion of any influence on the wider society. These issues are exacerbated for young people with learning difficulties and disabilities. For them the costs of dependency are commensurately greater in both human terms, with lowered expectations, aspirations and ultimate fulfilment, and in financial terms: personally and as a 'cost' to wider society.

The programmes that have been created which seek to improve the capacity of such young people to participate in work in an increasingly complex technological environment do not correspond sufficiently to the accompanying social complexity of either young people's lives or the perceptions of employers. To sharpen this observation, we might even say that vocational qualifications such as General National Vocational Qualifications (GNVQs) and the sheer mass of certificates currently available are of less importance to this group than the establishment and development of properly negotiated personal care and support services. These could be co-ordinated to meet different needs according to individual personality and the individual's social circumstances. Such is the complexity of most people's circumstances that to concentrate simply on vocational training alone only highlights one dimension of the disadvantages faced by students with learning difficulties and disabilities.

These students are socially disadvantaged at the point of developing a career for a number of reasons:

(1) Schooling may have been inadequate and the young person may be unmotivated to learn within a formal educational system. Some young people will be entering college with poor examination results or none at all. Some will have been drop-outs from secondary school and others will have come through a segregated special school system, for up to eleven years, that prevents them from sharing successfully in a complete range of educational and social experiences.

(2) Vocational training programmes can seem to disadvantage students and young adults with learning difficulties and disabilities, as can other pre-employment initiatives. Some young people can stay for years within a cycle of different but badly co-ordinated training schemes. They never actually achieve either adequate qualification or ultimate paid employment. Of those who achieve a qualification within the expanding programme of National Vocational Qualifications, the majority show only modest results at levels 1 or 2. Most who receive special certificates or records of achievement related to elements of their training find that these have little currency with employers. As a result, there are a number of unskilled and unqualified young people fit for low-paid employment and always under the threat of being laid off at short notice. Young women in this category are doubly disadvantaged, either staying at home on completion of their formal schooling, or obtaining a job that earns them so little that independent living is impossible. In order to come closer to this goal, they have to do overtime, night shifts or a second job.

In traditional, industrial society terms, the theory of a person's value within the workplace has been argued something like this:

employment potential is determined by an employee's efficiency
and productivity. People who are not capable of benefiting from
training are not likely to be economically efficient or profitable.
By definition, disabled people are less capable than non-disabled
people, so they are both at a disadvantage and more expensive.
These attitudinal barriers are deeply rooted and whilst special
training initiatives have expanded for all young people they have
also helped to provide a new justification for the subtle perpetuation of prejudices that limit the social and economic position of
an increasing number of disillusioned and alienated young people.
Tomlinson (1985) was amongst the first commentators to express
concern that special education was in danger of being redefined
in order to include a new population of young people who
are socially deprived rather than academically disadvantaged.
As jobs have disappeared and special education services have
been redefined to incorporate disadvantage, we are beginning to
see the expansion of special provision for those who have failed
economically and vocationally as well as educationally.

The failure of human relations has also disadvantaged many
young people who are able to look back on nearly twenty years of
life in which they will have been treated ambivalently. This often
manifests itself in an adolescence where one perceives oneself,
not only as different, but also as unable to adjust to social situations. This can result in the repression of effective relationships
in the home, college and the workplace. The inability to fulfil
the expectations of those around you, or the hopes of significant
others, is a large burden for these young people. Their reaction
can be withdrawal and depression, or the outbursts of vandalism
and aggression seen in many of our towns and cities (Campbell,
1993). But often there is also a disappointing rapport between these
disadvantaged young people themselves. For young men there are
few opportunities to establish and maintain intimate and mutually
respectful relationships with girls and women. The language of
sexual relationships in a post-feminist world has brought risks
of ridicule and flat refusals to young men who prefer the old
certainties of male dominance. Repeated rounds of frustration at
this level can lead to other outlets for arousal and an indifference
to courses of vocational training.

In such circumstances and with such fragile relationships,
young people do really need more contact with trusted com-
panions who are capable of forming a social 'umbrella' of
support; perhaps adults who can encourage them to form wider
social networks and friendships: these can cross the boundaries
of generations, social status and gender. Whether this is possible
at a time when most young people's social circle is small and

tightly formed around a peer group culture is another question.

Finance, or the lack of it, has already been indicated as a source of real hardship to all young people without qualifications. The wage earned in low paid open employment is little different from the amount paid to young people on training programmes or as social security. For young people with learning difficulties and disabilities, some of whom may be entitled to higher allowances due to their disability, welfare entitlement may far exceed their realistic earnings potential. Independence for them becomes an illusion. Either they remain living at home with their families or they become economically dependent upon others, perhaps a spouse, partner or the state. If they try to live alone or to join groups they can rapidly run into financial difficulties. Where the bureaucratic procedures of adult status are only beginning to be understood, it is important to be able to turn to somebody for knowledgeable advice.

(3) A failure on the part of society forces many disadvantaged young people and adults to live on the border of illegality, and this is reflected in the policing and control of this age group. As we have already seen, many students and young people with learning difficulties and disabilities have had to cope with an indifferent educational experience followed by under-, or more commonly, unemployment; they live in fragile, often disappointing relationships and are often confronted with mistrust and disdain. They have to live in restricted economic circumstances and their housing needs are often inadequately met. No wonder then that they are more often in trouble than the better-educated and more socially competent young adult.

(4) Young people with learning difficulties and disabilities are not familiar with handling the requirements of an expanding bureaucracy, so they try to avoid contact with official authority, be it an institution or an agency. They need help in getting hold of such things as birth certificates, identity cards, passports or registration certificates. They need advice on how to obtain insurance and how to cancel it if it is inadequate or too expensive. They may need technical support in public correspondence, for example in response to notices or demands, or on how to appeal against procedural decisions that may affect their lives. The ability to respond effectively can be a key factor in raising an individual's level of self-confidence and feelings of self-esteem.

(5) The physical health of such young people is often a factor in the accumulation of multiple disadvantage. Poor hygiene and poverty are not automatic correlates of learning difficulties but they clearly affect levels of physical and psychological self-confidence. At school, physical development and patterns of

health can be observed and monitored as part of the curriculum and school life. If necessary, medical services and treatment can be arranged. Whatever one thinks of the government prescription for more 'competitive' games, which do not usefully relate to the promotion of health, this at least recognizes their place in physical growth. The advantages of the curricular safety-net of the National Curriculum for the promotion of health and sport is unavailable outside the formal education setting of school. There is no mandatory requirement or prescribed curriculum in sports and health in further education colleges, neither is there any medical monitoring. The opportunities for organized sport may be reduced in post-compulsory education as individuals are left to their own devices, but it is now widely acknowledged that lots of non-competitive activities – e.g. dance, yoga, aerobics, swimming – are ultimately better for the development of health than are organized team games. These might be better considered in further education for all students, especially those with learning difficulties and disabilities.

It is clear from the above that many young people with learning difficulties and disabilities can become multiply disadvantaged by a lack of basic care in the areas of personal hygiene, laundry and sometimes reasonable nourishment. If you lack basic amenities and have only a temporary address you are immediately disadvantaged in terms of employment. No dwelling, no job is a basic rule for all people of lower status in society.

EQUAL OPPORTUNITIES IN VOCATIONAL TRAINING

Any discussion of the relationship between the expansion of youth unemployment, disabled young people, training and education should include a consideration of equal opportunities. However, unlike legislation in other countries such as the USA, which has the Americans with Disabilities Act, passed in 1990 (Morrissey, 1991), the United Kingdom currently has no civil rights legislation relating to people with disabilities. The Disabled Persons (Civil Rights) Bill failed to pass through parliament in May 1994, despite apparent all-party support. It was considered to be too expensive, particularly to employers. The government is now seeking views on how disabled people can achieve greater independence, including accessibility to the labour market (Enable, 1994). In the current climate of change to a vocationally driven further education system there is still a failure to acknowledge the needs, rights and aspirations of people with disabilities. Those who do not fit easily into recognized courses and programmes that incorporate an element of progression to employment are to all effect denied educational choice and opportunity.

The Disability Discrimination Bill addresses some of these issues. It certainly strengthens the entitlement of disabled students to vocational education in colleges (Skill, 1995). Nevertheless there is a strong body of literature which critically evaluates pre-vocational education (e.g. Ainley, 1990a, 1990b; Gleeson, 1990; Corbett and Barton, 1992) but it is only recently that researchers have paid any attention to the rights of young people with disabilities. The bulk of the literature to do with students on vocational programmes (e.g. FEU publications) tends to concentrate on curricular content, assessment patterns and case studies of practice without paying any real consideration to the socio-political factors that underpin all these contentious issues.

Corbett and Barton (1992) have pointed out that unless vocational education and training schemes can begin to incorporate an explanation and examination of the socio-political discourses and contexts from which they have emerged, they will fail to alter the levels of disadvantage experienced by many young people. The creation of disadvantage in society is a complex and multi-faceted process. If college lecturers and training providers continue to focus solely on the learning needs of individuals rather than challenging the social inequalities that are factors in the creation of disadvantage, they will tend to perpetuate the image of vocational failure as individual inadequacy.

In order for training programmes to become more acceptable as an appropriate way forward for young people with learning difficulties and disabilities, both the programmes themselves and the agencies or colleges that are responsible for them need to consider their overall framework or policy for equal opportunities. This includes the need to change staff attitudes and what they perceive their roles and purposes to be. For example, if staff continue to act on behalf of individual students or trainees, including intervening on issues of bias and harassment, they continue to perpetuate, not equality of opportunity, but paternalism. While undoubtedly well-motivated, such actions serve to shape and reinforce the outward expressions of behaviour perceived to be unacceptable, rather than posing a challenge to the underlying values that have created them. Far from preventing a recurrence of bias, such practices perpetuate the image of students/trainees with learning difficulties and disabilities as dependent, more vulnerable and ultimately more unconventional individuals than the non-disabled. These paternalistic and materialistic attitudes need to be rejected in both further education and training schemes. It is not only by putting an emphasis on equal opportunities in employment and vocational training activities that discrimination will be challenged. Providing students with learning difficulties and disabilities with real knowledge and information about realistic jobs and training opportunities is also important.

The opportunities for realistic work experience will not be met if students participate only in token experiences where the real choice is taken by the lecturer or instructor, e.g. where the young man or woman participating in a 'basic skills' cookery session finds that the work is done for them by an instructor.

The requirement of vocational progression that is anticipated for all students in colleges of further education, including those with learning difficulties and disabilities, confronts managers and lecturers with a number of tensions. These start with the widely held belief that current training policies are inevitably linked to government intentions to control the focus of and potential numbers in the labour force. Set against this view is the argument that such vocational reform is long overdue and that this initiative provides an opportunity to promote the needs of disadvantaged and disabled young people. The actual experiences of young people reflect both aspects of this discourse. The compulsory nature of youth training provision and the government steer towards training credits and modern apprenticeships has forced virtually all 16-year-old school-leavers into schemes where their real choices are extremely limited. In the opinion of Corbett and Barton (1992) choice may have actually been narrowed rather than broadened, and vocational horizons lowered.

Ironically, the rise in the availability of NVQs and opportunities to accredit students for what they can demonstrate that they can do may mean that progression is more accessible to people with learning difficulties and disabilities. However, when it comes to the range of work experience available, these young people are rarely placed in the most sought-after employer-led schemes on employers' premises; more often they are found in isolated and sometimes simulated workshop-based provision. It is also interesting to note that the Student's Charter (DfE, 1993a), training credits and the development of an independent careers service suggest that the government wishes to place the power to choose in the hands of individual young people. However, it is questionable if students are provided with adequate information and/or experiences on how to choose or exercise effective choice. Where the experience of education has been negative and damaging to self-esteem, trainees and students with disabilities can sometimes find that they continue to be discriminated against in a system that has low expectations of them and offers them little real choice of vocational experiences.

The effectiveness of vocational training schemes in colleges is also often influenced by the very language in which the outcomes of employment training are discussed. The whole issue of competency statements may not deter staff who have grown familiar with the terminology. But for students and some employers this understanding may be less than complete. More worryingly, the new training opportunities and the manner in which they are accredited may sometimes lead to unrealistic employment expectations on the part of both the students with learning difficulties and disabilities and the staff working in the area.

The unequal levels of status and empowerment of staff working in the area of vocational training programmes in colleges and other centres both accentuates and reflects the stigmatized status of the disabled people with whom they work. Such perceptions serve only to reflect the vulnerability of individuals trapped by the model of learning difficulties and disabilities as illness.

The marginalized status of vocational training for people with disabilities will be challenged only when the work can be seen to be part of an overall equal opportunities initiative. There are, however, inevitable contradictions. People with learning difficulties and disabilities do need help and sustained support. At the same time this support may involve confronting them with the extent of their limitations in terms of employment.

If these young people are to be supported properly in their search for employment, they will have to be allowed to experience risk; a risk that is within a support structure of realistic challenge rather than a passive acceptance of the status quo. As has been pointed out, there are a number of factors inhibiting this facet of vocational choice and training. Within the terms of an 'enterprise culture' that stresses national training priorities rather than local ones, the contribution of disabled people may be considered superfluous and the amount of support they require extremely expensive in terms of resources, both human and mechanical. As courses for students and trainees with learning difficulties and disabilities become squeezed by market forces, the issues of equity and social justice begin to disappear from the agenda of priorities. Vocational choice, like any choice, needs to be informed. Fundamentally it depends on power, so for a relatively powerless group vocational choices and the discourses through which the issues surrounding it are debated become ever more restricted.

RESPONDING TO CHANGE IN YOUTH TRAINING

In 1974 the Manpower Services Commission was set up by the Department of Employment to co-ordinate industrial training, under the provisions of the Employment and Training Act 1973. In twenty years there have been numerous changes of title to the Commission, now called TEED (Training and Education Employment Division), but its purpose has remained constant: to develop training initiatives in response to rapidly shifting economic needs. To begin with, job creation programmes were formulated as a response to 'temporary' unemployment amongst both youth and adult groups. The more firmly established programmes for youth unemployment such as the Youth Opportunities Programme (YOP) began in 1977, to be replaced by the Youth Training Scheme (YTS) in 1983. For young people with learning difficulties and disabilities aged between 16 and 19, these schemes offered, for the first time, a form of progression into work that combined an opportunity to gain both simulated and actual work experience combined with a period of off-the-job training in a local college of further education. This period of transition also allowed a young person a period of time in which to develop social maturity. During its time the Youth Training Scheme had a significant impact on the direction of further education for students with learning difficulties and disabilities.

> It has changed market conditions and has placed colleges in direct competition with other organisations for education and training contracts and it has brought young people of more widely differing attributes, motivations and needs into many FE establishments.
> (Stoney and Lines, 1987, p. 97)

The introduction of learners without formal qualifications and with a range of different learning needs required a flexible response from colleges. Through the somewhat uneasy relationship of the Department of Employment (in the form of the Training Council: MSC) and the Department of Education (in the form of the LEA-funded further education colleges), students were gaining entry into a post-school system that had previously ignored them. The guiding principles that lay at the heart of much curriculum planning, and were dear to the hearts of lecturers recruited from the school system, led to the proliferation of courses in 'social and life skills'. These sat uneasily in the craft-dominated traditions of the further education and vocational education system, where an emphasis on training for specific targets was much more in line with the expectations of the Department of Employment. The evident deficiencies of vocational education led by the Department of Education became apparent in 1986 with the establishment of the National Council for Vocational Qualifications (NCVQ). The Council was set up to simplify and rationalize the complex network of vocational qualifications that spread across various employment structures.

THE NATIONAL COUNCIL FOR VOCATIONAL QUALIFICATIONS

As concern with the decline in training has increased, vocational qualifications have come to be considered the new lifeblood of colleges. Nevertheless, from its early beginnings in the craft and mechanical institutes, further education has been centred on vocational qualifications. It was with this recognition that the government focused on colleges of further education as the vehicles of change in vocational qualifications in the 1990s. The 1980s had been marked by a growing concern about the United Kingdom's declining international competitiveness; studies designed to look for ways to achieve improvement had been legion. The vocational education and training system of the United States, West Germany (as then) and Japan had highlighted the correlation between investment in training and improved economic and industrial performance.

The National Council for Vocational Qualifications was established in 1986 by the Department of Employment in order to create a coherent framework for the development of vocational qualifications across the UK. It continued the drive towards an employment-based reform of youth training and further education as a whole. This marked the growing dominance of the Department of Employment over the Department of Education in the arena of 'practical learning'. Drawing heavily on initiatives developed under the Training and Vocational Education Initiative (TVEI) and by the MSC, it was charged with the task of rationalizing the vocational awards and assessment patterns of up to 600 separate awarding bodies which offered about 6,000 qualifications with considerable overlap and duplication. The Council's early work 'in bringing order to the jungle of qualifications has been widely welcomed' (Smithers, 1993). For those working in the area of vocational training with students with learning difficulties and disabilities these sentiments are equally true. The level of qualification achieved by these students could never be truly quantified within the clear divisions of academic qualifications, but now for the first time there was an opportunity to assess and monitor student progression against a statement of competence considered to be relevant to work-related activity. They were qualifications, moreover, intended to facilitate entry into, or progression within employment, further education or training, and they were to be issued by a recognized body.

A growing concern has nevertheless developed about the Council's philosophy and the values which underlie the notion of progression. Smithers (1993) has argued that this is based on behavioural principles of competence statements which suggest that what one knows can be inferred from what one does. This appealing but simplistic form of assessment is compounded by the assumption that these outcomes can be measured and quantified using reliable criteria.

There can be no doubt that competency-based assessment has its place in the armoury of assessment patterns available to trainers and educators. However, it is a different question entirely to build the whole edifice of vocational assessment around these behavioural principles alone. The most obvious example of the competency-based approach, for the purposes of comparison, is the driving test, and it has been scathingly attacked for its naïvety (Smithers, 1994). The driving test is an assessment of standards which is based on showing what one can do in terms of driving ability, rather than where or how the ability was acquired. It is argued by the NCVQ that the same approach is entirely appropriate to vocational education, which is also about successful performance in the workplace. It has already been argued that such simplistic logic is inappropriate for many learners, but particularly those with learning difficulties and disabilities who may have a history of reduced experiences on which to build their portfolio of competence and progression:

> the National Council for Vocational Qualifications has in effect adopted the driving test model without the driving test. The way NVQs operate is a bit like having your motoring instructor also acting as your driving test examiner and without any assessment of overall performance. There is verification but there is less to this than meets the eye. Since verification is treated as a generic skill it may be carried out by those with no particular expertise in the occupational area being assessed.
>
> (Smithers, 1994, p. 2)

The concept of progression, whilst important in relation to further education and the generation of funding from the Further Education Funding Council, becomes more questionable in relation to students with learning difficulties and disabilities. It is beginning to be apparent that the pressures of NVQs and output-related funding are influencing the judgements of adequate performance in competency-based assessments. The narrow TEC and FEFC interpretation appears to offer wide opportunities for abuse and the lowering of standards. For students with learning difficulties and disabilities, it should, however, mean progress in a number of spheres and not solely towards employment as the NCVQ suggests. It should acknowledge progress from school into youth training or other courses, progress from special school on to integrated college courses, progress from a special discrete course into an inclusive course in the mainstream, as well as progress from a college course into employment. The quality and effectiveness of this progression is not always measurable by the limitations of objectivity and rationality, but has an additional requirement: the subjective recognition of the value of developing a better quality of human relationships. If there is only a narrow interpretation of progression, related to the achievement of NVQ level 2, the questionable quality and effectiveness of this 'progression' is once more analogous with the Smithers driving test, whereby you only pay your instructor, who is also your examiner, if you pass!

The concept of progression is nonetheless important in further education for the purposes of generating funding from the FEFC. But the concept of progression for students with learning difficulties and disabilities is anathema to some commentators. Kedney and Parkes (1988) have suggested that one of the principal purposes of further education provision is 'parking', or 'provision for the deferment of decisions about adult life'. Progression, in their view, is the antithesis of parking, but the two may, in fact, not be mutually exclusive. Parking can form a breathing space for both young people with learning difficulties and disabilities and their parents, as they move from child-oriented to adult services. A period of further education in the more adult atmosphere of a college can then contribute some of the necessary development and maturation for students who have been denied these opportunities in school settings.

THE DEVELOPMENT OF TECs, NATIONAL VOCATIONAL QUALIFICATIONS AND STUDENTS WITH LEARNING DIFFICULTIES AND DISABILITIES

The political link between further education and training and Britain's 'place in the industrial world' is no better exemplified than in the rationale for the development of the TECs (Training and Enterprise Councils), NVQs and the emerging GNVQs. Since the mid-1970s overt concern has been expressed about the challenges facing 'UK Ltd'. The World Economic Forum has placed Britain in twentieth place in terms of a skilled working population out of the twenty-two 'advanced industrial countries' assessed (Harrison, 1993). The concern for education and training is also echoed in the establishment of national education and training targets: 'by 1996, 50% of the workforce should be aiming at NVQs or units towards them'. This has huge implications for the development of opportunities for students and trainees with special needs, learning difficulties and disabilities. (For further discussion see Muir, 1993.)

The historical divide that exists between the worlds of work and education and the decline in the numbers of young people gaining recognized training qualifications have also been well documented in the media. The lack of integration of education and vocational training is a national problem and it can affect access to NVQs for all individuals. In order to tackle this in 1988 the government announced that it would set up TECs in England and Wales and their equivalent bodies – local enterprise companies (LECs) – in Scotland. It is the role of the TECs/LECs to develop appropriate training and enterprise strategies and services in their particular geographical location. They are regional, incorporated, employer-led bodies responsible to the government through the Secretaries of State for Employment. Their function includes working with the Employment Department and the Departments of Trade and Industry and for Education. Increasing expectation is placed on the development of local links with a range of groups in a TEC region and the funding of specific training initiatives. One of the main training programmes funded by TECs is 'Youth training', in which young people with a range of special needs are entitled to participate.

In the guidance paper, *A Strategy for Skills* (Department of Employment, 1991), it was suggested that the necessary framework for re-skilling the workforce was in place. The key priorities for skill training were identified:

(1) Employers must invest more effectively in the skills their businesses need.
(2) Young people must have the motivation to achieve their full potential and to develop the skills the economy needs.
(3) Individuals must be persuaded that training pays and that they should take more responsibility for their own development.
(4) People who are unemployed and those at a disadvantage in the jobs market must be helped to get back to work and to develop their abilities to the full.
(5) Education and training providers must offer high-quality and

flexible provision which meets the needs of individuals and employers.

(6) Enterprise must be encouraged throughout the economy, particularly through the growth of small businesses and self-employment.

Thus, from the outset the NVQ framework was set for a clash of ideologies, purpose, and ultimately sources of funding, between various government departments. The historical legacy of a myriad craft certifications meant that qualifications were traditional awards from a variety of organizations, set to a variety of standards. Through linking with the private sector and local business, the TECs were charged with changing this tradition. TECs have now taken over from the former Training Agency and through the introduction of NVQs they are delivering national standards of competence. These initiatives are intended to counter the demographic change in work patterns across the United Kingdom. As the 'shake-out' in British industry has continued to alter patterns of working, it has created a mismatch between the supply and demand sides of the training equation. In other words, the new vision of training and retraining has been developed in order for the United Kingdom to be seen as a competitive player in both a national and global economic market. The economic survival of British industry is the rationale for driving the initiative.

Where, we might ask, does that place the real needs of students with special training needs or learning difficulties and disabilities?

WHAT IS AN NVQ?

The National Council for Vocational Qualifications was set up by the government in 1986 to develop quality assurance in vocational education and training. It had a responsibility to:

- establish 'Hallmark' qualifications to meet the needs of employers;
- locate these qualifications within a new structure which everyone can use and understand;
- accredit and approve quality assurance;
- ensure that National Vocational Qualifications develop people with the competences required in all sectors, in order to compete successfully in world markets.

Within this responsibility for rationalizing qualifications lies the function of the National Vocational Qualification. An NVQ is considered to be a kitemark and quality symbol describing a national standard of competence across all sectors of employment and at all levels of the workforce. Competence is identified as the ability to perform a job in employment, measured against standards laid down by industry. Learning and training for the qualifications can be done in any way, at any place and over no predetermined time scale. Candidates may also make as many attempts as are necessary to achieve the required standards. This feature is of particular relevance in relation to students with learning difficulties and disabilities. It helps to counter the suggestion that many of these young people reach the end of their school and college careers ill-equipped or unable to progress with basic vocational and technical skills.

> the low standards and expectations of special schools and the lack of effective teaching in mainstream schools is equally unsatisfactory and both represent a failure to assist young people in their development and serve to limit their life chances.
>
> (OECD/CERI, 1985)

The NVQs are made up of 'units' of competence; like building blocks or a jigsaw, they come together with account being taken of an individual's achievements and existing experience. NVQs are awarded at a specific level from 1 to 5 and will eventually cover all occupations in all sectors of industry. It is estimated that level 2 is roughly equivalent to five good GCSEs; level 3 is on a par with A levels. Such judgements raise immediate questions about the wisdom of attempting to compare or equate the products of academic A level and more practically based NVQ courses. This has particular relevance for students with learning difficulties, who in attempting a unit of basic competence at level 1 may be achieving a giant personal goal, but one that makes little impression on potential employers.

All NVQs are linked into a national framework and are recorded on a national database:

level 5: professional/senior managerial
level 4: managerial/specialist
level 3: complex skilled and/or supervisory work
level 2: a broad range of skills and responsibilities
level 1: foundation and basic work activities

The key characteristics of NVQs revolve around the expectations that they reflect a national standard, taking account of market and employment patterns. It is anticipated that they will be free from barriers to access and progression and that they will be available to all. This freedom from discriminatory practice and equal opportunities is explicitly directed towards gender, race and creed but makes no such specific statement to people with special needs or disabilities. The final characteristic of NVQs is the work-based method of assessment and the opportunity they provide for credit accumulation towards a nationally recognized record of vocational achievement.

The NCVQ was set the target of creating the NVQ framework, or at least covering 80 per cent of the requirements of the workforce, by the end of 1992. By that date it had achieved this target, 'with qualifications covering 83 per cent of the requirements' (Jessup, 1993, p. 14).

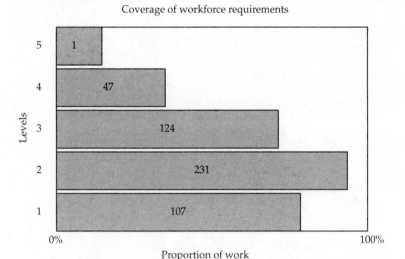

Coverage of workforce requirements

Figure 4.1 *NVQ framework as at 14 April 1993*

The NVQ framework indicates that there is a good spread of coverage at levels 1, 2 and 3, but that it is thinner at levels 4 and 5 (see Figure 4.1). At the present time there is only one NVQ at level 5, and that is in management. A fundamental feature of the NVQ framework is the unit system of accreditation. All NVQs are in the form of units that can be separately assessed and separately certificated. However, although the assessment model allows unit certification, awarding bodies appear reluctant to offer it either quickly or effectively in all areas:

> what we expect is that people will get certificates showing their units credited. Units are like mini-qualifications in their own right which certificate competence in particular functions. Units are not insignificant achievements. Even at level 1, a unit credit

represents something of tangible value and in the real world. If you take something like the driving test, which is a unit in the NVQ system, it is quite a significant level of achievement which people are motivated to gain.

(Jessup, 1993, p. 15)

Such comments relating the NVQ to the driving test are interesting in the light of the criticisms referred to by Smithers. Standards to be assessed are developed by representatives of employers and employer organizations that have been nominated as lead bodies and recognized as such by the Department of Employment. Lead bodies are not necessarily legally constituted as such, but are usually either an umbrella organization or a loose federation of separate employer bodies connected with a particular sector of industry. These are often based on the former industrial training boards such as the Agricultural Training Board for the development of agricultural services and commercial horticulture. Assessment is carried out in any one of thousands of approved centres, including employers' premises, colleges of further education and training suppliers. It is not necessary for NVQs to be assessed in the workplace, although in some cases it may make sense to do so. What is required is that the assessment should make sense, taking into account the outcomes that are to be achieved. Assessment requires the presentation of evidence of competence. Competence can be demonstrated through projects, assignments, prior achievement in work or in life generally. It can also emerge from oral or written tests of knowledge. The characteristics of NVQs are to legitimize any form of assessment that provides valid evidence of competence. They are intended to open up access to everyone, including those with learning difficulties and disabilities/special needs.

In 1991 the newer qualification, the General National Vocational Qualification, was planned for introduction into schools and colleges. This programme is intended primarily for 16- to 19-year-olds. Whilst NVQs are intended to be vocation specific, the GNVQ provides a more broad-based approach to vocational education. In addition to acquiring basic skills and understanding of the underlying principles that form the basis of a vocational area, all students gaining a GNVQ will be expected to achieve a range of core skills. It is anticipated that the combination of vocational attainment plus core skills will provide a foundation from which students can progress to either further or higher education, into employment or further training.

The rationale for GNVQs is to provide a more vocationally oriented alternative to A levels (the Gold Standard referred to by the DfE) for the increasing numbers of 16-year-olds staying on in full-time education (e.g. the GNVQ at level 3 is intended to be equivalent to a pass at A level). During the first year of take-up (in 1992) the programme had a limited impact in occupational areas and in the numbers of schools and colleges involved. However, by 1994–95 the qualification has become available in a range of occupational areas and a GNVQ at level 1 will become available. These developments link closely to the expectation that all awarding bodies monitor their approach to equal opportunities in relation to special needs. It is interesting to note that data in 1993 suggested that 3.5 per cent of students taking GNVQs categorize themselves as having some kind of special need (Jessup, 1993, p. 17).

The introduction of NVQs and GNVQs is an attempt to develop an overall framework of coherent progression to qualification. It builds upon the government White Paper *Education and Training for the 21st Century* (DES, 1991a), which attempted to outline a vision of linked education and training. All young people will be expected to have experienced the National Curriculum between the ages of 5 and 16 in school and then progress to the three primary routes for qualification: the academic A/AS level, the GNVQ middle road or the NVQ route. As with NVQs, GNVQs will be specified in the form of outcomes to be achieved and will be made up from a number of units. Credits will be awarded for each unit separately. The accumulation of credits may be used in the building of the award of a full GNVQ. The idea is that everyone aged 16–19 is expected to go through one of these three routes (see Figure 4.2).

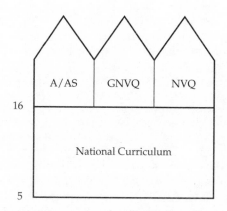

Figure 4.2 *Three routes post-16*

The potential of the NVQ as a means of raising equal opportunities in access to employment rests in the acknowledgement that, even with support, some students with learning difficulties and disabilities will have to work harder and longer to obtain the same vocational qualifications as their non-disabled colleagues. The individual needs of students with learning difficulties, physical and/or sensory disabilities are fairly readily apparent, but there are also the needs of students with psychological and emotional difficulties. These can make progression towards desired objectives more problematic. The NCVQ claims to recognize the need to incorporate flexibility into their programmes. This means an allowance for alternative forms of assessment, provided they generate valid evidence of competence, and provided there are no inbuilt restrictions on the duration of education and training or the timing of assessments. This suggests a recognition that whilst no concessions should be sought on the grounds of *disability*, there does need to be a positive and flexible response in terms of both the range of qualifications available and the support needed to achieve completion. The selection criteria for point of entry and the assessment and evaluation procedures nevertheless fail to recognize the impossibility for some people with disabilities ever to achieve full competence within the present NVQ framework. For example, a blind person is never likely to achieve a full NVQ in office skills. Opportunities for different routes to qualification have certainly been opened up by the development of NVQs, but so too have routes to the ultimate frustration of ambition!

This issue raises a number of considerations in respect to attitudes to the competences of disabled people. The whole role of disabled people in society is at present under scrutiny. Disability as an equal opportunities issue is concentrating public concern in the same fashion as it has forced attention upon issues of race and gender. Nowhere is the debate more concentrated than in the development of vocational qualifications. Hutchinson is adamant:

> It is clear, in the field of vocational education and training, that impairment and disability will present difficulties for the individuals involved. What we should be concerned with, at the outset, is that impairment and disability do not become a handicap as a result of the environment within which the individual finds him or herself.
>
> (Hutchinson, 1992a, p. 165)

The National Council for Vocational Qualifications is well aware of the need for an attitudinal change, within an overall framework of equal opportunities, towards students with special training needs. The Employment Department defines 'special needs' as the needs arising from any personal disadvantage which significantly impairs the ability of the individual to participate successfully in training for work. The department defines 'special training needs' as the training needs arising from disability or other personal disadvantage which significantly impairs the trainee from undergoing successfully a course of training. This seems to imply that the concept of special need – closely allied to learning difficulties and disabilities – is about individuals and their distinctive needs for support. 'Equal opportunity', on the other hand, is more about the development of policy for groups of individuals with common characteristics. The link between the two is obvious, but they are not the same thing. This concept of 'special training need' nevertheless suggests that the Council is recognizing a broader range of social disadvantage than the tightly confined concept of 'learning difficulty and disability'. The definitions 'special need' and 'special training need' acknowledge that some individuals and/or groups of individuals may experience forms of social disadvantage separate from or in combination with a learning difficulty or disability. Muir (1993) has usefully distinguished three categories within the concept of special training needs:

(1) access-related needs; these are related to the removal or overcoming barriers to training and employment, which face some groups disproportionately. This may involve the provision of child-care, special aids, transport or flexible training times for people living in remote areas.
(2) need relating to training content and duration; this might mean the provision of preliminary or extra training in order to arrive at the same starting point as other trainees. An example might be English language training for those for whom English is not their first language, or mobility training for a blind person.
(3) need unrelated to occupational training; this might involve counselling for people to become sufficiently motivated to enter and thus benefit from a training programme. People with disabilities might require advice and counselling on such issues as personal finance and social security in relation to benefit entitlement and entry to employment.

In summary, there are a number of advantages claimed for the NVQ framework and the system of credit accumulation that appear to have particular benefits to students with learning difficulties and disabilities:

- easier access to qualifications;
- units can be built up over time;
- students can be motivated by the immediate recognition of their achievements;

- different parts of a learning programme and different modes of learning can be integrated;
- more flexible learning programmes can be designed;
- a clear statement of the student's competence can be made in language familiar to an employer.

Such characteristics are immediately attractive for any development of the education and training of young people who have left school with no formal qualifications and have been less able to take advantage of educational and training opportunities than their non-disabled peers. There are nevertheless a number of obstacles to access; the major ones being scepticism and reluctance to change. Levels of resourcing are also a constant theme as the goalposts for future funding continue to change. The income per student is driven down and the targets set are driven up. There is also still a large number of people who argue that people with learning difficulties and disabilities are not capable of achieving the same as others in the world of work. This is exacerbated when employers and members of TEC boards claim that level 1 NVQ units have no credibility, immediately undermining and failing to take account of where some students are starting from. As has been pointed out, 'For many people level 1 is not only a major milestone in their lives but it gives them the opportunity to go on to level 2 and 3' (Weinstock, 1993, p. 8). To this end the development of performance indicators and endorsed certificates for some people with disabilities cannot come soon enough.

TRANSITION TO ADULTHOOD AND THE ROLE OF SUPPORTED EMPLOYMENT

The majority of people with learning difficulties and disabilities are dependent on a combination of low-paid, part-time employment and benefits, in order to meet their living costs. This is not because they do not want to work full-time, but more because they are unable to maintain an acceptable quality of life without income from benefits. The recent introduction of the disability working allowance has attempted to address the wage/benefits trap, but evidence is already emerging that loss of benefits remains a major disincentive to moving into full-time employment.

Another fundamental barrier to the employment of people with learning difficulties and disabilities lies in the ideology of 'dependency'. Lane (1980), in his early study of employment and training, characterized the employment training pattern of a group of people with Down's syndrome as 'social education'.

There was little realistic anticipation that people with Down's syndrome in a training centre would ever achieve the target of open employment. Courses in social education, social and life skills and 'significant living without work' consequently formed a significant focus in the newly developing further education curriculum for students with learning difficulties. More recent studies have come to recognize the fallacy of the social education movement and instead acknowledged that employment is the ultimate goal of all young people. It is, therefore, also considered to be a legitimate aspiration for young people with learning difficulties and disabilities (OECD/CERI, 1988; FEU, 1990, 1992). A job is one of the ultimate marks of adult status, a rite of passage, and for most people it forms a substantial part of the framework of their lives. As Hegarty (1990) has pointed out, one of the most ordinary things about adult life is employment and many of our formative childhood and 'pretend' experiences are related to jobs. In the same fashion school education and training prepares for the job market by developing personal skills, craft skills and qualifications, all of which are prerequisites for securing employment.

The benefits of employment can be usefully summarized as follows:

- a job provides economic independence and a better standard of living;
- a job empowers people by enabling them to become self-determining rather than living their own lives as others dictate;
- a job provides status that influences positive attitudes and public visibility: 'by demonstrating that they can be accepted, productive and an integral part of society, by working in integrated work settings people with learning difficulties increase the likelihood of being accepted by the non-disabled community' (Henstock, 1989);
- workplaces in integrated settings provide opportunities for social interaction and friendships;
- a job is one of the ways in which the majority of people continue to learn and develop skills, competences and intellectual abilities;
- work gives our lives a routine and structure. Successful employment and job satisfaction give people a sense of fulfilment, achievement, confidence and dignity;
- developing employment opportunities is cost-effective. A job involves people exercising their independence and choice to become self-supporting, rather than remaining dependent upon a lifetime of support services.

So, just as it is recognized that all young people can benefit from employment, it is also recognized that those with learning difficulties will require support if this employment is to take place in the wider, more competitive community. Griffiths (1990) speaks for all those with learning difficulties and disabilities when he claims that too often, too little is expected of them and a more informed and open estimation of their abilities is perhaps their greatest need. This suggestion echoes the responses of the National Development Group for the Mentally Handicapped (1977) which stated that many, then called 'mentally handicapped' people, given suitable training and help, are capable of working in both sheltered and open employment.

There are, nevertheless, significant factors which appear to act as barriers to open employment, the most fundamental of which are the supply of jobs and the number of suitable people available to do them. The supply of jobs available is related to the structural characteristics of the local economy, but it is also dependent upon the nature of the work itself. The tendency of employers to have a homogeneous view of disability means that trainees with learning difficulties and disabilities and people with learning difficulties in particular are placed in low regard. Too often they are thought capable of undertaking only repetitive and 'simple' tasks and if such work does not exist then such a person will not be considered as employable. Such issues are particularly pertinent in connection with jobs where 'initiative' is seen as a prerequisite for work. In the same way that special provision in schools and colleges can mean segregated provision, special work placements can become discrete enclaves set in sheltered settings where initiative on the part of the employee is neither required nor encouraged. Attendance in these 'closed' settings limits the necessary social experience and knowledge of employment that is an anticipated part of the normal everyday life of those working in non-segregated settings.

TRANSITION AND STUDENTS WITH LEARNING DIFFICULTIES AND DISABILITIES

There are numerous interpretations of the term 'transition'. It can include passing from one classroom to another, as well as being a comment upon shifts in status and position throughout a life cycle. Significant markers or transition points occur throughout one's life, such as the establishment of an adult identity, establishing a family, career progression and retirement. The impact of these phases in one's life is influenced by a range of variables and 'rites of passage'.

The 'rites of passage' for most young people in Western society are not clearly defined. For adolescents with learning difficulties and disabilities setting out on their journey towards adulthood they are even more poorly developed. The decision-making and choice that is a normal part of the period leading up to a child's sixteenth birthday is often less available to them than for their counterparts of average ability. There is evidence to suggest that at the point of leaving school, old and known certainties begin to change. The long-established systems of support for both young people and their families are placed under new stress. Many young people with learning difficulties and disabilities clearly show the need for a properly thought-out programme to help them to overcome the gap between compulsory schooling and work (Fish, 1990). There is also the possibility that it is only on leaving school that some students begin to see the relevance of continued education.

As Fish (1990) points out, successful transition to adulthood should result 'in a satisfactory life style and a sense of personal value in the family, neighbourhood and the community. The same opportunities for independence, access and choice should be available to all.'

There are also economic, value-for-money reasons why the concept of supported transition needs to follow smoothly from ten to twelve years' investment in education. Long-term dependent care is ultimately much more expensive than supported independence and useful work. Not only will such support cost the country less in the long term but it will accord individuals with learning difficulties and disabilities the status and dignity of contributing adults in the society in which they live.

The inequality of access to the labour market for disabled people is reflected in the unequal distribution of reward. Among those who are employed there are typically fewer on high earnings and in good conditions of work and many are working longer hours for lower earnings. Griffiths provides an illustration of how changes in employment patterns and the rise in technological efficiency can affect the employment prospects of young people with learning difficulties, seeking unskilled occupations:

> For example, a laundry which provides 50 jobs may close and instead two estate agents, three specialist retail outlets for electronic goods, a restaurant and a solicitor's office may open in the same area. There will have been no statistical job loss, but most of the ex-laundry employees may become unemployed because they cannot be recruited for the new jobs. New arrivals or commuters from another area fill them.

(Griffiths, 1990, p. 12)

Whether this is a restatement of economic reality or a confirmation of political and economic inequality, the result is a restriction upon people with learning difficulties and disabilities in their attempts to achieve adult status.

Fish (1990) has outlined some of the issues that restrict the quality of life for disabled people in Western society:

(1) Just as negative stereotypes and labels often limit the opportunities of individuals in their move from childhood to adulthood, so does their age and the starting point on this road to transition. Stereotyping implies some fundamental questions about the influence of schools and colleges in relation to their curriculum offer to young people at the more severe end of the disability spectrum: e.g. are people with severe learning difficulties really able to benefit from transitional choices? Is supported open employment considered an outcome of transition? (Fish, 1990, p. 5.)

(2) Time is an important feature of the preparation for transition to an adult working life. As Fish (1990) points out, 'in a number of countries it is recognized that the transition of those with disabilities may take much longer than their contemporaries'. This entitlement to extended education and training is now acknowledged in the United Kingdom as a feature of the Further and Higher Education Act 1992. As has already been noted, until the 1970s it had tended to be only the more able (and financially solvent) students who had been entitled to delay entry into employment, as they went through university. The increase in further education and training for the less academically gifted raises new questions about the adequacy of support over an extended period. The availability of support has to balance between the development of personal and vocational independence and the concerns of employers and the prejudices of wider society.

SUMMARY

The increased awareness of the importance of national vocational training for all young people has coincided with an increase in youth unemployment. The absence of effective political strategies for creating jobs has drawn more attention to the purpose of further education. Young people, disadvantaged by unemployment, have been encouraged to enter vocational training schemes intended to help them develop flexible skills and introduce them to the work ethic. For young people with learning difficulties and disabilities the chance to participate in flexible vocational training seems at best contradictory, if not deliberately cynical. Young people who have spent their school years being differentiated from their more academically capable peers and being made to 'know their place' are unlikely to become the highly mobile and quick-witted workforce that the country really requires. The introduction of National Vocational Qualifications (NVQs) and General National Vocational Qualifications (GNVQs) provides narrow competence-based measures which have the potential for crediting all workers, including those with no previous qualifications. It is too early to know if they will also allow students and employers to develop *all* their potential and aspirations.

5

Curriculum influences and models of teaching and learning

This chapter is about the ways in which teachers teach in further education. To this end, it will present models and teaching strategies that are taken from a number of sources, many of which are already well known. The chapter is also about teacher development in the rapidly shifting area of equal opportunities in further education for students with learning difficulties and disabilities. It sets out to question an education system that must beware of becoming constrained by a mechanistic conservatism within the National Curriculum and the mystique of specialism that has clung to those who work in special education. Our point of departure is the central precept that all learning in further education is not simply the acquisition of skills and knowledge but about valuing relationships. Thus, for all learners and not only those with learning difficulties and disabilities, an emphasis on the partnership between student and teacher is likely to enhance learning. This consideration means that the student is at the centre of the negotiations and that any strategy for the development of teaching is, ultimately, about learners and teachers developing together.

Such notions are not new – Rogers (1965) clearly established the characteristics of a student-centred approach to learning. More recently the ideas have been explored by Faraday and Harris (1989). Through such an approach the teacher/tutor acts as both a facilitator and a resource person. For their part, students/trainees are responsible for sharing the planning and construction of the curriculum, or at least participating in making choices. Learning is self-initiated and often involves enquiry and discovery. The learner is also responsible for evaluating outcomes and reflecting on the results. For students with learning difficulties and disabilities and their teachers, such notions may well accord with student-centredness. For others who are more subject- or skill-focused it may at first be a difficult concept to grasp, for such an undertaking involves changes in teaching strategies and organizational adaptations and that at heart means changes in philosophy and values.

SOME BASIC CONSIDERATIONS IN THE EVOLUTION OF THE NEGOTIATED CURRICULUM PROCESS

The FEU (1986) model of curriculum development shown in Figure 5.1 suggests that styles of teaching and appropriate strategies for learning are but one part of a totally interdependent curriculum process. So integral is each of the sum of the parts, that however well resourced the implementation phase of the process may be, this cannot, for example, make up for inaccurate needs analysis or inappropriate programme planning at the design stage. The model also suggests that versions of all four processes are necessary at whatever level provision is being planned: from the level of the locality, via individual institutions, down to and including those concerned with individual programmes. The model also reminds us that at each level

> the clients as well as the providers need to be involved, whether the former be identifiable sections of the community or individual learners, vocational sectors or specific companies. Clients and providers need to be involved in the analysis of needs and judgements about priorities, the negotiation of learning programmes appropriate to those needs and priorities, and the evaluation of the extent to which the latter have been met. Implementation must also involve the active participation of the learner, and be flexible enough to adapt to different learning styles.
>
> (FEU, 1989, p. 6)

Research would tend to suggest that whilst some individual teachers and lecturers would support such a radical reappraisal of the teaching role, for teachers as a whole the realignment of power and responsibility will be hard to accept. For many of them it is the teacher who has the ultimate responsibility for the day-to-day management and presentation of the curriculum to the learner. However, as children grow to adulthood teaching becomes a more collaborative exercise, with planning being shared between colleagues and students. The culture of teaching and the role of the teacher will have to change.

Research also suggests that the role of the teachers in schools and further education colleges is essentially conservative, present-oriented and individualistic (e.g. FEU, 1989). Teachers have tended to avoid long-term planning and collaboration with their colleagues and have resisted involvement in whole-school

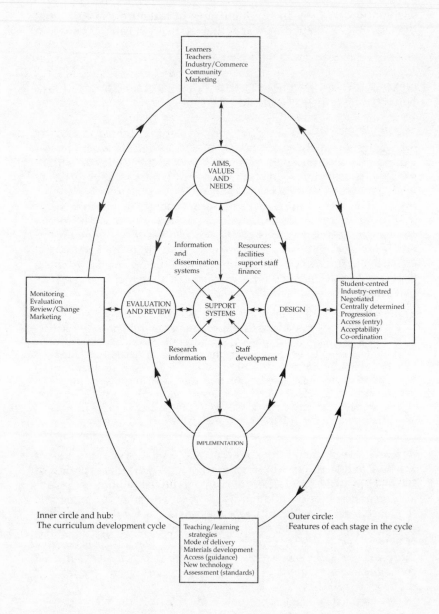

Learners
Teachers
Industry/Commerce
Community
Marketing

AIMS,
VALUES
AND
NEEDS

Information
and
dissemination
systems

Resources:
facilities
support staff
finance

Monitoring
Evaluation
Review/Change
Marketing

EVALUATION
AND REVIEW

SUPPORT
SYSTEMS

DESIGN

Student-centred
Industry-centred
Negotiated
Centrally determined
Progression
Access (entry)
Acceptability
Co-ordination

Research
information

Staff
development

IMPLEMENTATION

Inner circle and hub:
The curriculum development cycle

Outer circle:
Features of each stage in the cycle

Teaching/learning
strategies
Mode of delivery
Materials development
Access (guidance)
New technology
Assessment (standards)

Figure 5.1 *Process of curriculum development*

Source: FEU (1986)

decision-making in favour of gaining marginal improvements in time and resources to make their own individual teaching circumstances easier. This teaching-room-centredness is a characteristic shared by all teachers, and its importance is an issue of particular relevance to those providers working in the area of 'special education' (in whatever phase of education). What a teacher thinks, believes or assumes is bound to have a powerful influence on the way in which they formulate a philosophy of teaching. This, in turn, influences their organization of learning and how it is translated into action.

The world of learning difficulties and disabilities is often perceived as a small social system within the wider orbit of mainstream further education. Status and the intensity of personal/professional interaction is by eyeball-to-eyeball contact rather than departmental memo. For some this has created a confusion about the value of professional status, a confusion that has coincided with the decline of the 'deficit model' explanations of learning difficulties, whereby the purpose of the teacher in the special education service was to identify individual deficiency and remedy it, rather than to recognize proficiency and develop it. The educational and moral notions of equality, further opportunity and curriculum progression into the mainstream have increased. However, so have ambiguities about the nature and value of the contribution of teachers and lecturers within this more negotiated environment and common curriculum framework of NVQs and integrated classes.

DEVELOPING THE CONCEPT OF STUDENT-CENTRED LEARNING

The fundamental principles for the development of a student-centred approach can be summarized as follows:

- learners are of equal value, regardless of their individual strengths and weaknesses;
- learners have access to appropriate programmes and resources in the locality, within the physical and financial constraints prevailing at the time;
- learners have the opportunity and positive encouragement to maximize their own potential achievement;
- all learners are treated equally and benefit from certain common experiences, regardless of the nature of their learning programmes.

Thus, although the concept of learner-centredness is, for our purposes, being applied as a key feature in the teaching of students or trainees with learning difficulties and disabilities, it is part of an overall curriculum philosophy of 'entitlement'. This framework of entitlement can and should be implemented with all learners. As the FEU points out: 'no-one should be denied access to successful learning strategies and enriching curriculum elements and they should form part of the educational entitlement for everyone over the age of 14' (FEU, 1989, p. 8). The constituent parts of curriculum entitlement can be outlined in the form of seven phases:

(1) **learner-centredness**: this involves the arrangement and management of educational provision, in order that learners are involved in negotiating the content, style and targets for their programmes. Thus, learners are to be encouraged to become involved, even at the formative stages of programme planning.
(2) **maximized accessibility**: this is about ensuring that there are no artificial barriers to programmes, such as unnecessary entry requirements, and that every effort is made to provide for all the potential learners in a locality;
(3) **integrated curriculum**: this involves making connections between the various elements of learning; between the subjects, or academic aspects of the components of a programme, between activities in an institution and outside it, and between past, present and future experience;
(4) **guidance and counselling**: this comprises a wide range of support for learners including educational, vocational and personal guidance provided as a part of both learning programmes and the institutional infrastructure;
(5) **personal development**: an important consideration in the design of programmes is to ensure that there is both opportunity and encouragement for the development of personal qualities such as effectiveness and role awareness;
(6) **optimized progression**: all learners should have the opportunity to achieve their own personal targets and maximize their progress on a particular programme in order to advance to another programme or employment;
(7) **equality of opportunity and experience**: this is a starting-point and implies that institutions should move from equality of access, through equality of treatment, towards equality of outcomes.

(FEU, 1989)

In order for us to incorporate these phases of entitlement in the context of teaching and learning, it is necessary to understand why and how people learn at all. Learning arises from activity. Teaching approaches need to reflect the management of this activity if learning is to be successful. For students with learning difficulties and disabilities, it is worth remembering that a wide variety of teaching methods have probably already been employed in the belief that effective learning depends upon matching tasks to individually different learning styles. These learning styles will need not only to be accommodated but also developed. The effective management of learning on the lecturer's/trainer's part therefore becomes the key to effective personal development on the part of the learner.

SYSTEMATIC AND INDIVIDUALISTIC APPROACHES AND THEIR APPLICATION TO STUDENTS WITH LEARNING DIFFICULTIES

At the heart of the debate on all aspects of special education, at any stage of personal growth and development, is the consideration of personal difference and the measurement of difference. This raises ethical considerations about the extent to which it is legitimate for teachers to impose on or set the limits to the learning experiences of students. However, there are a number of fundamental features at the heart of learning. These are not very different from the commonsense planning that we all employ for individual survival, such as in carrying out such simple tasks as making a cup of coffee or remembering where one has left the car! The key to the application of learning is its deliberate intention to bring about either temporary or permanent changes in behaviour. Organizing the management of teaching for groups of students with learning difficulties and disabilities follows the same deliberate, systematic approach that the concept of planning implies. This is often in marked contrast with the realities of the learning activity that takes place in many college classrooms and workshops.

Any deliberate organization and imposition of learning is to some extent a denial of a learner's natural capacity to seek out activity and information that is considered to be personally worth while. A number of commentators on teaching approaches in schools (Ainscow and Tweddle, 1979; Shipman, 1985; Ainscow, 1994) have highlighted some of the assumptions and objections that are inherent in any attempts to impose management of learning as a totally prescriptive activity. Such models assume that all learning, whether teacher directed or open-ended, is, in fact, enhanced by the teacher actually creating and taking charge of both the learning exchange and the environment in which it takes place. These models also assume that it is possible for teachers to know and plan, in relation to the knowledge, skills and attitudes of learners in a class. Even in the comparatively controlled environment of a school, such assumptions are open to challenge. In post-school settings they are even more open to question.

Any marginal intervention by teachers/lecturers could be interpreted as a form of exploitation or distortion of individual development. Such an argument has as its premise the notion that any attempts to match learning environments and teacher-devised learning sequences with the supposed capacities of learners is a tacit or overt form of discrimination on the part of teachers.

Such charges of discrimination or exploitation raise a number of issues. As previously mentioned, the challenge of student-centred learning is to encourage learners to become more responsible for developing their own learning styles and less dependent on teacher-only direction. Yet it can also be argued that for students with learning difficulties and disabilities the organization and direction of learning is more, not less, necessary. If part of the purpose of education and training is to encourage students to take responsibility for and to recognize the consequences of their own action, these students will require more guidance in appropriate strategies for managing both themselves and their own learning tasks.

That people may interpret the special considerations for students with learning difficulties and disabilities as a form of exploitation has been taken up by some educational philosophers. Bayles (1966), examining the issue of differential rights to education, argued that people with learning disabilities are entitled to special opportunities in order to compensate for their disabilities. However, such 'positive' discrimination does little for the promotion of equality of opportunity as it provides handicapped and disabled learners with more rights than their non-handicapped peers. To consider this issue in terms of curriculum planning and teaching methods it is probably more fruitful to go beyond that which is ethically fair. It may be better to look at that which is morally desirable. If, as a society, we are to consider ourselves as civilized, helping individuals with special needs to obtain an appropriate education that leads to suitable employment would seem a morally desirable goal.

PROMOTING THE MANAGEMENT OF LEARNING

A number of issues arise from this ethical and moral position. In the area of post-compulsory education, people with learning difficulties and disabilities have to build this sense of responsibility. Teachers and lecturers have to play a part in promoting and building a pathway to independent learning and the sense of adult responsibility. Four phases emerge that require consideration:

(1) What characteristics and previous knowledge do learners bring to a learning exchange, or planned activity?

An analysis of the characteristics of the learner is fundamental. It can range from a rapid review of previous learning related to the present exercise and the enthusiasms for the work, through to a detailed analysis of learning styles and social background. The basic issues to be addressed are as follows:

- whilst not all learning is sequential or linear, it is safest to assume that it is. So how can connections be established with earlier work?
- have all the learners the necessary prior knowledge to benefit from the new task?
- what steps will be necessary in order to establish a sufficient basis for learning?
- do the entry characteristics of learners, in relation to the task, point to individual, small-group or whole-group work?

(2) What are the central features of the task or activity?

In similar fashion to analysing the characteristics of the student, there needs to be an analysis of the activity to be undertaken:

- is work matched to the learner? Ideally work should stretch learners, but not be beyond them. Attempt to match the levels of ability and the task requirements.
- is the work properly focused for the levels of ability in learners, moving from the more able to the less able?
- is it the intention that learners will do the work at the same speed, or at their own individual rates?
- how is the work to be organized to allow for different rates of progress?

(3) How are the activities to be organized in order for the task/exercise to be mastered by the learner?

The organization of activity is not an end in itself, but is dictated by the aims established at the planning stage of a teaching sequence. An aim might, in fact, be to initiate learning. But, whether the aim is to promote new learning directly, or to promote the skills that will enable the learners to explore ideas and practices themselves, the means employed will be directed at aims that have previously been specified.

(4) What are the emotional characteristics of the learner and how might they influence the learner?

The crucial variable in this context is motivation. Learners tend to approach work with different degrees of enthusiasm. Students and trainees may be emotionally disturbed by it or see it in ways that differ not only from those of other learners but also from the teacher or lecturer.

- is there anything about the work that will be offensive to any of the learners?
- are there any material, psychological or social factors that may interfere with successful learning?
- is the learning organized so that all learners can and will achieve personal targets?

A final consideration, closely related to all four phases, is the understandable need to take into account contextual or environmental factors. By way of a reminder, the following may serve as a checklist of considerations for preparing a teaching sequence for any learner of whatever age or ability and whatever the task. It is worth considering the following:

Preparing the learner for the task
Do learners know the purpose of the activity?
Do they know what they are supposed to be doing?
Does the work that has been organized have some purpose?
Keeping the work rewarding
Is the work organized in such a way as to provide feedback to students on how well they are doing (without excessive dependence on the teacher)?
Is there sufficient reinforcement of successful learning, through speedy rewards or feedback?
Is there sufficient realization that negative responses to student attempts will act to stop or hinder successful learning?
Are there sufficient opportunities for learners to think for themselves, express their thoughts and have them valued?
Controlling the quality of work
The cost-effectiveness of teachers in the allocation of their time

and energy to individual students, or whole groups requires examination. The role of the teacher as both a resource and a manager of resources suggests that much time can be used up in preparation and delivery of short-term goals. Too little time is given to reflection and the evaluation of individual or collective learning experiences. To this end teachers and lecturers need to have considered the following:

- how should the teacher's time be allocated between being a resource for learning and being a manager of learning?
- with so many pressures on teachers/lecturers, what is the optimum use of the teacher's time?
- how should criteria for success be established for the activity?
- how can evaluation of the activity be built into the planning of the activity in order to provide feedback on pre-specified criteria?
- how can evaluation criteria be established for indicators or stages that arise during and/or after the activity?

THE FEATURES OF THE ACTIVITY

Any analysis of learning can range between casual and informal planning of 'the back of an envelope' sort, to the most detailed and intricate planning of task analysis. The following steps, adapted from Shipman (1985), are an indication of some of the features to take into account:

Defining what is to be learned
What are the learners expected to learn, practise or experience?
Is the learning concerned with knowledge, skills, attitudes, or some combination of these?
Is the intention to introduce new ideas, skills or values or to lead learners towards discovering these?
Is the intention to practise or revise?
Deciding on the resources required
Will the task require special facilities inside or outside the teaching room?
Will the task require any special arrangements in the teaching area?
Will the task require written or audio or visual resources?

How might the teacher act as a resource?
Deciding what is a measure of successful learning
What will be accepted as evidence that intended learning outcomes have been achieved?
Is it possible to spell out criteria of acceptable/competent performance?

This brief checklist of planning and management strategies serves to remind us that although teachers as a group may have similar professional problems and undergo similar training patterns, the teachers of students with learning difficulties and disabilities may not share this identity. For just as some learners are 'picked out' from their peers as having special needs, so are special needs teachers 'picked out' from their colleagues. By nature and role they consider they are different from ordinary teachers (O'Hanlon, 1988) – in focus, practices and clientele. O'Hanlon paints a picture of an individual and original person, who does not depend on 'outside' direction or policy; a person who is inner-directed through sensitive responses to individual needs. O'Hanlon concludes that as they see their learners, so the teacher of learners with special needs see themselves: as special, unique and nonconformist. It is probable that the same applies in further education and training.

The ways in which teachers of students with learning difficulties and disabilities operate gives rise to a central dilemma. Many of the lecturers in this work are employed part-time; they have a more person-centred than academic focus to their role and as such their status is not clearly defined. Status tends to be accrued through specialist subject knowledge and the acquisition of technical skills – it is rarely ascribed to skills in learner-centred relationships. The potential for value conflicts between the tutor of students with learning difficulties and disabilities who is filled with learner-centred humanitarianism, sensitivity and intuition, and the technically minded skills-based specialist and expert practitioner, is constantly apparent. The tensions that emerge may tend to compound and exacerbate the difficulties of bringing about effective teacher change and developments towards student-centredness.

SOME CENTRAL FEATURES OF TEACHING AND LEARNING IN FURTHER EDUCATION

Despite these concerns about the management of learning, good practice in the teaching of students with learning difficulties and/or disabilities is not necessarily a qualitatively different type of further education. It is, put simply, good further education practice applied to students with a range of needs arising from individual circumstances. This leaves the definition of what constitutes 'good further education practice' hanging in the air. Among the factors which mark out the distinctiveness of further education is the manner in which it accepts and responds to the local community that it serves; the range and choice of courses; adaptability of response to student demand and patterns of attendance and, finally, the increased opportunities for participation in inter-agency initiatives.

Applying these principles to the teaching of students with learning difficulties and disabilities has sometimes run the danger of denying these students full curricular access. Dee and Corbett (1994) echo some of the concerns of O'Hanlon (1988) in their suggestion that staff, who in the 1970s were recruited from the special school sector, brought with them not only their expertise but also their expectations of segregated professional activity. By perpetuating the notion of separateness within the full range of college activity and maintaining the belief that a proper educational response to meeting individual needs was through specialist provision, much good further education practice was being denied to a new and potentially vulnerable group. Colleges have now begun to move towards embracing the concept of learning support with its greater emphasis on a more comprehensive and coherent system of supporting learning across the whole college from a central resource. This means that all college staff are being encouraged to become involved in furthering the opportunities for all students. They are beginning to move away from the separate forms of assessment, curricular goals and teaching methods highlighted earlier in this chapter. These had supplied some of the mystique surrounding the teaching of learners with special needs, learning difficulties and/or disabilities.

It is in this context of rapid change, in both the funding structure and the management of further education as a sector, that the former verities of teaching approaches for all students are being questioned. Dee and Corbett (1994) have described the current climate as a period of transitional change where practitioners in the new tough world of special needs entitlements have to know how to fight for what they want. It is reminiscent of an observation overheard at a Skill annual conference in 1987, when a group of lecturers were discussing their newly emerging roles as learning support co-ordinators. One described his key function as having to develop 'guerrilla tactics' in order to survive the market culture that was beginning to emerge in further education. By this he meant gaining insider knowledge of the politics of a college, developing the capacity to confront authority and retaining the strength to keep coming back for more. As the educational climate has shifted towards the reality of internal markets, the literature of further education has moved towards a rights focus that is strong in the rhetoric of entitlement, but uncertain about the practical realities. The FEU has led the way in their definitions of entitlement and empowerment:

> all learners are entitled to a range of learning opportunities which will enable them to fulfil their learning goals and ambitions and improve their life chances. Some learners will require specific, additional support in order to help them meet these goals and to allow them to achieve fully.

> (FEU, 1993, p. 11)

In the same publication 'empowerment' is defined in the following terms:

> The underlying purpose of the learning support services is to help staff take more responsibility for the educational progress of all their students and for students to take responsibility for their own learning. In effect, the learning support service should be aiming to eliminate the need for itself.

> (ibid.)

Such considerations place a heavy emphasis on the ability of individuals to deal confidently with a system that is becoming more competitive. In some cases the system will have deliberately excluded young people on the grounds that they are not sufficiently sophisticated to know how to become self-directing, or to demand their entitlements. To expect all such students then to be able to take responsibility for their own fully participative place in society is at best fanciful and at worse dishonest. It is certainly not empowering for teachers to abandon students to the whims of market forces. Harris has developed this critique of the ethical and professional tensions underlying teaching approaches for empowerment and entitlement, when he claims that a teacher's reluctance to intervene in a student's autonomous decision-making can, in fact, be far from empowering: 'such aversion, rather than being empowering, could be more likely to have the effect of providing endorsement for, and thus reinforce conservative, oppressive and reactionary modes of thought and practice' (Harris, 1994, p. 82).

DEVELOPING A MODEL OF INSTRUCTION

Two fundamental models of teaching and learning still dominate teaching strategies for students with learning difficulties and disabilities: the setting of instructional/behavioural objectives and the more process-oriented, humanistic approach. They are sometimes presented as mutually exclusive, but they will be discussed here for what they really are: two complementary aspects of the teacher's armoury of teaching skills.

The essential components of a successful teaching and learning strategy for students with learning difficulties and disabilities in further education has already been summarized. The strategy manages to accommodate many of the differences between humanistic approaches and direct instruction. When they are set out as follows, it becomes clear that there is greater emphasis on the humanistic elements of student self-determination and education as a process.

Roles of students and lecturers

Students are active in directing their own learning.

Students are involved in choices of materials, methods and pace of learning.

Lecturers and instructors serve as resource persons rather than as directors of learning activity.

Diagnostic evaluation

Observation, written histories and samples of student work (rather than conventional tests or grades) are used to evaluate progress.

The purpose of evaluation is to guide instruction, not to grade or rank students.

Materials and sources

Diverse materials are used to stimulate student exploration and learning.

Emphasis is upon use of materials students can touch and explore; real-world activity and natural settings are preferred to worksheets and books alone.

Individualized instruction

Instruction is based on individual needs and abilities. Students proceed at their own rate.

Materials and circumstances can be adapted to provide for differences in students' preferred modes of learning.

Students are set individual goals for learning.

Instruction tends to be given to individuals/small groups and rarely to large groups.

Team teaching

Two or more lecturers will plan together, share resources and mix with students.
Two or more lecturers may choose to combine student groups in a large area.
Other volunteers are often used as assistants to both students and lecturers.

BEHAVIOURIST MODELS OF TEACHING AND LEARNING

This approach is derived from psychological learning theory based on behavioural and task analysis. Its application to work with students with learning difficulties and disabilities particularly applies to working with students with more severe learning difficulties. The approach involves the following features:

- Maladapted behaviour, like well-adapted behaviour, is considered to have been learned. It can therefore be unlearned and substituted by the teaching of adaptive behaviour.
- The lecturer/instructor can teach new behaviour, just as new skills are taught. All behaviours (both academic and social) are susceptible to being changed by the manipulation of the learning environment.
- Irrespective of other possible 'causes' of the undesired behaviour (for example poor home conditions, relationships, health, neurological functioning, etc.), it can be brought under control and changed by modifying the immediate environmental conditions (i.e. by modifying learning events so as to elicit desired behaviour and systematically changing the consequences that follow a learning activity).
- This approach can encourage positive thinking about a student because it focuses on *desired behaviour* in a context of praise and success instead of on failure and misbehaviour in a context of criticism.
- It should lead to a restructuring of the classroom/workshop environment so that the student (and the instructor/lecturer) is given clear immediate feedback about the results of his or her performance and behaviour.

Behaviour modification techniques are sometimes described in other ways, for example as programmed learning, or personalized systems of instruction (PSI). This development of an aspect of applied behavioural analysis was first developed by Keller in 1968. It is in effect a form of teaching to objectives that lends itself to mastery learning. Learning theory clearly emphasizes that an effective teaching–learning process for *all* students, not solely those with learning difficulties and disabilities, must incorporate this element of student-centred over-learning, e.g. rehearsal and repetition; teaching must involve the learner actively and instructional effectiveness must be evaluated in terms of what the learner actually learns.

For students with learning difficulties and disabilities PSI has a number of merits. It is based upon well-documented techniques for effective instructional strategies. The technique of behavioural teaching to objectives was developed in the late 1950s and 1960s by Skinner and his associates (e.g. Skinner, 1968). Their principles, derived from the experimental analysis of behaviour, were applied to the writing of systematic text material. The concepts and principles of a particular subject/aspect of training were identified and behavioural objectives were written for them.

A behavioural objective is a precise statement of what the student should be able to do by the end of a given segment of instruction. Effective behavioural objectives include a statement of behaviour in observable terms, the conditions under which the student should perform the specified task and some criteria for an acceptable level or standard of performance. By way of illustration, a student in the process of completing a reading or comprehension assignment may be expected to do or say certain things as a result. It would be possible to state these expectations in terms of behavioural objectives. As an example: a student is set the task of reading an instruction manual (the context and conditions under which the student is asked to perform and be assessed) and the student should be able to define a concept (the observable behaviour) using terms in a technically accurate written sentence or discussion (the standard of acceptable performance).

After deciding on behavioural objectives, these targets can be broken down into smaller steps, supplemented by study questions. These study questions can in turn be structured in such a way that they can cluster behavioural objectives into manageable chunks or combinations of steps. At the most fundamental level each step of a behavioural objectives approach can be broken down into frames, wherein students might, for example, be expected to read a few sentences and then answer a question based upon them. Having answered, the student would receive immediate feedback by checking his/her answer with the one provided. This form of programmed instruction has achieved success in many spheres in elementary and secondary education and can be seen to be emerging as a preferred strategy for competence training in the development of NVQs.

The concept of teaching to objectives is perhaps the most significant contribution to 'expertise' amongst those who teach in special education settings. At the same time it is one of its greatest weaknesses. Proponents of the strategy will argue that it trains for success by making students aware of positive expectations and by giving them immediate rewards that are both tangible and reinforcing. Where it is done well, it is both successful for the learner and a positive reinforcer to collaborative planning for teachers and lecturers. Furthermore, by setting behavioural objectives it is possible to implement carefully graded, appropriate teaching programmes for students who have difficulties with (and may previously have shown no interest in) planning their own learning. The supporters of behavioural methods point out that one of the most consistent and educationally significant characteristics of students with learning difficulties is their reduced capacity for unplanned, spontaneous and incidental learning. As children, they may have experienced the freedoms of discovery learning, open-plan classrooms and a stimulating, well-planned and attractive school environment. However, for some children these environments are a contributory element to learning failure. Too much freedom and a high-stimulus environment have association with hyperactivity and learning difficulty in adolescence. Indeed, the greater the learning handicap the greater the need for a carefully planned intervention or strategy (Ainscow and Tweddle, 1979). No matter how well motivated the teacher, how technically competent or sensitive the teaching-room atmosphere, the vital ingredient of successful learning is planning. Supporters of teaching to behavioural objectives with students who experience learning difficulties will maintain that the lecturer/instructor needs to have worked out in detail and in advance what is going to be taught, how it is to be taught and how the results are going to be checked in order to determine what has been learned. In summary, the major case for having clear objectives concerns lecturer effectiveness, control over the content of learning and accountability for the measurement of learning outcomes.

Opponents would argue that the technique is time-consuming, too cold, dehumanizing and teacher-centred. The limitations of the approach were well summarized by Ainscow and Tweddle (1988) when they came to re-evaluate some of their earlier enthusiasms for the objectives approach to teaching students with learning difficulties. The problems they identify are not exclusive to the objectives approach but they are possibly best exemplified by the techniques. Through over-reliance on behavioural objectives, a mechanistic and narrowly constrained form of teaching tends to emerge. Their objections to behavioural objectives are that it results in:

a narrowing of the content of learning;
segregation of learners;
teachers and lecturers feeling inadequate;
passive responses from students and trainees;
a static curriculum that fails to respond to changes in individual needs.

There are obvious dangers if teaching approaches set up rigid structures that lead to mechanical responses from students or trainees. It could be argued that the period of life associated with further education should be leading students towards the development of more spontaneous and self-directed responses. For those lecturers who consider themselves as supporters of learning for individual needs, rather than as continuing an educational ambulance service for slow learners, this flexibility of response is a key feature. For them it is not enough for young adult students to be exposed to a series of explicit objectives, as this simply reduces opportunities for both creativity and teacher autonomy. There needs to be a focus on the more affective responses within human endeavour too.

HUMANISTIC AND PROCESS APPROACHES TO TEACHING IN FURTHER EDUCATION

The objectives approach to teaching focuses on increasing aspects of a student's specific knowledge and skills and draws heavily on direct instruction: the focus is upon outcomes that can be measured. The humanistic approach is more about learning how to learn, enhancing creativity and concentrating on the process of learning. It was the dominant force in American and UK education in schools and colleges in the 1970s and draws heavily on the research of humanistic psychologists such as Maslow (1970) and Rogers. It has, perhaps, been most notoriously chronicled in the work of A. S. Neill (1960) in his educational experiments at Summerhill. The philosophy of Summerhill was summarized by Neill himself, as follows: 'The child is innately wise and realistic. If left to himself, without adult suggestion of any kind, he will develop as far as he is capable of developing' (Neill, 1967, p. 4). The abandonment of guidelines may take the risks of process too far, but this encapsulates the developmental nature of learning as a shared and experiential activity.

The humanistic movement is a natural successor of Dewey's progressive movement of the 1920s and 1930s. It emerged as a direct reaction to the regimented rote learning of the Edwardian English school system. The innate appeal of humanistic approaches such as Maslow's hierarchy resides in their fundamental common sense. Child (1987), in summarizing Maslow's psychoanalytic research, outlines his hypothesis that certain basic human needs can be arranged in hierarchical order, the needs becoming more human as one proceeds through them. Using the pyramid shape shown in Figure 5.2. Maslow has distinguished not only the basic needs that have to be satisfied before 'higher order' needs, but also their hierarchical arrangement.

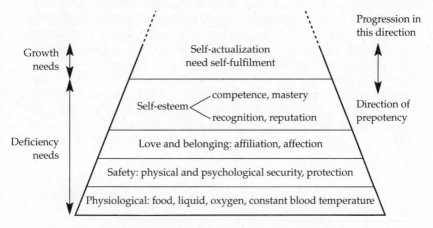

Figure 5.2 *A hierarchy of basic needs*

Source: based on Maslow (1970)

Once fundamental reflex and organic needs are capable of being satisfied, Maslow posits that 'higher' needs begin to emerge and assert themselves. Progressing towards the apex of the pyramid, one passes from esteem needs (the desire to attain competences, skills, mastery and recognition) to the desire to fulfil one's potential, or 'self-actualization' and 'self-realization'. Maslow is indicating here that connected to basic needs there is a desire for knowledge and cognitive understanding both of ourselves and of our environment: 'What someone can be, they must be.' However, in order to achieve this state of being, it is necessary to have some idea of our potential for growth and to have some understanding of the limits and boundaries to what we can do. To this end we search for knowledge and seek to express ourselves in a variety of ways (e.g. through art, music, mathematics, athletic endeavour). It is this search for knowledge and the attempts to systematize and structure our perceived understanding that marks out much of student activity in late adolescence and the time of further education. For students with learning difficulties and disabilities, these 'growth needs' may only be emerging at the time of entry to further education college and the opportunity for this exploration should not be denied to them.

One of the most important ideas inherent in the humanistic approach to teaching is that students should have a substantial responsibility for directing their own education, choosing what they will study and to some extent when and how they will participate in learning (Slavin, 1991). The central purpose is to encourage students to become more self-directed, self-motivated learners rather than passive recipients of information. This feature of developing choices is in keeping with learning goals that are more to do with increased student motivation and preparedness to work, if there is some choice in what they will be studying.

Humanistic educators usually lay as much stress on affective goals as on cognitive outcomes. The argument is that it is of more educational value and importance to students to become responsible, caring, feeling adults than to score points or acquire grades in standardized tests of attainment. Such standardized testing and formal methods of evaluation are not part of the repertoire of a humanistic approach. The concepts of co-operation, consideration, mutual respect and valuing learning for its own sake are more typical. Davis (1983) lists some examples of values considered appropriate to humanistic education:

Honesty: e.g. not cheating; being trustworthy; understanding and respecting authority; not vandalizing;

Respecting rights of others: e.g. respecting individual rights; not vandalizing; listening; accepting and respecting individual differences; empathizing with others; helping others;

Energy, environmental consideration: e.g. caring for property (own and others); conserving electricity, gas, natural products;

Manners: e.g. sharing; being courteous; behaving well in public; doing favours; being considerate to others;

Study, work habits: e.g. being prompt; accepting leadership or participant roles; observing safety rules; following directions; valuing education; being industrious;

Personal development: e.g. accepting responsibility; developing self-respect; appreciating beauty; valuing physical health, hygiene; controlling one's temper; developing one's talents; being courageous, honourable.

Whilst it would be easy to criticize such ambitions and targets as these, on the grounds of subjectivity alone, there is an implicit understanding of mutual co-operation in the desired attributes referred to by Davis. His goals have certainly formed the basis for much of a student's earlier 'moral' education in his/her school years.

All lecturers and teachers hope that their students will develop positive attitudes towards both learning and identifying with the needs of others. The humanistic approach particularly emphasizes the use of a variety of experiences and resources to obtain information. In the development of educational provision for students with learning difficulties and disabilities there is the need to give students a wide range of opportunities. They need to experience choice and risk-taking rather than under-expectation and over-protection. This calls for the design of instructional materials and learning situations that are built around solving real problems and exposure to risks and choices that are sufficiently challenging to be authentic. At the same time, they should not be threatening to physical or personal dignity. It is in facilitating and helping these students to learn to live with the consequences of their own actions that the lecturer in further education is adopting some of the more humanistic approaches to teaching.

In helping students to develop a positive regard for their own contribution to learning, the lecturer is underlining the part a student can play in working out the solutions to his/her own problems. This concept of 'client-centred' counselling first conceived by Rogers (in e.g. Kirschenbaum and Henderson, 1990) places the teacher/counsellor in the role of collaborative, non-threatening figure. Rather than telling students what to do, how and when to do it, the function is more that of an encouraging, sympathetic and non-judgemental listener. The intention is to assist the students to understand the incongruities between their identification with a personal egocentric world and their ability to learn to empathize and show respect for the feelings of others. The learner is encouraged to broaden personal experience and gain satisfaction from serving and helping others. It is these skills that mark out the successful humanistic role model of the 'teacher as facilitator' in this area of further education.

The positive reception of humanistic teaching approaches within the new contract culture and climate that is currently favoured in further education is sometimes hard to understand.

As the scarcity of jobs begins to hit school-leavers particularly hard, it is those young people who have experienced difficulties in learning who are at the greatest disadvantage. As Hegarty (1993) has pointed out, the number of unskilled and semi-skilled jobs is in decline and there is more competition for those that are available. Students with learning difficulties and disabilities are in competition with their more able peer group in a shrinking job market. In a world that still places the highest value on academic achievement, the weakest go to the wall. Dyson *et al.* (1994) have suggested that the curriculum for the learner approaching adulthood should be based on the traditional notions of a liberal education, recognizing the intrinsic worth of the pursuit of education in its own right. Their driving concern is with the quality of life for learners with disabilities and the function of education as a transforming agent. The underlying philosophy is essentially rooted in the humanistic tradition: it values people for what they are, rather than what they can do; the process of learning rather than its outcomes. In an economic climate of uncertain futures for the world of work, such an approach means designing educational programmes that motivate. Hegarty suggests that it also means recognizing education as a lifelong process:

> It means helping young people to discover all their capacities and start on the lifelong task of developing them. It means freeing them from domination by their immediate surroundings and unlocking new worlds of experience, feeling and insight. It means replacing work preparation with preparation for constructive use of time, community involvement and personal relationships.
>
> (Hegarty, 1993, p. 192)

Hegarty's spirited rhetoric captures much of the essence of humanistic approaches to teaching and learning. It also highlights a central dilemma that faces teachers and managers within further education. Should the curriculum be made more vocational in order to best equip young people for the available jobs, or should it, as is the case in some other European countries, reduce the emphasis on vocationalism in favour of preparation for a lifestyle where paid work is considered less important than it is today? The current preoccupation with competitive vocational preparation for all school-leavers places the majority of the further education curriculum firmly within the more mechanistic domain of behavioural objectives. However, as has been pointed out by critics of this approach, it is flawed by a failure of logic and the central reality of too few jobs. As a general strategy within the education system, vocational preparation is doomed to failure. If all educational settings are preparing young people effectively for the labour market and no jobs are available, then 'nothing will have changed – except that the unemployed will be better qualified (for work, not necessarily for unemployment)' (Hegarty, 1993, p. 192).

The more humanistic – some would say realistic – approach is to prepare young people to live with the reality of a lifestyle not shaped by the prospect of regular paid work. The desirability of the education system being used as the agency for informing young people that they are likely to face possible periods of unemployment is in itself somewhat questionable. Certainly, it requires some rethinking of curriculum strategies in order to counter the negative thinking, disillusion and alienation that are so often associated with the time of school-leaving for young people with learning difficulties and disabilities. It may become more appropriate not merely to alert young people to the likelihood of limited employment possibilities, but to concentrate on the development of knowledge, attitudes and outlook that can reform old concepts of adulthood. Rather than linking the status of adulthood to the status of the work ethic, all students, particularly those with learning difficulties and disabilities, could be challenged with socially useful work and thus achieve a status that would be determined and conferred by co-operation within the community.

Both strategies have their strengths and weaknesses. As school-leavers move more towards becoming adult learners, it becomes apparent that lecturers and students will have to develop negotiated understandings. This negotiation involves relationships, responsibilities and choices. It includes discovering the style of learning that is the most appropriate to a given situation. In such circumstances, the roles of teacher and learner become interchangeable. This is perhaps when learning is at its most satisfying and productive and is a basis for moving forward the opportunities in further education.

DILEMMAS OF ASSESSMENT

In the United Kingdom there is a strong disability rights movement which is conscious of the need to eradicate the use of labels that 'stereotype' disabled people. For example, since 1980 there has been increasing use of the term 'disabled person' rather than 'handicapped', which is now considered both pejorative and misleading. Children are no longer described as having a 'mental handicap', or suffering from 'mental retardation', but as 'experiencing learning difficulties' (indeed in 1994 the British Institute of Mental Handicap (BIMH) relaunched itself under the new title of the British Institute of Learning Disabilities, or BILD).

The legacy of the medical model of disability has been a range of terms that are part of the professional shorthand of teachers in special education, but it is uncertain if these terms are considered acceptable either to disabled people as individuals or to the collective voice of the disability movement. At the present time in the UK the methods of assessment and measurement of student outcomes are being placed under greater scrutiny. It is important that professionals working in further education and training recognize the power they have to create and apply terminology which can be unintentionally oppressive. The power they exercise in the assessment of others should be acknowledged as a shared activity with those who have the greatest stake in the activity – the students with learning difficulties and disabilities themselves.

This section reviews some aspects of the assessment procedures that are currently in operation for learners with learning difficulties and/or disabilities in education and training in the United Kingdom. The concentration will be upon the language of 'equal opportunities' and 'choice' that is now being used more often in the post-compulsory sector. The issues that arise reveal interesting examples of how linguistic misunderstandings can emerge in relation to the language of special education, less in the meaning of individual words than in their implied conceptual underpinnings.

As an example, Adams and Whittaker (1994) indicate that the term 'learning difficulty' has different meanings in different cultural contexts. As used by English and Scottish educationalists, 'learning difficulty' encompasses the whole range of learning disabilities, but it can mean something that is very mild to people who are unacquainted with the education system in the United Kingdom. On the other hand, the phrase is more widely associated with the concept of 'mental retardation' when used outside the United Kingdom, in northern Europe and the United States. Perhaps this is as a result of the influence of the definitions of the World Health Organization and terminology employed in North America. At their best these different terminologies may be indicative of nothing more than slight differences in mutually agreed and accepted understandings. However, they may also be indicators of more deep-seated values and fears about disability and the purposes of education and training for a group of people in society who are unlikely to be economically productive. These prejudices are perhaps most marked in relation to people with severe or profound learning difficulties.

These considerations have practical, ethical and political consequences for teachers and students alike. Bryans (1993) has succinctly outlined three broad phases in assessment since the 1940s, which chart the developing sensitivity of approaches to assessment in the United Kingdom. In the first phase most attention was directed to the supposed within-child deficits related to a range of eleven categories of 'handicap' (e.g. physical handicap, mental handicap, partially hearing). This period of assessment closely linked educational disadvantage to the judgements of medical officers and doctors.

The second phase, which heralded the publication of the Warnock Report (1978) in the United Kingdom, saw the focus on the nature of the interaction between the learner and the task. This incorporated judgements of task content, its presentation and in addition the method and style of teaching. Special educational methods of instruction, many derived from the United States Headstart urban recovery programmes (Cicirelli *et al.*, 1969) and the techniques of operant learning pioneered by Cruickshank *et al.* (1961), influenced assessment methodology so that greater consideration was given to a more focused criterion-referenced as opposed to norm-referenced assessment (Keogh and Becker, 1973). Another effect of the vast array of intervention programmes in the United States and the Educational Priority Area work in the UK was that the special education labels and categories began to break down, as it became clear that some categories of handicap or need were not normatively distributed across whole populations of pupils (Barton and Tomlinson, 1984), but rather could be construed as one of the effects of low socio-economic status. At the same time special education was in danger of entrapping itself through the creation of, or its association with, the alienation and 'felt powerlessness' of the working-class child, the immigrant, the unemployed and the underprivileged (Bruner, 1975; Tomlinson, 1985).

The last phase of assessment, from the mid-1980s onwards, has focused more globally on the characteristics of the learner and the student's total learning environment – the so-called interactionist view. This has coincided with the development of the concepts of 'special educational need', 'inclusive education' and the establishment of a funding methodology for educational provision that is locked into assessment methods and questions about the most appropriate place for education and training. The assessment perspective has shifted over a fifty-year period from the 1940s from that of fitting pupils into provision via prescribed categories of disability or handicap, to the directing of resources via assessment, to meet perceived needs. The assessment of students with learning difficulties and disabilities in further education is therefore quite clearly linked to matters of funding.

Bryans (1993, p. 20) has already noted this link in relation to the assessment of children with special educational needs: 'One consistent thread running through all assessment practice and procedure is the expectation that all assessments will have some observable outcome in terms of extra resourcing, change of provision or placement and/or change of status of the child.' Such an observation reinforces the essentially political nature of assessment procedures in further education, for although there appears to be a change from assessment for placement of a student, to an assessment to meet needs, this is always going to be dependent upon the financial limits of budgets. As Bryans goes on to point out about the present state of special education in the United Kingdom, the volume and quantity of rhetoric about it has often obscured what is actually happening 'on the ground'. It is, after all, worth bearing in mind that, despite some changes, at heart special education assessments are about the identification of learner characteristics in order to separate the learner: either from the majority of his/her peers or from the curriculum/teaching approach currently employed with the majority of students.

DIAGNOSIS AND ASSESSMENT IN SCHOOLS

This section will briefly outline the approach to assessment of children with special educational needs in school settings. Under the 1993 Education Act, the assessment arrangements for young people with statements of special educational need at the age of 14 should incorporate a transition plan, 'which will draw together information from a range of individuals within and beyond the school in order to plan coherently for the young person's transition to adult life' (DfE, 1994a, para. 6.45). 'The transfer of relevant information should ensure that young people receive any necessary specialist help or support during their continuing education and vocational or occupational training after leaving school' (ibid., para. 6.43).

Some pupils with statements of special educational needs will remain in school after the age of 16 and LEAs retain responsibility for such pupils until they are 19. Others with statements will, nevertheless, leave school at 16 and move to a college of further education or to social services provision. It is therefore anticipated that the first annual review after the young person's fourteenth birthday will involve those agencies that will play a major role in the course of the young person's post-school years.

The detailed arrangements for the development of a transition plan build on the targets set at earlier reviews and are intended to focus on a young person's strengths as well as weaknesses. The intention is to establish clear guidelines for the varying responsibilities of different agencies and professionals in the development of the young person with a disability. The Code of Practice (DfE, 1994a) indicates that where it is anticipated that a young person with a statement of special educational needs is transferring to a college of FE, the LEA should ensure that a copy of both the statement and the transition plan should be passed to the college that the young person will be attending.

For those young people with special educational needs, but without statements, it is anticipated that LEAs will provide a variety of detailed information and advice at the age of 16. This must include help and guidance about local and national voluntary organizations which may help both them and their families to exercise more choice about transition plans. Amongst the support services that are of the greatest help to parents and young people alike is the careers service. The specialist careers officer with responsibility for students and young people with learning difficulties and disabilities should be in a position to offer vocational guidance in the wider context of information about further education and training courses. In some circumstances, the careers service may wish to involve other specialist help, such as an occupational psychologist, in order to develop a more detailed vocational profile. Increasingly it is expected that ways of involving young people themselves in the assessment process will be developed. This procedure is intended to include strategies for addressing any behavioural or other problems that might otherwise adversely affect a student's further education or future employment.

The initial identification of children with special educational needs at school will, typically, be carried out by the use of a screening test, in accordance with the expectations of the 1993 Education Act. This initial screening or register will be conducted by a class teacher in consultation with a school's SEN co-ordinator. The information will be gathered from class records, the parent and from the child him or herself, as well as other sources already available in the school. As a child moves through stages 1 and 2 of assessment a record of educational achievement will profile developmental and individual achievements under a variety of headings.

The Code of Practice (DfE, 1994a, pp. 21–2) has determined a model which can be summarized as follows:

Stage 1: initial identification

This stage aims to gather information about a child and tries to determine the differentiation within the normal classroom setting. At this stage the classroom teacher:

- identifies a child's special educational needs
- consults the child's parents and the child
- informs the SEN co-ordinator, who registers the child's special educational needs
- collects relevant information about the child, consulting the SEN co-ordinator
- works closely with the child in the normal classroom context
- monitors and reviews the child's progress in such things as standardized test results, the child's health and development, expressive and receptive language competence, the child's own perceptions of any difficulties.

Stage 2: developing an individual educational plan

At this stage the SEN co-ordinator takes responsibility for establishing and co-ordinating a child's special educational provision but is expected to work closely with the child's teachers:

- marshals relevant information, including, as appropriate, information from sources beyond the school
- ensures that an individual education plan is drawn up
- ensures that the child's parents are informed
- monitors and reviews the child's progress
- informs the headteacher

The class teacher will complete the profiles of assessment at stage 1, often in conjunction with the parent, and from the points score on this profile it will be decided whether the child is indicating a special educational need. If, after discussion between the class and the headteacher of the school, it is decided that the child has special educational needs, or is at risk educationally, further diagnostic testing will be arranged through the head of learning support in the school and the Psychological Service and the child will move to the next stages of the assessment procedure. Following these interventions, a special report programme will be devised, to be implemented by a school's SEN co-ordinator, but often carried out in conjunction with an external learning support service for specific programmes, materials or equipment.

Effective assessment procedures for children at risk educationally will attempt to ensure that all of the following factors are addressed (Griffiths, 1994):

- early detection of difficulties is documented;
- objective observation of behaviour is recorded;
- recordings of strengths as well as weaknesses are made;
- there is a sharing of full information between schools and families;
- formal testing is undertaken only when the real purpose of it has been agreed and understood;
- where diagnostic assessment is required in order to develop planned programmes of study, this should, wherever possible, be provided within the school's existing resources;
- there should be a clear referral procedure for internal school purposes as well as when working with outside agencies.

With all of this in mind, it is worth considering where the shortcomings in the system of assessment are most likely to become apparent. Although the fuller involvement of parents and teachers in the assessment process is to be welcomed, the reality is that this may lead to the false raising of expectations that 'something can be done'. Diagnosis is not the same as provision, and the effective meeting of needs in educational terms is still comparatively low in contrast to the high level of diagnosis. There are also too few 'key workers' or 'named persons' in the sense of the Warnock Report (1978) to help parents and teachers to co-ordinate effective educational provision. For example a child with a visual handicap and a learning disability from a poor socio-economic background may be visited by an educational psychologist, a support teacher for the blind, and a social worker. All three professionals may recommend different things with little or no liaison between them or explanation. A key worker or named person, who could minimize such confusion, could be the class teacher, or the co-ordinator for special educational needs; however, time needs to be made available for this to happen (Griffiths, 1994). Whoever takes on the role must ensure that relevant information is passed on to appropriate people and that effective records are maintained. This point links to a weakness in the training of all teachers about the skills and teaching techniques required in both assessing and making effective provision for children and their special educational needs. It may be quite difficult to find the happy medium between under-specialization and over-specialization, but mainstream class teachers need to be given as much knowledge and information as possible about individual difference, special needs and equal opportunities.

ASSESSING NEEDS IN POST-COMPULSORY EDUCATION

In this section I am going to address the assessment procedures that are currently in place for learners in post-compulsory education and training in the UK. I shall begin by examining three major legislative influences that illuminate the pace of change in this sector and are likely to have an impact on the intensely political nature of the assessment procedures in further education and training. The first is the White Paper *Education and Training for the 21st Century* (DES, 1991a), followed by the Further and Higher Education Act 1992, and *Choice and Diversity* (DfE, 1992b). All merge into one another as a single surge in the championing and promotion of market forces in education and the desire for consumer-led outcomes (Corbett, 1993).

The White Paper published in 1991 formally indicated to colleges of further education that they would soon be expected to publish a summary of their results in a similar fashion to schools in order that the two sectors could be compared. The government's justification for this formality was that: 'Young people, parents, employers and the schools and colleges themselves, will then be able to make more informed judgements about the quality of their provision, overall and in individual courses' (DES, 1991a, p. 26). Such a narrow view of the purposes of assessment fails to take account of the dangers inherent in all assessment systems, whether in schools or colleges. If they fail to take account of, or acknowledge, the very real differences between students and their social and economic circumstances, assessment fails. Above everything else, there is the danger that the concept of assessment is being distorted into a process of outcomes that are mechanistic, detached from personal need. Instead they appear to be determined by external pressures and prevailing financial and economic conditions.

As curriculum researchers have pointed out, a key component of all effective assessment at any level should be the link it makes back to an overall learning programme. 'In this way it can indeed be owned by those who are being assessed, if they are aware of its centrality' (Corbett, 1993, p. 114). The same point has been emphasized by Brown (1991) commenting on the development of modular schemes of study in Scottish further education, where assessment is integrated into the teaching methods, content and management of programmes of work. If this view of assessment, as an integrated facet of the whole teaching and learning process, were to be held by all post-compulsory education it would help the assessment system to develop shared ownership with those who are being tested. The system would become fairer and there would be a reduction in the power monopoly that underlies relations between pupils, students and teachers in the education system as a whole.

However, the issue is never so simple when we involve our basic prejudices about people with learning difficulties and disabilities. As Corbett (1993) has pointed out, these values inevitably inform our observations as assessors.

It is this balance between the ways in which students assess their skills and potential and the different approaches offered by their tutors which can challenge the whole concept of ownership and create an uncomfortable tension. This may lead one to ask, 'whose equal opportunities are they anyway?'

(Corbett, 1993, p. 125)

Under the Further and Higher Education Act 1992, the responsibility for the funding of further education was transferred from local control by LEAs to the Further Education Funding Council. Funds for the assessment of students have been transferred from the LEAs to the Council, so in theory, colleges should be able to offer continuity of provision. However, within the rapidly shifting scenario of post-compulsory education there are some threats to the delicate balance of assessment for young people from marginalized groups. This includes those individuals with needs which require careful support, in the transition from school to adulthood. Changes in the nature of vocational qualifications appear to be increasing the influence of employers in determining the assessment frameworks and narrowing the contexts in which assessment takes place. This threatens to exclude students deemed superfluous to requirements. As assessment is becoming the territory more of employers than of educationalists there is a very real threat to the adequacy of both educational provision and employment opportunities for students at the more severe end of the disability spectrum, or to those with behavioural and emotional difficulties. For example, if the assessment of student need suggests high expenditure, for example on toilet facilities, personal care support or communication aids, this has clear funding and staffing implications during a time of competing expenditure priorities and measured accountability in training targets.

Corlett and Dumbleton (1992) have indicated that the FEFC is continuing to use similar terminology to earlier educational legislation with regard to the assessment of students with learning difficulties. The Council is to 'have regard to the requirements' of students with disabilities, and/or learning difficulties. To assist them in this task, the Council's specialist committee, under the chairmanship of Professor John Tomlinson, has made a call for evidence of the perceptions of students with learning difficulties and/or disabilities and from all who have an interest in this area of post-compulsory education. The committee is due to report its findings in 1996.

The final document that has influenced the climate of assessment in the UK is the White Paper *Choice and Diversity* (DfE, 1992b), the recommendations of which are now enshrined in the 1993 Education Act. This legislation has brought a number of changes to the statementing procedure for pupils with special educational needs in school settings and emphasizes the transition plans at 14.

The effect of these legislative changes has been to place the measurement of achievement and outcomes at the centre of the assessment process (of schools and colleges as well as students). The FEFC (1992b, 1992d) has stipulated that funding is to be related to the three stages of assessment; pre-course, on-course and final outcomes. Assessment in all areas of education, including special education, now reflects just one element within a blatantly consumer-oriented interpretation of accountability:

> Assessment and testing are the keys to monitoring and raising standards in our schools. Teachers realise that testing encourages the greater involvement of parents in our schools – tests supply the information which informs parents and are entirely consistent with the aims of the Citizen's Charter.
>
> (DfE, 1992b, p. 9)

This stress on choices and rights is a powerful endorsement of the notion of choice, student entitlement and the concept of assessment as an integral aspect of the learning support framework that has been promoted by the Further Education Unit. It is also increasingly being seen as the influential model for the support of all learners. This focuses on a more generic system of learning support for all students who may require services and is significantly different from the concept of the special needs unit which formed the basis of provision in the recent past:

> Entitlement is related to the individual and describes what a potential student has a right to expect on acceptance into the educational institution . . . institutions will have implicit or explicit notions of entitlement and of standards. A market approach demands that colleges make student entitlement explicit. They should also make their

standards clear as well as the means by which they are assessed.
(FEU, 1992, p. 26)

Sutcliffe (1992) has noted that in one college she visited, learning support across the curriculum incorporated assessment as but one aspect of full student entitlement. The model of support she described encompassed the following:

Information
Guidance
Accreditation of prior learning
Assessment testing
School liaison
Community outreach
Careers education
Access development

So assessment in post-compulsory education in the UK is becoming a dimension of a wider equal opportunities issue. This raises its own dilemmas of both an ethical and practical nature. Allowing students to struggle on their own on the grounds of equal opportunities is indefensible. However, it may be more responsible to dissuade a student from studying on an academic course if the end result is that there is little opportunity of gaining employment. In such circumstances equal opportunities have served little purpose, other than to exacerbate the conflicts of perception between staff and students' personal judgements of a course of action. As has been suggested about the issue:

> We tend to assess how it feels to us, not how it feels to the person being assessed, as we can only guess at that. Assessment is about feelings and values as well as about measurement.
> (Corbett, 1993, p. 126)

Unfortunately, despite the rhetoric of equal opportunities, it is becoming clearer that not all students will be able to compete equally in the new competitive climate of further education in the UK. Equal value is not placed on all courses, nor upon all students in post-compulsory education and training. An overall pattern of discrimination is emerging in further education and training propelled by the competitive climate of the market-place. As Warnock (1991) has aptly noted, the market mentality has infiltrated every area of education, including special educational needs, and has promoted a hardening of attitudes. Warnock's observation was a bleak warning for students with learning difficulties and disabilities that in such a climate the underdog does not overcome adversity; he or she simply goes under.

SUMMARY

The exploration of models of teaching and learning with students who have learning difficulties and disabilities is itself a voyage of discovery. The use of a wide variety of methods allows different learning styles to develop and this may be essential in order that people with learning difficulties and disabilities may learn in the most effective way for them. The chapter emphasizes that good learning arises from activity and direct experience. The behavioural models of teaching often experienced in school settings are tempered with more humanistic encounters in colleges. The discussion of supporting learners in the more independent settings of further education raises new questions for assessment of outcomes. The education and training of students with learning difficulties and disabilities poses special concerns for the small minority of students with particularly challenging disabilities. This forms the focus of the next chapter.

6

The tensions of inclusive practices and specialist colleges

During the late 1970s and early 1980s a challenge to the separateness of special education began to be posed by a combination of factors emerging in a number of countries across the Western world. These factors came together under the broad banner of inclusive education and community. The action arose in a number of countries which were beginning to reinterpret the concepts of equal opportunities. Ironically, some of the very organizations that had first helped to legitimize the need for and recognition of a separate educational entitlement for young people with disabilities and learning difficulties were amongst the most vociferous in fighting to dismantle the systems that had been the products of their early successes.

FROM INTEGRATION TO INCLUSION

The link between progression, transition and inclusion has often been overlooked in the debate on entitlement in further education. However, one of the fundamental purposes of further education for students with learning difficulties and/or disabilities is essentially linked to the negotiation of adult services rather than perpetuation of child-oriented and protected provision. The development of inclusive education, as distinct from integration, has been built on the notion of equity and rights for marginalized groups who have traditionally been excluded from educational and community services. Put at its simplest, the concept celebrates the value of an individual for those qualities which he/she brings to a situation or human encounter, rather than attempting to place conditions upon their acceptance. Thus, whereas integration is in many ways an ultimate goal (all people are accepted equally), inclusion is a step along the way in which people with disabilities are accepted and accorded recognition for their contribution to any human transaction, precisely because of their differences.

The concept was most widely discussed first in Canada in its fullest educational and community sense, particularly in the Catholic school boards of Waterloo, Ontario and New Brunswick. The notion of educational integration has become a priority for a variety of advocacy groups in these school districts (Richler, 1991). The need to develop an alternative model to the isolation of segregated services gained wider acceptance as normalization principles became more widely understood. It was clear that simply improving segregated services would do little to provide the tools for eliminating the wider barriers to inclusive living.

It is almost certain that the majority of those who are employed in the education system, at whatever level, are attempting to improve people's lives. This underlying philosophy is apparent amongst those who work in what is broadly termed special education. For this reason, if no other, the enthusiasm for integration amongst some teachers, parents and administrators is difficult to interpret and evaluate. The initial and fundamental 'gut' reaction would be to agree with any cause that professes to have at its heart improved access to social and educational opportunity. It is nevertheless a matter of some confusion for those who work in settings especially designed and equipped to serve people with learning difficulties and disabilities to find their efforts being criticized on the basis that they are continually creating services that segregate people and exclude them from full participation in social activities. For teachers who have worked in segregated special education systems for a number of years it can only come as a shock to realize that they are considered by their critics to be perpetuating a kind of educational apartheid; that despite their best endeavours to serve they have, in fact, been preparing children and students for segregated lives in the future. In other words the experiences that the education system has created for children and young people with learning difficulties have 'systematically disengaged them from natural connections, and from the mainstream of life in their communities' (Tyne, 1993).

The popular movement towards inclusive education has grown out of debates on the effectiveness of mainstreaming and questions about the validity of special classes. Reviews of studies in the United States carried out in the 1950s and 1960s with mildly mentally retarded children (e.g. Johnson, 1950, 1962; Ainsworth, 1959; Dunn, 1968) concluded that although special classes did not harm the social adjustment of mildly mentally retarded children, they were of little advantage in terms of academic achievement.

Research evidence for the complete effectiveness of mainstreaming throughout school years is nevertheless inconclusive. There is some tentative evidence to suggest that regular class may be better than special class placement for both the academic and social growth of higher-ability learning-disabled youngsters, but that this is less evident for children and young people at the more severe end of the ability spectrum.

When the concept of integration was gaining momentum in the early 1980s it met with mixed reactions. It had few complete supporters. What has happened in the years since then has been a reflection of the growing awareness of normalization principles that were first developed in Scandinavia and in Canada by Wolfensberger. (The concept of normalization is more widely discussed in Chapter 9.) The rapid increase in enthusiasm for inclusive education in recent years, in the United Kingdom, on the other hand, has coincided with the growth of further education and the rhetoric of citizen rights. This is understandable and inevitable, for supporters of inclusive principles have argued that post-16 education is the most appropriate stage for the movement's fullest realization. Advocates of inclusive education and community living have also maintained that if further education is anticipated to be part of an education for 'emerging adulthood', it surely has to involve all students in the fullest participation in both realistic and mainstream activities (Whittaker, 1988). As in the arguments in favour of integration advocated in the 1970s, there is a strong moral imperative that persuades in favour of inclusion and yet behind the 'rightness' of the case there appears to be little hard evidence that it will always prove the most appropriate educational, or even social, outcome for the young people concerned. Ultimately, however, the central issue at the heart of inclusion is similar to that which lies at the heart of other causes that are strong on rhetoric, but less solid on practical reality. It is a question of empowerment and the lifting of restriction on people's lives; it is about the power to choose.

Special education, as we saw in other chapters, emerged as an alternative system in response to the failure of mainstream education. The latter had either failed to meet the needs of a particular group of pupils, or it excluded children on the grounds of bureaucratic and administrative convenience. Supporters of inclusion have attempted to describe the ways in which educational and welfare services for disabled people continue to systematically exclude:

> By 'exclusion' I am not talking of articulate people making a clear choice of a 'disabled culture' nor of groups of disabled and non-disabled people choosing to share a somewhat separate life in

a purposefully-formed idealistic community. Nor by 'systematic' do I mean that anyone necessarily intends people to be excluded. I am though, talking of a system which offers few or no options to disabled children, and whose inevitable consequence is that children grow into an adult life of exclusion.

(Tyne, 1993, p. 151)

Thus, the issue at the heart of most discussions about inclusion and exclusion is not really that of the failure of special education, but an attack on the visible instrument of exclusion, which is the special school. By aiming at a target that is itself a product of the failure of the mainstream education system the critics of exclusion reduce a complex analysis of wider social, economic and political considerations to a somewhat simplistic debate: ordinary schools are good; special schools are bad.

On the basis of this argument the concept of inclusion, as a celebration of difference, begins to emerge as a more problematic construct. The initial response to a movement that seems to be promoting ideals associated with integration and equality of opportunity is a positive one; inclusion is a process that most people would find it hard to disagree with. However, the reality of experience suggests that this initial enthusiasm is not universal. The movement reflects the value systems of different teachers or educational sectors through whom its meaning will be interpreted. Neither, of course, is a static entity which can be achieved by simply following established procedures. Inclusive education is often described in the same fashion as integration – as the education that takes place in the same class or setting as mainstream pupils/students – but this fails to guarantee the regular association with the integrative exchanges and interactions that such a definition often assumes. Integration and inclusive education should be seen as a matter of access to and regular association with the same range of opportunities and institutions as others have (Fish, 1988). The widest usage of integration is the process of combining different elements into a unity. With reference to students with learning difficulties and disabilities, it is the process of total inclusion at as many social and educational levels as possible. This requires continued and planned interaction with other people, including the contemporaries of students with learning difficulties and/or disabilities, and the freedom to mix with other different groups.

The inability to meet the needs of increasing numbers of young people, who are being excluded on grounds of failure to learn, or to maintain disciplinary codes, has led to the emergence of specialist provision in terms of both place (either special class or special school) and curricular support (adapted materials,

specialist equipment or additional teacher support procedures).
To abandon these continually evolving and carefully considered
practices and to sacrifice them on the altar of inclusion is for
many tantamount to suggesting that those involved in special
education have, like the Emperor who wore no clothes, been
deluding themselves; and perhaps they have. The simulated
practice environments in the classrooms, plastic money and card-
board cut-out supermarkets that were a feature of the infant
classroom or playgroup continue for some groups of disabled
people to be a part of the learning environment into adolescence
and beyond. These situations contribute nothing to the concept
of 'education for adulthood', but do a lot to confirm separateness
and preparation for the long years in the day centre.

INCLUSIVE LIVING AS ADDITIONAL CHOICE

For many, colleges of further education are the 'natural' places
for the development of inclusive practice (e.g. Whittaker, 1991,
1993). At present they are undergoing uncertainty and change
in a new managerial climate, but they also offer the opportunity
to bring together a fuller range and diversity of people and skills
than can be found in any school. Their policies for equality of
opportunity drive forward the values of a culture that is intended
to unite rather than to exclude and to celebrate diversity rather
than to stigmatize on the grounds of personal differences.

The rhetoric and ideological language that is associated with
any discussions of inclusive education has certainly been influenced by the contemporary debates around the wider remit of
equality of opportunity. Indeed in terms of the debate, it can be
recognized that equal opportunities are cited as the single greatest
incentive for promoting the concepts of integration and inclusion.
The equal opportunities of all students have, inevitably, to be
considered within this wider ethical framework. For example, a
student may be assessed as having sufficiently severe difficulties
and needs to adversely affect the sensibilities or study habits of the
other students and staff around him/her. In such circumstances
it may prove difficult to encourage a truly inclusive/integrationist
educational approach. The encouragement of inclusive living and
education for individuals with disabilities should not be at the
expense of others' equally valid educational opportunities. The
development of equal opportunities within a civil rights code
for disabled people will, hopefully, influence future policy and
practice for inclusive living. This will incorporate the concerns
of students with disabilities and learning difficulties. However,

so far civil rights legislation has not been forthcoming and so the advancement of rights has not kept pace with the expansion and rhetoric of inclusive practice.

Given the conflicting opinions and the limited number of studies on the effectiveness and respective merits of inclusive and segregated special education, it is worth considering that before it became the practice to place students and young people in segregated forms of special education, *all* children were either in mainstream or they were excluded from school. It was because they failed in regular classes that special classes were established for them. In other words, unless special provisions are made that take account of individual needs, we may be putting children and students back into a situation which we already know they are not able to handle.

Bleakley (1993), in piloting a more integrated approach to her teaching in drama, considers that the key to developing effective inclusion is the identification of a syllabus that can accommodate adult learners of all ages and not only those within a restricted age range. In order to progress to an externally validated qualification Bleakley expressed concern about the restrictions imposed by any syllabus that focused on the formal requirements of written work as evidence of skills acquired. The more experiential use of drama is one example of an alternative teaching approach.

THE ROLE OF SPECIALIST RESIDENTIAL COLLEGES

The arguments in favour of specialist residential provision are not easy to articulate in a climate where the search for quality is expected to be accomplished as economically as possible. Without doubt it is more expensive to send students to a residential college than to place them in their local neighbourhood college of further education. However, this oversimplifies a complex consideration based on the assumption that all local colleges can adequately meet the legitimate demands of students with a wide range of disabilities. It also tends to imply that what is going on in colleges is worth offering and is acceptable and appropriate to students with a range of complex needs. This assumption may not always be well founded, particularly where colleges are building the basis for their learning support provision on an intake of students with more moderate learning difficulties and disabilities. By so doing, they are resisting the challenge of students with more severe physical and/or sensory disabilities, or more challenging behaviours. This reluctance to extend provision may arise either from fear of losing output-related funding from the FEFC, or may result from inadequate resources or sheer lack of specialist staffing.

At a time when the spirit of competition and cost-effectiveness is running strongly and when there is a widespread belief in the benefits of mainstream college placement for students with learning difficulties and disabilities, it is worth considering what the advantages of residential provision might be. Kent (1986) and McGinty (1993) have argued that there are advantages for both the students and their families. The colleges and centres have been built up over many years with specialist facilities, including buildings, equipment and staff who are highly skilled in a range of academic and therapeutic disciplines: 'an expertise which is not only unrivalled but has been acquired over many years of constant contact with the problems of young people with severe physical handicaps, sensory disabilities and/or learning difficulties' (Kent, 1986, p. 3). Clearly, some mainstream colleges have been able to respond to the demands made of them by a small number of students with a range of more severe physical and other disabilities. They have managed to make both the college environment and the curriculum more accessible. There are, nevertheless, individuals and groups of students who, through geographical isolation, complexity of need or personal preference, are unlikely to be able to attend college on a daily basis. For them a period in a specialized residential college may be the most appropriate choice as a way of meeting their needs.

For the student there is the opportunity to live in a setting where needs can be met and understood in a dignified manner, respecting an individual's need for privacy as adulthood emerges. There is also the unfortunate reality that specialist colleges may be better able to meet the needs of students with deteriorating medical conditions, or seriously challenging behaviour. Specialist colleges may also provide some students with their only opportunity to experience maximum freedom of movement in a purpose-built or adapted environment. Some young people, disabled from birth, recently disabled, or who have a deteriorating condition, may find that living with their disability means they require the specialist support of a 24-hour curriculum. This may be from medical necessity, or in order to try new experiences away from the often confining conditions that exist at home (where, of necessity, much of the family life has been organized around meeting the physical care needs of the severely disabled individual). Residential specialist colleges can help parents and other members of the disabled student's family to reassess their own relationships and to rediscover some of their own shared identities. Perhaps, above all, residential provision permits parents to appreciate the essential normality of their children growing to adulthood and leaving home. It is with this realization that they discover that a severely disabled young adult does not mean a lifetime of perpetual and unshared care.

The distortion of family life that emerges for both the disabled person and other members of the family in such circumstances tends to prolong the state of childlike behaviour and a sense of perpetual parenthood. Parents often feel that they ought to let their disabled son or daughter perform more tasks for themselves, but the organization and effort involved, coupled with the need to arrange other aspects of their lives, makes this practically impossible. Development is retarded as a result. In the environment of a residential specialist college, it is argued, programmes can be arranged to promote the full realization of an adult personality. Kent (1986) suggests that this is possible because of the availability of a wide range of specialist staff, not available in mainstream further education colleges. Such staff often include physiotherapists, occupational therapists and other para-medical staff with knowledge and experience in meeting the special needs posed by particular conditions. It is highly unlikely that this range of expertise could be provided on a full-time basis outside the realms of a specialist college setting. However, it is questionable if such specialist services are cost-effective in an educational setting that is often small in size and isolated from the larger community.

The specialist colleges claim to be able to provide a number of additional facilities not normally found on a day-to-day basis in mainstream further education and training. Some of their arguments are increasingly tenuous, e.g. it is not only in residential colleges that it is possible to be assisted and taught to drive a specially adapted car, or to be individually assessed for the most suitable items of microelectronic equipment for more complete participation in both education and wider community activity. The opportunity to have direct access to on-site vocational training could indeed be considered a positive disincentive to the object of open employment. There are nevertheless some major advantages to residential provision over non-residential further education. These include the opportunities for extended contact between staff and students, which has the potential for developing skills and knowledge at appropriate times of day, in real situations, rather than as simulated, artificial classroom exercises. This is a powerful argument, as students can be taught to dress themselves or to prepare their breakfast when they would not normally do these things, thereby gaining improved understanding of how much effort and planning is involved in managing such fundamental aspects of daily living in addition to the routines of the normal college or working day.

In order to sustain and promote the perceived advantages of these specialist and mainly residential colleges, with their long history of making provision for disabled students, the Association of National Specialist Colleges (NATSPEC) has been formed. This federation is made up of eleven colleges, all of which are nationally known and primarily within the voluntary sector. Members of the Association are fully supportive of the principles of inclusion and integration but would claim that there are a number of students who are unable to move directly from school to a mainstream college. For them, a period of residential further education serves as an essential bridge into community provision. As NATSPEC points out, underlying many statements about the integration of students is the assumption that somehow it is better simply because it takes place in the community in which the student has grown up. This sidesteps the issue of those young adults who have not been accepted by their local community. As a care worker at Singleton Hall (a NATSPEC college on the outskirts of Blackpool) informed me, 'every specialist college could tell tales of the students who only really began to develop once their "differentness" was no longer a problem'. NATSPEC also argues that residential colleges are far ahead of the community in the attitudes and expectations they hold about the opportunities, rights and life chances of young adults with severe and complex disabilities.

To promote the opportunities for further education available to students with more complex learning difficulties and disabilities, the specialist colleges have developed within a national framework. This has made the matching of college, course and student more effective in terms of competing with the quality of any specialist provision offered by a local college of further education. No local college can easily provide facilities which will be of comparable quality for every student with learning difficulties and disabilities in its catchment area: the number of students involved would be too small to justify such a vast increase in resources. If for no other reason, this issue of access to appropriate resources in itself justifies the existence of further education in these specialist residential colleges.

Residential colleges are often run by voluntary sector organizations and pride themselves that they are able to provide a range of services, such as physiotherapy, speech and occupational therapy, rarely available outside these specialist settings. Some have a long tradition of provision, like the Spastics Society (now renamed Scope) or the Royal National Institute for the Blind. Others were founded as communities with their own spiritual or religious philosophies. A national survey of residential provision by Lillystone and Summerson (1987) shows that they are, in the main, small but expensive. They cater for the wide range of students' needs and personal circumstances and their curricular focus tends to be on a generic 'independence' as well as academic and vocational qualifications.

Hereward College in Coventry is well known for the pioneering work it has been carrying out since 1971, to provide for physically handicapped young people of average ability or above, from all over England and Wales. The college provides further education and training opportunities for disabled and non-disabled students and 24-hour care for some 110 residential students, male and female, living in three hostels. The age-range is normally between 16 and 30 years, with the majority of students being in the 16–19 age group. Courses vary from one to three years, the majority lasting two years. The college has four important advantages: specialist buildings that are purpose-built for students with physical disabilities with the appropriate equipment to match; skilled academic staff who can provide appropriate curriculum challenge; competent medical, nursing, physiotherapy and care staff who are sympathetic to the needs of disabled people; and its position adjacent to and on the same site as a larger college of further education. Hereward was set up as a national college, but it is moving towards a regional focus as well. Originally it was an experiment concerned with extending the educational horizons and aspirations of severely physically handicapped young people. As Panckhurst and McAllister (1980, p. 9) have commented about these early years: 'All colleges of FE have skilled academic staff, some have adapted toilets and buildings, but very few have ancillary staff to do what the Hereward care staff do. Hereward may be seen as the embodiment of what can be achieved by the able severely physically handicapped.'

A fundamental aim of the college is to assist students to achieve high levels of competence and independence. This implies a number of responsibilities and concerns. The college has to ensure that students are helped to achieve the goals that they have set for themselves on entry. Alongside this there is the need to promote and facilitate independence in daily living and personal care. That the college has been largely successful in promoting these aims is thanks largely to resource allocations. As Panckhurst and McAllister have said, the Hereward solutions to providing further education for physically handicapped young people are not the only alternatives. 'With the provision of ramps and converted toilets, access to a lift where one is available and goodwill from staff and fellow students' the small number of physically handicapped students in ordinary colleges can normally get by. Hereward College and the other specialist colleges are not for these people, but for those who need something more. They are the students with good potential but who also need some help with elements of self-care, like washing and toileting, independence and mobility. The college aims not so much to do things for or to a disabled student, but to help 'the student to manage and in the process, move towards self-understanding and independence'. It is debatable if such independence is best achieved in the segregated and specialist environment of a specially adapted college, but there can be no question about the success that Hereward College brings to the transition from child to adulthood for young people with physical disabilities.

Beaumont College in Lancaster has a number of similarities to Hereward, with specialist buildings, well-qualified academic and care staff and residential facilities. The college was established in 1977 and continues to be managed by Scope. It meets the needs of 60 to 70 less socially mature, physically disabled young people. The majority are cerebral palsied school-leavers and young adults in the average and slow-learning ability ranges.

The shift towards provision of further education in ordinary colleges has raised a number of questions about the place of the independent residential colleges as business propositions. In the same way that universities and institutions of higher education have had to become more 'client'-centred in their approach to the higher education of students with disabilities, the specialist further education colleges are having to attempt their own marketing too. By establishing specialist accommodation in halls of residence it is apparent that newly independent colleges have opportunities to begin to market residential provision for new client groups in a mainstream context. As an example Blackpool and the Fylde College have established a residential facility for physically disabled young people between the ages of 16 and 26 in the development of Singleton Hall, which they took over from the LEA with incorporation.

However, Singleton Hall suffers from the same problems as its better-known sister colleges. Comparative isolation – physically, geographically and socially – still prevents a more thorough sense of integration. It is some miles from the main college building, not easily reached by public transport, and it has evolved from its former purpose as a school with many of these rather oppressive undertones still present. Personal privacy is limited by dormitory living and shared study-bedrooms. The goal of personal space is still a comparative luxury for students, at a time in their lives when dignity is an important aspect of the development to adulthood. The concept of independence training is central to the curriculum, in the daily routine of college life. At the same time, it is regrettable that the opportunities for developing a full range of social relationships in a segregated hall of residence have not been more fully addressed.

SUMMARY

The enthusiasm for inclusive education, building on the practices in Canada and Scandinavia, is shared by a number of teachers and lecturers who see it as a way of reforming special education. It is supported as a guiding philosophy by a number of colleges of further education. As one element on a continuum of provision it deserves to be an alternative choice of educational provision but not necessarily the only choice. For students with more complex and/or multiple needs the provision of support from the other end of the inclusionist continuum also needs consideration. A specialist residential college can provide resources and emotional support to both students and their carers/parents. The respective merits of inclusion and segregation have been discussed and it was suggested that their purposes are not as diametrically opposed as might at first be imagined.

7

Staff development: problems and possibilities

It is temptingly easy to produce criticisms of staff development work, without providing clear suggestions as to how the situation might be improved. It is one of the purposes of this book to offer an explanation for this and to argue that there are ways of minimizing staff cynicism. First, however, it is necessary to examine the root causes and to discuss some of the possible reasons for ineffective staff development.

Staff development in further education settings is a comparatively recent phenomenon. In their early study, Bradley *et al.* (1983) pointed out that during the 1950s and 1960s when further education was enjoying a period of rapid expansion, 'very little thought was given to staff development'. The notion of developing skills already acquired in the workplace seemed unnecessary; for lecturers and teachers working with students with special educational needs, it was even further from consideration.

THE EMERGENCE OF STAFF DEVELOPMENT IN COLLEGES

Further training and other staff development initiatives now form an unquestioned part of the professional development of teachers in further education. It is readily accepted as an important element in enhancing both individual and collaborative skills. However, what Bradley *et al.* (1983) called 'the uncomfortable compromise' has tended to emerge between the 'management' or top-down approaches to staff development and the more grass-roots bottom-up, 'democratic' approaches initiated by staff in direct contact with students. This is seen particularly clearly in the drive towards system-led management and organization strategies that are emerging in further education colleges. These are alien to the more 'people-oriented' intuitions of teachers and tutors of students with disabilities and learning difficulties.

The Warnock Report (1978) offers a useful reference point against which to assess provision for students with special needs and consequent staff development. In terms of access to the curriculum, content and the context in which it is provided, the Report suggests that special educational need is likely to take the form of one or more of the following:

(1) the provision of special means of access to the curriculum through special equipment, facilities or resources, modifications of the physical environment or specialist teaching techniques;
(2) the provision of a special or a modified curriculum;
(3) particular attention to the social structure and emotional climate in which education takes place.

In the years that have followed Warnock, attitudes towards and provision for students with learning difficulties and disabilities have changed. It has become more readily accepted for students with disabilities to be in college. HMI (1989) confirmed that a range of courses had emerged to meet the diversity of needs presented by these students. Necessarily, the rapid expansion in further education for students led to an increased demand for staff development in this area.

Staff development initiatives on special education in further education have taken a variety of forms and have been developed by a range of organizations. Skill (formerly the National Bureau for Students with Disabilities) was one of the first voluntary organizations with the needs of this population of students and their tutors in mind; but the major force in promoting and sponsoring staff development activity has been the Further Education Unit. Like many non-governmental organizations, the FEU was established in the 1970s and was formed with the express purpose of developing effective routes for the vocational preparation of young people between the ages of 16 and 21. In the early days it worked in close collaboration with the Department of Employment, in the form of the Manpower Services Commission and the DES. The FEU has been more effective than many other units in initiating and responding to the management of change in the area of a new student intake. The sheer volume of FEU publications has acted as a form of staff development in its own right. However, a major weakness of all the FEU's good work has been its failure to facilitate any form of progressive and co-ordinated staff-development from initial qualification to post-graduate professional development.

The first abortive attempt to address this important issue of progressive professional development with different groups of administrators and tutors was made by a DES working party in 1987. In *A Special Professionalism* (DES, 1987) the DES seemed to be recommending training that targeted staff in colleges and in senior management positions in LEAs. There was a particular emphasis on initiatives that would facilitate inter-agency co-operation and communication. The programme anticipated was ambitious, consisting of a combination of short courses and conferences, locally, regionally and nationally for different staff with different responsibilities. The different modes of delivery and target audiences are outlined in Figure 7.1.

PATTERNS OF STAFF DEVELOPMENT IN COLLEGES

The well-thought-through objectives and implications of *A Special Professionalism* for improving the quality of participation of all involved in the further education of students with learning difficulties and disabilities deserve further consideration. The Report sets out a pattern for the structure of staff development opportunities for extending and deepening mainstream staff's understanding of the process of working with students with learning difficulties and disabilities. The framework identified offered the chance to extend teaching skills and approaches for key members of staff, including non-teaching assistants and managers. Although now nearly ten years old it still offers a coherent framework for short-term to long-term progression to a qualification in an area that has generally been overlooked as a priority in terms of career structure. Several universities have continued to provide full- and part-time diploma courses in the field of curriculum development in this area of work (for example the University of Greenwich, Wolverhampton University and Bolton Institute of Higher Education) and they have used some of the programme elements in *A Special Professionalism*. However, the opportunity to use the Report as the impetus for developing the professional competence of all staff, and thereby promoting the self-esteem and status of people working in a comparatively undervalued area, has been missed. The array of workshops and seminars run nationally and locally by organizations such as Skill, the FE lecturers' union NATFHE and the FEU have not really compensated for this lack of development in properly accredited career development. These shorter courses have targeted curriculum development, the dissemination of information and the facilitation of exchange networking between colleges and individuals.

Some other successful examples of staff development are the staff resource pack *From Coping to Confidence* (DES/FEU/NFER, 1985) and *Learning Support* (Faraday and Harris, 1989). Both were

Programme content	Possible modes of delivery				
	Regional		Local		In-house
	Conferences	Short courses	Conferences	Short courses	Short courses (including induction)
Programme 1. Awareness-raising for managers	i, ii, iii, iv		i, ii, iii, iv		
Programme 2. Awareness-raising for staff with no direct special needs involvement					x, xi
Programme 3. Awareness-raising and support for staff with some special needs involvement					vii, xi
Programme 4. Curriculum development and implementation (introductory)				vi	vi
Programme 5. Co-ordination of special needs work		v			
Programme 6. Staff development strategies		v			
Programme 7. Curriculum development and implementation		v			
Programme 8. The FE system				ix	ix

Source: **adapted from DES (1987)**

Key   (i) Senior officers
(ii) Advisers, inspectors and staff developers
(iii) Senior college managers
(iv) Staff with co-ordinating responsibilities of a general nature
(v) SLDD co-ordinators/course tutors
(vi) Mainstream teaching staff with major SLDD involvement
(vii) Mainstream teaching staff with some SLDD involvement
(viii) Part-time teaching staff with a SLDD involvement
(ix) Teaching staff recruited to colleges from other sectors, e.g. schools
(x) Mainstream teaching staff with no direct SLDD involvement
(xi) Ancillary and support staff
(xii) Teachers in initial training

Notes Part-time staff (category viii) would take programmes
relevant to their individual needs.
Teachers in initial training (category xii) would take
elements of Programmes 2 and 3 as part of their normal
training course.

Figure 7.1 *Possible modes of delivery*

produced to support staff development for further education teachers working with students with moderate learning difficulties. It was anticipated that they would provide a stimulus and support materials for curriculum-led staff development at regional, local and national level. The packs acknowledged the move towards the concept of staff development based on self-help rather than on a one-year course leading to a qualification. Lecturers are encouraged to work on a co-operative basis with colleagues to find their own solutions to the problems they experience with students with special educational needs. Neither pack offered any form of qualification or accreditation towards one.

The focus for staff development, inevitably influenced by the accumulation of documents from the FEU, was on the curriculum as the area for change. This influence of curricular 'choice' emerged as a driving force of the FEU. Such documents as *A Basis for Choice* (1978), *Experience, Reflection, Learning* (1981) and *Developing Social and Life Skills* (1980) all emphasize that tutors must recognize the need for a shared exchange. It may not be an easy matter to discover the type of learning opportunities that have already presented themselves in a young person's life outside college, but the best way to find out may be from a dialogue with the young person concerned. Staff development programmes to help tutors to improve and plan these skills formed much of the stuff of staff development in the 1980s. The model for change built on the belief that a cascade dissemination of practice could work its way through a complex system of operations and personnel and break through the rigidly compartmentalized structures of further education and training. The motivation for achieving this ambition was unfortunately never anything more than enhanced professional satisfaction. In the new internal market-place of further education such ambitions appear rather naïve. The chief criticism of staff development without inducements for participants, or opportunities to implement what is learned, is that it gets lost. The end-product, far from being the enriching, absorbing experience that it was designed to be, tends to become abandoned amongst vast tracts of information that is mechanically reproduced from the very packs and reference books that were intended to move staff away from such procedures in the first place.

One contributing factor to this limited success of curriculum-led staff development is identified in *A Special Professionalism*. Staff development initiatives in further education for students with learning difficulties and disabilities have traditionally been uncoordinated and have worked from a low base of provision.

This suggests that a prime reason for the ineffectiveness of much of this work is simply that staff developers do not possess the skills necessary to perform efficiently the activities involved. It seems appropriate to suggest that the majority of these skills might be classified as 'professional social skills', albeit fairly complex ones (e.g. negotiating and running meetings and workshops or training sessions, understanding the dynamics of group behaviour). With the threats to changes in the structure of teacher education, there is a strong chance that these skills will, unfortunately, continue to be given even less attention in initial teacher training. It is hardly surprising, then, that teachers and lecturers should exhibit weaknesses in those areas, in which they are unlikely to have been given sustained advice or instruction.

It is self-evident that teaching students with learning difficulties and disabilities is not the simple exercise which many lecturers had first appeared to think. Without co-operation and support, few members of a department will be able to cope with it on their own. All staff need detailed guidance and instruction if they are to manage to negotiate a teaching sequence, acquiring and exercising the requisite skills. They will also, as the FEU (1989) points out, need assistance with the detailed organization and planning of the work, especially if this involves collaborating with others, sharing resources and planning timetables. Just as many students find these aspects difficult and require guidance, so too do staff who are often expected to perform with an inadequate grounding or support structure.

Another reason for the ineffectiveness of much staff development seems to be the lack of purpose with which it is commonly approached. Both from the staff developer's and the lecturer/teacher's point of view 'staff development' often seems a rather vague activity. Many of the FEU publications, now stacked on the library shelves of nearly every FE college, bear testimony to this; they are seldom read and less frequently used. Staff development is more frequently used as a context for *ad hoc* help and discussion, rather than systematic guidance in specific skills. It is, in other words, a somewhat haphazard experience. If teachers are not given systematic guidance in how to participate in staff development activities, it seems unlikely that they will gain much from them other than a collection of a few unrelated impressions and facts.

Teachers also seem to approach staff development in special needs work with rather vague purposes. Very often their only brief is a desire to 'find out about' something – a specific condition such as Down's syndrome, behavioural approaches, or the latest thoughts of the FEFC, for example. Whilst this has its place, it is unlikely to initiate real development unless the purpose is refined into something more specific. Staff are also unlikely to be satisfied by the experience.

This vagueness seems to have two major causes. The first is the over-generalized nature of initial purpose, which makes achievement of the purpose very difficult indeed (it is obviously impossible to 'find out' everything; about Down's syndrome, for example). Having, therefore, set themselves an impossible task, staff cannot feel, or foresee feeling, any sense of achievement from completing the task, and so their interest quickly wanes. The process can rapidly become a somewhat vapid experience.

Several other possible reasons for ineffective staff development work could be suggested. Chief among these would be the question of available resources. If teachers and lecturers are expected to use staff development time efficiently, then obviously the staff development resources have to be suitable for that purpose. Bradley (1989) suggests that often, in the case of students with learning difficulties and disabilities, they are not. She criticizes staff development in this area for being too concerned with awareness-raising rather than the establishment of a satisfactory theoretical base from which to develop effective teaching skills. A further, fairly obvious reason for the slow growth in effective teaching of students with learning difficulties in FE is that teachers and lecturers lack the skills necessary to deliver. Largely this is because they have received cursory training in the area of special education. In turn, those with knowledge of special education frequently have no knowledge of the further education and training system.

For teachers unused to the working of the system, post-compulsory provision for disabled school-leavers is also extremely complicated. Further education colleges grew as a local response to the needs of a particular region or group of students. They prided themselves on their strength in meeting these specific and often *ad hoc* needs; part of the diversity of the local response. As such, there were no nationally agreed aims and objectives for students described as having special needs. There was no National Curriculum and no clear definition of statutory responsibility. The removal of colleges from LEA control in 1993 has brought new pressures on the funding for staff development. All funds, including money for staff development in the area of learning support for students with learning difficulties and disabilities, now take their place in the open cockpit of market forces in competition with other departments and concerns.

Tomlinson (1982) was one of the first academics to seriously explore the concept of 'transition to adulthood' with reference to the needs of students with learning difficulties and disabilities. Tomlinson had noted that handicapped young people seldom reach adulthood without considerable problems and this issue was taken up by Hutchinson and Tennyson (1986). Their staff development work on transition with physically handicapped students confirmed that it is not only young people with disabilities who are beset by tensions. Parents and carers are similarly faced with the prospect of developing new roles and relationships with their children, with little guidance or advice. The adolescent years are uncharted waters, but for those involved with young people with disabilities, the temptation to ignore changing circumstances and to maintain a state of perpetual childhood (and at the same time perpetual parenthood) is an additional difficulty.

Staff development work needs to consider some of these wider aspects of transition. All young people seek to expand their networks of social contacts in the years between 16 and 25. Students with learning difficulties and disabilities also need to discover opportunities to experiment which can hardly be offered, but have to be taken. The experiences for promoting independence within curricular structures such as *A Model for Future Need* (Hutchinson, 1992b, p. 11) acknowledge that choice has to be interpreted in relation to the changing political and economic realities of students' own lives.

Staff themselves need to learn how to help students to choose. This might involve comparatively mundane choices – what to wear, who to visit, what to do and how to structure daily activity. Nevertheless, this is an unfamiliar experience for many young people, especially those with more severe learning difficulties and disabilities. Childhood dependence has limited most opportunities for decision-making, with responsibility for social and vocational arrangements being taken by and remaining with an adult in authority.

Staff development needs to address these shifts in authority. Proper staff development in further education recognizes this, and that all participants bring different skills and expectations to the process of working with students and young people with learning difficulties and disabilities. All have different roles to play. It is worth considering the diverse range of personnel involved in establishing an appropriate strategy of staff development policy. This focuses on the need for the active involvement of senior college managers. As was noted by the DES, 'their role focuses essentially on ensuring that policy is both effective and relevant to student needs and on supporting those colleagues who are working to convert this policy into practice' (DES, 1987, p. 7).

City and Guilds courses have been an important route for

many staff seeking career advancement in the area of learning difficulties and disabilities. Through courses such as the Certificate in Continuing Professional Development (Special Needs) and the newly emerging Certificate in Learning Support, staff are able to gain recognition of the skills and knowledge they already possess in this area. New knowledge is accrued via a combination of both theoretical and practical assignments. Other advantages of these part-time programmes are that they bring new opportunities for staff to reflect upon established working practices and the chance to exchange ideas.

SOME DILEMMAS OF STAFF DEVELOPMENT

Research carried out by Skill in the 1980s indicated that at that time only about a quarter of college staff working with students with learning difficulties and disabilities had received any specialist teacher training (Stowell, 1987). The part-time City and Guilds qualification on Special Needs in Further Education was the main vehicle for the introduction of awareness and further professional development, together with in-house staff development, which at its best involved all staff. Since the original Skill survey and over a period of some fifteen years, the FEU has become the key player in shaping and refining the curricular framework for teaching and learning in post-compulsory education. The FEU sees both student and staff development as part of a more negotiated approach to the post-16 education of all students. The starting point for the FEU is that curriculum entitlement places an obligation on providers to develop an appropriate learning environment for everyone. At the heart of the development the FEU has suggested that there is the need for strategic planning with the aim to provide:

- appropriate learning opportunities, regardless of gender, race, age and ability;
- opportunities for all learners to establish and develop a recognised competence base of knowledge, skills and experience, sufficient to facilitate progression into employment, further education, training or other roles;
- an understanding of the local and national economic and social environment, to promote an appreciation of the variety of available adult roles in society;
- a basis for learners to increase their self-awareness, to appraise realistically their potential and prospects, and to become progressively responsible for negotiating their own personal development.

(FEU, 1989, p. 7)

This agenda for entitlement put forward by the FEU is an attempt to try and break the belief that for many learners, and particularly those with learning difficulties and disabilities, a deficit model of education applies. In other words, the purpose of the education they have received has been to identify deficit and to remedy it rather than to recognize proficiency and to develop it. By promoting the concept of entitlement and a common curriculum framework, the FEU stresses that all learners should be treated equally and that they should be able to benefit from certain common experiences, regardless of the nature of their learning programmes or of their individual strengths and weaknesses.

Such ambitions are in line with the original education and training procedures proposed by the FEU for vocational preparation. These stressed the need for improved curriculum negotiation; the provision of counselling and guidance; the opportunity to acquire relevant and work-based skills; formative and profiled assessment; and, above all, valuing the experiences of the learners, or consumers of the programmes of study. Just as these procedures were intended for the benefit of a new group of learners with a variety of disadvantages and complex learning needs, so it has raised the need for a more thoroughgoing and co-ordinated form of training for staff unused to working with a client group that had previously been unprovided for in further education colleges and training.

Skill has echoed the emphasis of the FEU and its numerous publications by maintaining that the most important way of ensuring that provision is made for those with learning difficulties and disabilities is to follow a straightforward three-stage process: (1) assessing needs; (2) establishing a policy for meeting needs; (3) monitoring progress made. The assessment of need is frequently best accomplished by a working party consisting of some or all of the following: college staff, specialist careers officers, people with disabilities, parents, advisers and others who may have a special professional or local knowledge. Cooper (1993) has suggested that the questions that generally need to be addressed include the following:

- what provision exists or is planned in the college or in the area?
- how many young people leaving special schools and units each year do not currently have opportunities in further education?
- how many adults are there with learning difficulties and disabilities in the local community who could benefit from further education?
- can these needs be met within existing courses?
- what resources are available?

- what are the priorities for making provision in the light of existing resources?
- what opportunities are there for staff to receive training in the identification of student needs and the adaptation of curricular materials?
- how will any plan for provision be implemented?
- how will this plan be regularly reviewed?

Putting this policy initiative into practice is not a short-term operation. It can take time to convince staff and middle management that the approach is worthwhile. A NATFHE (1993) survey enquiring into the provision of staff development made in 138 colleges (almost 50 per cent of those in the FEFC sector) for students with learning difficulties and disabilities indicated that 78 per cent of colleges responding to the questionnaire had developed written policies relating to students with special needs in the institution. In 76 per cent of colleges this was incorporated in a general equal opportunities statement. As Cooper (1993) has indicated, 'this is wonderful but it also implies that 22 per cent of colleges do not have policies'. It appears that realistic change in developing staff is still painfully slow.

The Further and Higher Education Act 1992 makes no requirement on colleges to have any form of written policy in this area. However, there is a requirement for every college to have a strategic plan as a condition of grant and this is being closely monitored by the FEFC in relation to students with learning difficulties and disabilities. The NATFHE survey also suggested that the organization of staff development as a nationally co-ordinated activity has improved since an earlier NATFHE survey in 1986. The variety of award-bearing courses undertaken by specialist staff in the 'special needs' area varied from MEd programmes and advanced diplomas, to qualifications in first aid. Many colleges are encouraging staff to complete the City and Guilds qualification 740.1 relating to the teaching of students with learning difficulties and disabilities in FE. The use of staff development funds for this small group of staff has meant an increase in the range and variety of short in-service courses provided in-house and by organizations such as the Basic Skills Unit (ALBSU), Skill, FEU, MENCAP and RNID. Through these activities, the survey identified a range of staff development concerns that had been addressed including: curriculum development, assessment and profiling, behavioural development, NVQs and learning difficulties and disabilities, deaf-awareness, IT updating, Braille tuition, self-advocacy and classroom management.

Staff development for mainstream staff, who may or may not have dealings with students with special training needs, suggested that many colleges had developed 'awareness-raising' courses: 'Over one third of the replies actually described the staff development programmes for "mainstream" staff specifically as "awareness raising" and many of the other examples could have been given that classification' (NATFHE, 1993, p. 26).

It is worth recalling the concerns expressed about courses that move no further than awareness-raising. It is evident that many of these staff development activities are held at odd times, such as lunchtime workshops, one-day or half-day events and that topics covered include issues such as dyslexia support, physical disability, and epilepsy. Interestingly, not many respondents drew a distinction between academic and support staff for purposes of priority of attendance. This could be interpreted as an encouraging sign of co-operation or alternatively as a reminder that the different roles played by staff within an institution under the broad heading of 'learning support' are often misunderstood or not yet properly determined. Surveys, on the other hand, tend to be passed to and completed by teaching staff alone. Inevitably, there is a wide variety of opinion about the effectiveness of staff development. Sixty-nine per cent of respondents in the NATFHE survey considered that the programmes of available staff development did not meet their needs. The areas that were considered as yet unaddressed included the following:

mental health, dyslexia, behaviour problems;
the difficulty of reaching those who don't want to be reached;
integration into the mainstream;
evaluating learning/teaching styles, systems of learning support, assessment methods, and accreditation.

More recently it has been suggested that real staff development needs to return to its roots, the coming together of people to unpack their own 'needs' grounded in both personal and professional concerns. Talking about staff development at a NATFHE conference in 1993, the director of Skill argued that the key to the development of real quality was in co-operation and networking in order to ensure that 'opportunities are not lost and [that there is] co-operation between providers, colleges, LEAs, social services departments etc. to make sure that provision is continued and provides a seamless garment. After all, a chain is only as good as its links' (Cooper, 1993, p. 43).

SUMMARY

Staff development events have come to be part of work in colleges of further education. Not only is it incumbent on staff to be seen to be updating their own skills and knowledge, but it has also become part of a college's income generation to provide and host courses from which other groups can learn. Staff in the area of learning difficulties and disabilities need to network with others in order to develop and keep abreast of changes and guidance from the FEFC. However, it is also important to keep in touch with the informal links back to schools and on to local employers. As the college experience is a short-term interlude for young people on the road to adult responsibility, employment or occupation, college staff need to regularly revise and update their own skills and to stay aware of the needs of all students. For those young people in college who have learning difficulties and disabilities, still a relatively new student group, this developing awareness is even more essential.

Young people who are transferring to colleges from the relative shelter of special schools or small units have had little exposure to the speed of change, length of day and sheer boisterousness that can be part of college life. These considerations can bring new challenges for the staff involved and raise old anxieties for the parents and carers who have borne the brunt of the responsibility for unshared care during the years of childhood. These considerations form the focus for the next chapter.

8

Those who are left behind: parents and carers

This chapter considers the impact that further education has on the development of relations between parents/carers and young adults with learning difficulties and disabilities as they move from childhood to adulthood. The established guidelines for being a care-provider/parent are never more blurred than during this period of transition as young people seek an element of autonomy in their lives and yet are encouraged by economic and political circumstances to remain the responsibility of families. This dilemma is even more acute for the parents of young adults with severe and profound learning difficulties, who may be faced with extended periods of home supervision as colleges become more selective in their student intake. Anderson and Clarke (1982) noted in their extensive survey of physically disabled adolescents that parents are an important influence on a child's ultimate physical and emotional independence. The need to keep in touch with parents during the final years of school life was clearly stated. However, there is a lack of supportive follow-up services for disabled school-leavers or their parents. A major problem appears to be that once a disabled child leaves school there is no clear indication of who takes responsibility if difficulties arise. As increasing stress is placed on a return to 'family values', it is ironic that the 'parenthood' of adolescent children seems to be turning into a more isolated and thus potentially more difficult experience for all families.

This chapter also briefly focuses on the impact of the self-advocacy movement and the Student's Charter on the rights, entitlements and concerns of parents/carers as their sons and daughters with learning difficulties and disabilities move into the adult services provided by statutory and voluntary agencies.

THE GROWING CONCERNS OF PARENTS/CARERS OF YOUNG PEOPLE AND STUDENTS WITH LEARNING DIFFICULTIES AND DISABILITIES

Whilst the development of a better working relationship between parents and professionals has been growing in recent years, relatively few studies have concentrated on the additional challenges that face the parents and carers of handicapped and disabled children in their adolescent years. Nevertheless, a consistent theme of the research is the increasing level of parental anxiety about the future as the time of school-leaving approaches (e.g. in early research the importance of consulting parents, as the main providers of care, was stressed, in order that young people could rehearse practical social skills: Glendinning, 1983; Cheseldine and Jefree, 1982). The development of post-school opportunities for young people with learning difficulties and disabilities can help to relieve elements of parental anxiety, but there are a number of reasons for continuing to seek out the views and opinions of parents since the original notions put forward by Cheseldine and Jefree (1982):

- parents and carers have some of the greatest influence on any young person's development;
- the time that a young person spends in a home setting tends to be greater than the time spent in school or college;
- when adolescents with learning difficulties and disabilities are faced with the changes in the transition from school to post-school settings (changes to familiar faces, friendship groups) parents/carers may form the only stable link;
- for the more severely disabled adolescent a parent or carer remains a crucial decision-maker in relation to the young person's future. The quality of life for all concerned is dependent on the parents'/carers' ability to cope.

Because disability is so often perceived in negative terms, the families and carers of people with learning difficulties have themselves frequently felt marginalized in common with their sons or daughters. Their social circle and experiences of daily life have been linked with the large numbers of professionals with whom they have come into contact through their child's disability. Research shows that many parents/carers feel oppressed and have a distrust of the professional care services that enter their lives from the time when a learning difficulty or disability is first diagnosed (e.g. Horobin and May, 1988; Richardson and Ritchie, 1989; Short, 1992). These, too often negative, experiences have shaped and reinforced the distrust of parents/carers as their children grow. It has been argued that this form of 'learned helplessness' both emerges from and subsequently strengthens the low expectations of people with learning difficulties, disabilities and communication disorders. It is possibly for this reason that students with learning difficulties were for so long denied access to further education. As it has been argued, if people are treated as if they cannot, or will not, learn, then this can over time become a self-fulfilling belief. Because of a parent/carer's extensive and intimately intensive contact with their son or daughter, they are in a key position to either combat or reinforce such learned helplessness (Hutchinson and Tennyson, 1986; Short, 1992).

The emotional ties that exist between parents/carers and their disabled children can become increasingly difficult to sever. Just as young people have been dependent upon their parents during childhood, so a parent has derived varying degrees of satisfaction from meeting the needs of their son or daughter. Through this retention of 'control' parents/carers have managed to evade the need to renegotiate their relationship with an emerging adult. On the face of it, this would appear to be emotionally driven behaviour. Such action may, however, be quite rational. For example, if the alternatives have been to teach the child to cope for him/herself, or for the parent/carer to carry out the tasks on the child's behalf, the second alternative carries less risk than the former in terms of short-term emotional (and possibly financial) costs. Parents/carers who are unable, or unwilling, to plan for the long-term future of their disabled youngster are unlikely to develop the long-term strategies of risk-taking and citizen advocacy that real independence and autonomy imply.

There are many more opportunities for contact between parents/carers and professional services in the early years of a child's life than during the years of adolescence. The advice and assistance is both comprehensive, anticipated and usually well-meaning in both formal and informal forms. Whether it is the doctor, health visitor or Aunty Nelly, there is usually plenty of support for most young parents. It is noticeable that these systems operate with less certainty and availability as children grow older and/or begin to indicate that there might be signs of difficulty or a disability that will take up disproportionate amounts of time or expenditure on the part of service providers. For many parents/carers, children moving into young adulthood present a double challenge. The issue of changing roles and 'letting go' with dignity is not only difficult for both parties, but also confused by the conflicting messages of community care and the concept of 'normalization'.

The principles of self-advocacy and normalization that began to influence the curricular planning of many colleges of further education in the 1980s were developed with particular regard to their impact on the lives of people with learning difficulties. These have been well documented elsewhere (e.g. Wolfensberger, 1972; Williams and Schoultz, 1982; Wertheimer, 1986; Brechin and Walmsley, 1989; Clair, 1990) but at their heart was the simple belief of moving from a system-centred to a more student-centred education service. In a system-centred institution, evaluation schemes, tests and marks, for example, tend to be more norm-referenced. This means they are based on the abilities and achievements of 'average' or 'normal' students. Students have to adapt to fit the system; if they do not, or perhaps are unable to, they suffer the consequences.

A more student-centred approach adapts the teaching approach and structure of the curriculum to a more 'criterion-referenced' needs-based evaluation, matched more to the abilities of individual students. In this way, students with learning difficulties and disabilities can be given work at their own level and evaluated against individually set criteria. The concept of criterion-referenced assessment fits well with the concepts of self-advocacy and equal opportunities. Undoubtedly, both principles have the potential for radically altering the life experiences, community attitudes to and expectations of people with learning difficulties or disabilities. Positive results are already much in evidence in terms of increased acceptance of disabled people on work placements, college courses, centres for independent living, coalitions of disabled people and larger advocacy movements such as People First.

However, such radical change has tended to occur without the unanimous approval or understanding of everyone. Ultimately, the movement towards self-advocacy leaves an unanswered question: where is the voice of the parent/carer in all this? In the past decade and a half, the prevailing political orthodoxy has been to reaffirm the family as the primary unit in society and to encourage families to take responsibility for their members. This has led many observers to doubt if the political endorsement for 'community care' means anything more than a reassertion of care within the family. When this is linked to the uncertainties of the economic climate, public expenditure in a downward spiral and demographic change that reminds us that we are living longer, it would appear that the strains of caring for adults with disabilities and/or learning difficulties will increasingly be borne by parents and carers at home.

Parents of young adults are normally in the middle years of life themselves. It would be unusual to find many parents or carers with these responsibilities under the age of 45. Their views and attitudes to 'caring' have been formed over a number of years and many of them will have been influenced by the accepted positions of the professional service providers of, perhaps, a generation earlier. Parents are also at a time in their own life cycle when they feel that they should be able to begin to draw back from some of the more arduous tasks of parenting. It is the usual period for sons and daughters to establish the beginnings of their own independence. However, for the parents of young adults with learning difficulties and disabilities, the duty of care continues and the role takes on an often uncomfortable reminder that it is a 'job for life', in some cases akin to providing nursing care. The parents interviewed in Short's study (1992) confirmed earlier studies (e.g. Johnstone, 1986, 1987; Brimblecombe and Russell, 1988; Richardson and Ritchie, 1989) that most parents/carers had very low expectations of their child's potential for independent living and as a result tended to place even greater restrictions on their child. There were few indicators of anything approaching what could be described as a 'normal adult life'. The low self-esteem and loneliness of the young disabled adults interviewed was echoed in many of the responses from the parents.

The responses of parents/carers to the implications of changing family relationships as their children grow to adulthood are predictable and essentially involve practical considerations. Key issues revolve around concerns for the physical and moral safety of their child. There are also worries about what will happen when they are no longer physically capable of providing current levels of care, or after they have died. Other important concerns are voiced about the poor level of respite care available. For many parents of children with learning difficulties and disabilities, the impact they have on their lives is an accepted reality and something to be endured or coped with. Although most parents are keen to point out that there are positive aspects to the caring role, this is accompanied by a good deal of stress as they learn to cope with the new demands made of them.

Much of this strain appears to be as a result of the need for ongoing practical support in the home, in terms of meals, lifting, cleaning and housework. Many of the parents of young adults with learning difficulties, in particular, have also indicated from their responses that they believe much of the popular discourse about people with learning difficulties, notably in respect to the perpetuation of childlike behaviour (Short, 1992). This has led to the result that many young adults continue to be treated much as one would respond to younger children, with numerous restrictions upon their activities. Many parents in Short's study worried about their child's safety whenever they were out 'unsupervised' and complained of the general strain of having a younger adult with different expectations continuing to live at home. For many older parents the development of self-advocacy is seen as a challenge to their control over both their own and their son's or daughter's pattern of life. This is important, for 'control' has frequently served for some as the only tool in the development of their personal 'coping' strategy. The decline in respite care support for parents/carers as a child grows is also a major factor contributing to the strain experienced and reported in many studies. So it is not surprising that many parents feel vulnerable and suspicious of the motives that underlie the growth of self-advocacy in day centres and colleges of further education.

PARENTS AS CO-WORKERS

For parents who have been used to the day-to-day communication with school-oriented services the transition to the world of further education can leave them feeling isolated and with no trusted point of contact. For young people who have attended special schools especially and their parents, the structure of the school day brought an assurance that was comforting, but ultimately destructive to the development of self-advocacy. Some parents/carers, resenting the ways in which social and self-advocacy skills are being developed as a part of the curriculum, consider that the new ways of working in colleges are a backward move. Although the majority of parents may favour community integration they wish to see this set within prescribed limits and with improved communication and consultation about post-school policies and activities (Johnstone, 1986; Clair, 1990; Short, 1992).

This raises a crucial issue for policy-makers, curriculum co-ordinators and self-advocates. Consultation may be desirable – but with whom? Parents/carers or the emerging young adults with disabilities and/or learning difficulties? Whilst it may appear sensible to place an emphasis upon the student in college or emerging young adult with learning difficulties in the day centre it is neither sensible nor fair to abandon consultation with parents and carers. They have had and continue to have a significant part in defining the role that a young person will play in life and as such need to be involved in supporting self-advocacy if its full potential is to be realized (Mittler and McConachie, 1983; Wertheimer, 1989; Clair, 1990).

Since the 1970s it has become more popular to recognize parents and carers as 'partners', especially in the school sector.

This recognizes that parents not only have a legitimate right to participate in the development of services for their child, but that they have practical skills to bring to this shared activity. However, as Russell (1991) points out, many parents do not know how to utilize their unique knowledge of their child and do not understand the principles behind the practices of college courses or self-advocacy programmes. Although the majority of service providers for families acknowledge the need to encourage active partnership with parents, such a partnership cannot be assumed to be present simply because professionals are working with parents. As a young adult with learning difficulties and disabilities moves from childhood to adulthood, many parents feel marginalized by procedures which they do not fully understand and are uncertain of how (or even if) they can express their views in the larger and often overpowering setting of a college of further education. Partnership, or co-working, in post-16 settings is another potential form of consumer-participation. It should not be seen as merely a cheap version of respite care or an alternative to the provision of appropriate aids, equipment or services.

PARENTS' RESPONSES TO SELF-ADVOCACY

The majority of parents/carers have little understanding or knowledge of the issue of self-advocacy. Short (1992) suggests that younger parents are more prepared to challenge stereotypes and prejudice and to encourage their child towards greater independence, but the opportunities for marginalization are clear as concentration is placed upon the development of individual autonomy.

It has already been argued that the teaching of self-advocacy to students and adults with learning difficulties and disabilities is likely to lead to conflict at home. Many parents and carers establish very restrictive boundaries to the limits of independence that their sons and daughters are anticipated or encouraged to achieve. At the same time many express the desire to see their son or daughter leading a more independent life. This paradox seems to suggest that while most parents may support self-advocacy as a concept, they are unable to develop the appropriate coping strategies for readjusting to the changed circumstances of its practical reality.

Self-advocacy lies at the heart of a good deal of work in colleges and day centres, with people with learning difficulties in particular. It is therefore surprising that so little information about such an important policy initiative is passed on to parents. The perceptions of those parents who have heard of self-advocacy and normalization is still quite limited: often they confuse the concept with independent living and work placement (Clair, 1990; Short, 1992). For some parents self-advocacy is the equivalent to 'going shopping on your own', or 'living independently or in groups. Certain of them working in the community' (extracts from parental interviews: Short, 1992, p. 100). Although this work on life skills and independent living is important in its own right and can be seen as complementary to the development of self-advocacy, they are not the same thing. However, for some parents, the two ideas appear to be synonymous.

So it is worth asking, is the fulfilment of self-advocacy possible in this climate of parental uncertainty and conflicting messages? One parent has voiced an opinion that is shared by many when he states that a self-advocate is someone who speaks out for themselves, but that in relation to some young people – those with learning difficulties –

> they haven't got that ability – by definition. They haven't got the intelligence to think that far ahead for themselves . . . I think it's a non-term . . . they haven't got that initiative to be able to say 'I like watching football, can I watch it on TV?' They just try to do it and try to accept it . . . knowing him and his pain. I can't see them coming in here and banging the table and saying 'I want this'. . . . It's not in their nature.
>
> (Short, 1992, p. 101)

This somewhat fatalistic view linking the ability to think for one-self with innate intelligence is almost inevitably associated with the conflicts and threats of disruption to home life. As we saw earlier, self-advocacy and the assertion of independence appears to manifest itself first in the refusal to conform to parental wishes at home. This is particularly problematic for parents who have built up rigid routines for themselves and their children in order to cope with the stresses of caring for a young adult with learning difficulties or a disability. Any challenge to this established routine therefore has the potential for opening up a veritable Pandora's box of disruptions to routine, as parents have to reconstruct their lives. Not surprisingly, many parents will prefer to try to stick with what they know.

THE STUDENT'S CHARTER

The Charters for students in both further and higher education (DfE, 1993a) have been developed within the broad framework of equal opportunities. The Charter is a force for change within a further education system that is in the process of redefining itself. It sets out the entitlements to fair treatment that can be expected by students while studying and the entitlement to efficient service from a college, an employer or a member of the local community. It thereby challenges colleges to ensure an appropriate and accurate consideration of how they inform both students and the wider community. The emphasis in the text of the Charter is still upon how an individual student can gain access to provision. This, at first sight, appears to be unfortunate for the emphasis would more usefully be to encourage a consideration of how the further education system as a whole is *enabling* access. This would be especially relevant to the needs of students with learning difficulties and disabilities, who are not specifically mentioned. This could be viewed as a reasonable and genuine demonstration of equal opportunities, but it is more likely simply to have been that they were overlooked.

The second edition of the Charter for Further Education will be published in 1996. The revision will give special consideration to the service standards and information needs of students with learning difficulties and disabilities, prospective students and third parties.

SUMMARY

The concerns of parents of young adults with learning difficulties and disabilities are often overlooked. Parenthood and caring at home is associated more frequently with the early years of life, when networks of informal gatherings centre around self-help at the school gate. These ties become weaker as children grow and strike out for independence, and as parents themselves take on more concerns in their daily activity. Nevertheless, the time of leaving school and moving from childhood to adulthood brings tensions for all parties concerned in the transition. The more severely disabled son or daughter places a severe burden of responsibility upon parents, and mothers in particular. When compared to their peers young disabled adults report feelings of loneliness as a big problem, along with lack of social confidence and poor self-esteem. There appears to be a decline in the transitional support arrangements for parents, and more experiential shared-group work for them may be of advantage and needed at this new stage of life.

9

Developments in the management of learning

The torrent of reports and reforming legislation that has cas-
caded on to the educational world during the past two decades
has had a number of purposes. For some, the intention has been
to stem and control the 'rising tide of mediocrity' that seems to
have affected the educational systems of the Western world. For
others, the intention has been guided by economic considerations
and a commitment to counter the growing skills shortage by
investment in education and training. The legislative framework
created by the tensions between these philosophies has brought
its own challenges. Rowan's (1990) review of the literature has
distinguished between the emergence of 'control' and 'commitment' strategies for the implementation of educational policy in
the United States, and the analysis of the mistakes and inconsist-
encies in reform echoes many of the developments in the United
Kingdom in further education in the 1990s:

> In a first wave of reform, many large urban districts and several
> state legislatures responded to the problem of low achievement
> in schools by increasing bureaucratic controls over curriculum
> and teaching. . . . However, a reaction to this approach formed
> when it was argued that bureaucratic controls over schools are
> incompatible with the professional autonomy of teachers.
>
> (Rowan, 1990, p. 353)

DETERMINANTS OF POLICY AND PRACTICE

Policies for change in schools and colleges in the United Kingdom
have tended to follow a similar two-phase pattern, with the reaction to the first enthusiasm for educational reform through
'control strategies' being followed by a more conciliatory second
phase of reform based upon strategies for shared 'commitment'.
Commitment strategies are based on achieving high levels of

agreement amongst organizational members about purposes, beliefs, norms and assumptions (Leithwood *et al.*, 1991). They place an emphasis on helping to develop and improve problem-solving strategies from a common values base. By way of comparison, 'control strategies' are an attempt to prescribe what people do in an organization on the assumption that the most productive things to be done can be determined centrally. Rowan (1990) has pointed out that both strategies can be useful, with the former contributing to the solution of complex open-ended tasks and the latter to simpler routine tasks.

The financial investment in educational innovation and change in the United Kingdom has heightened expectations of improved performance. Not only is this expected from central and local government but also from industry, corporations and individuals. Yet for all of this effort, evaluation of the reforms indicates only minor changes either in educational/teaching practice or in achievement (Dyson *et al.*, 1994). For the most part, the methods of teaching and content of instruction in colleges are little different from what they were twenty years ago. Much of the critical discourse around these disappointing results has attributed them to the characteristics of 'top-down', 'more of the same' management styles which were initiated by forces outside the college environment. Attempts to improve and reform educational inputs were initially aimed at curricular reform and the quantification of the competence and performance of lecturers (e.g. NVQs, new contracts of employment, changing conditions of service including annual reviews, incentive payments, etc.).

Whereas in the past special education, which by definition was confined to a small and specialist population, was relatively immune to sharing this attention, it has now become embroiled in change. This includes the determination of policy and practice to promote and protect the interests of the most needy in society within a framework of learning support and equal opportunity. For students with learning difficulties and disabilities and the people who work with them, this shift towards inclusion and equal opportunities suggests that a more democratic style of management has begun to develop. Yet, for this to be realized, it is necessary to create a coherent environment within which colleges, trainers and lecturers can best perform their jobs and at the same time protect and develop the best interests of all students, including those with learning difficulties and disabilities. At present there appears to be a concentration upon the development of communication of ideas at the expense of purposeful co-ordination of effort, ideas and responsibility. Different political agendas and the changing positions of special interest groups have had the effect of dissipating the energy that would best be channelled towards a focused goal or the planning of coherent, progressive, long-term strategies for achieving challenging, yet commonly agreed outcomes.

The potential consequences of incorporation and the expectations of rapid growth in further education are having their effect on colleges and their management systems. The management of change in the further education context has borrowed many of its ideas from business. One of the main consequences is that colleges are being expected to adopt more businesslike approaches to management of finance, accountability and quality control. However, there are some important differences between a manufacturing business and the business of further education. These differences need to be appreciated, especially in relation to the educationally desirable but relatively unlucrative business of recruiting students with learning difficulties and disabilities.

If a manufacturing concern has a product line that does not sell sufficiently well to make a profit, it is likely that the item will be dropped from the production line. There would need to be strong arguments in favour of retaining a product unless it was a deliberate 'loss leader' (perhaps because it happens to capture a caring image that the business wishes to cultivate with the public, or because it attracts additional business). In similar fashion colleges may be prepared to see some parts of their course portfolio financially supported by other areas. As Burton has acknowledged:

> there are real dangers that in some misguided race for status, some incorporated colleges may wish to shed work which is not seen as having the highest academic status. This may be particularly the case if the college is successful in enrolment terms and in the position of not being able to cater for all who wish to attend because financial, physical or human resources simply will not permit it.
>
> (NATFHE, 1993, p. 54)

It is also worth bearing in mind that the political pressures on educational administrators, elected officials and college managers is to produce measurable 'or at least memorable' results in short periods of time and that this can lead to a 'projects' mentality (Smith and O'Day, 1990). For instance, a new strategy for assessment and testing, an in-service day on disability etiquette, a shared project with local schools, or new computers for dyslexic students (but little appropriate software) are all familiar concepts to people who have worked in schools and colleges. In such a climate, the emergence of learning support should be seen in a similar light and treated with a degree of caution. Hopefully, support in this sense is not going to be merely a short-term fad. It will not become yet another name for 'special educational needs', this time in a further education context. Nor will support be seen as a subsidy for a few at the expense of the majority. Learning support is what all teachers should be in a position to supply as part of their professional commitment to any student. It is about providing a more systematic response to the individual needs of all learners.

THE EMERGENCE OF LEARNING SUPPORT

The recognition that learning difficulties or other disabilities can arise at different points in any student's educational career has helped to underline the need for appropriate levels of support. The rationale for learning support is closely allied to the notions of entitlement, integration and inclusion. It also implies co-operative ways of working for all staff, sharing responsibility for the development of provision between mainstream subject-oriented teaching and the more process-oriented concerns of staff working with students with learning difficulties and disabilities. It is, therefore, not the same thing as special education as an alternative curriculum. Instead it encompasses the wider recognition of the original Warnock (1978) belief that a continuum of need requires a carefully managed and assessed response. An essential element in the delivery of successful learning support is the provision of specific assistance on an individual or a group basis in order to achieve targeted learning objectives. The organization and co-ordination of this support can have internal cross-college implications as well as involving a variety of external agencies. The aims of learning support are to ensure that an appropriate management and organizational structure is in place and accessible to all learners, particularly those with learning difficulties and disabilities.

The concept of learning support in colleges continues to be burdened with some of the confusions identified in the development of 'whole-school' responses to special needs in secondary education (Dyson, 1991; Dyson *et al.*, 1994). The effectiveness or otherwise of learning support in schools rests first on the notion of learning as a fully participatory process, and secondly on challenging the concept of learning as a progressive acquisition of a hierarchy of knowledge. As Dyson *et al.* suggest, the emergence of real learning support is part of a 'continued movement in the direction of increasingly responsive provision and an almost complete abandonment of the "category" of special educational needs as a basis for the structuring of provision' (Dyson *et al.*, 1994, p. 312). Thus, the emphasis for positive teaching is upon building participation and placing a sharper focus on learning as a process in which all students can actively engage. Nevertheless, learning support and its development have also been influenced by the same contradictions that have traditionally been associated with the tensions between 'special' and 'ordinary' education (Booth, 1983). 'Special' and 'ordinary' are not simply opposites, but stand in a more dialectical relationship with each other; on the one hand learning support is 'ordinary', formed on the basis that students with learning difficulties and disabilities have more in common with all other students, and on the other it is 'special', requiring additional resources, extra support and specialist teaching (Dyson *et al.*, 1994). Strategies for the development of learning support also incorporate the establishment of a more effective identification and an acknowledgement of student entitlement to participate in learning, rather than emphasizing the measurement of knowledge outcomes. It is built on the belief that a reconceptualization of equality and entitlement is integral to educational management.

However, as has been suggested, the managerial response to students' needs and learning support tends to be shaped by a business ethic. Learning difficulties and disabilities have, in effect, become but one aspect of equal opportunities and part of a general marketing strategy. This marketing response might involve the development of some or all of the following forms of provision for learning support:

- discrete courses, with an appropriate reduction in group size to enable closer attention to the individual needs of a group of students;
- withdrawal for extra tuition, individually or in groups;
- discrete core groups for the teaching of basic skills;
- individualized learning programmes that enable students to build upon their strengths as well as providing opportunities for extended support in areas which need to be developed;
- team teaching between subject and specialist support staff, thus encouraging an alliance and sharing of different skills and enabling attention to be given to individual learning needs. This development can also contribute to a form of staff development and extend the range of teaching approaches;
- a roving 'peripatetic' support tutor, with a managed caseload, to work with students and tutors in order to meet any difficulties that may arise and to provide short periods of one-to-one support;
- volunteer supporters or using co-student tutoring to provide

support in workshops or teaching rooms, or with mobility. Such volunteers need induction and support of their own;

- using specialist equipment and information technology both to enhance communications and to improve opportunities to participate in a range of activities;
- the use of specialist staff brought in to develop and assist course planning, curricular or materials adaptations to facilitate the learning of particular students, e.g. in speech therapy.

These approaches have been criticized as ineffectual (Dyson *et al.*, 1994) in bringing about real change. It is argued that too narrow a focus on the manipulation of forms of provision under the guise of additional equipment or in-class support fails to acknowledge the need for perhaps more radical changes in ways of understanding how students learn.

A consideration and assessment of individual needs within the process of learning has begun to be recognized as an essential bridge into any well managed form of further education. Such an assessment will need to take into account all of the above factors, but also the wishes and aspirations of students and their families. Learning support is not simply about helping students in classrooms; it is also about staff development and facilitating teachers and lecturers. Above all else it means acknowledging that individual learners may make choices which conflict with the opinions of teaching staff and other professionals. As Dee and Corbett (1994) point out, this is the challenge of real support and empowerment, and what it means in reality. They cite the example of a student who can recognize the complexity of his or her physical needs and choose to go to a residential specialist college in preference to the local mainstream college where facilities may be inferior, but less costly. Unfortunately the educational ambitions of students may fall victim to the resource-led mentality of managers who use the rationale of inclusive education and integration to justify the blocking of placements that they consider too expensive.

WHOLE-COLLEGE MANAGEMENT OF LEARNING SUPPORT

Although the approach to the development of learning support tends to be specifically aimed at the needs of students with learning difficulties and disabilities, it is also focused on the needs of all students. It has also been influenced by the higher demands for quality assurance surrounding the passing of the 1988 Education Reform Act, the 1992 Further and Higher Education

Act and the establishment of the FEFC, which, itself, had been built on the White Paper *Education and Training for the 21st Century* (DES, 1991a). Other factors influencing change included the government-endorsed call for national targets for education and training (NTETs). These were set out as target numbers for the achievement of nationally recognized qualifications by the year 2000, formulated from the results of a CBI report, *Towards a Skills Revolution* (CBI, 1989). These initiatives are linked with the expectation that colleges should be aiming to expand their student enrolment numbers by 25 per cent over a three-year period (1994–97). When these factors are taken together, it is clear why managers of colleges are concerned to market themselves and further education to a new client group.

The consequence of these initiatives has meant a reappraisal of the curriculum provision offered to all students in colleges. The FEFC has stated that strategic planning is more likely to be effective if institutions also recognize their wider curricular responsibilities for quality control, staff development and student progression. The first FEFC circular (1992a) made specific reference to the importance attached to both provision for students with learning difficulties and disabilities and to strategic planning for the development of support. Guidance on planning includes the requirement that colleges should begin their approach with a corporate mission statement and then incorporate a needs analysis of their local catchment area. All colleges have been specifically requested:

> to include within their needs analysis considerations of:
> – provision for those with learning difficulties and/or disabilities, including the identification of organisations consulted, such as special schools, local authority social services departments and careers services.
>
> (FEFC, 1992a, p. 4)

A number of initiatives have focused on these considerations. The Education Reform Act 1988 required LEAs to produce a three- to five-year strategic plan for further education, and individual colleges were further required to produce their own development plans. As part of this guidance on planning it was anticipated that colleges would ensure that they incorporated the design of effective learning support. This, in turn requires colleges to carry out a risk analysis of the effects of any possible external or internal factors on planning. This might include any changes in the recruitment patterns of schools and sixth-form provision, raising the levels of awareness of the senior management team with overall responsibility for implementing policy across the college, the awareness of admissions tutors and the effectiveness of networks with schools, careers service and other agencies.

Whilst the primary responsibility for quality control rests with the management of colleges, the day-to-day management and co-ordination of educational provision across the college remains the responsibility of a designated named person. The involve-ment of senior management in line management is essential if a clear college position is to emerge for the establishment of criteria for the successful monitoring of quality. The setting of aims for assessment, accreditation and progression routes for students with learning difficulties and disabilities is required to ensure curricular coherence and continuity. In order to do this colleges cannot afford to act alone but must network with other agencies. Colleges need to become influential in those bodies that accredit and award qualifications: 'a college may be independent but it cannot afford to be an island' (Burton, 1993, p. 54). To this end, the encouragement from the FEFC to colleges to prepare a strategic plan that includes specific reference to students with learning difficulties and disabilities is of fundamental importance.

Strategic plans will undoubtedly include policy considerations of equal opportunities, within which students with learning diffi-culties and disabilities are an integral part. The NATFHE survey of provision (1993) indicated that 78 per cent of colleges had an equal opportunities policy linked to a strategic plan and that this was an essential starting point for developing a structure for collaborative teaching and learning support. To sustain the effective management of support it is suggested that an advis-ory committee or sub-committee be established (Lancashire LEA, 1991) including representatives from across the college, local schools, college governors, careers service, health and social services. This sub-group should be able to establish links with professionals in the community who can advise on the resourcing of support services and the calculation of the additional support costs or units which a college or institution may claim for pro-viding additional support to a student.

ADDITIONAL UNITS

Part of the central purpose of the FEFC is to drive up the quality of further education while remaining mindful of the costs. As such, it was inevitable that attention would centre on the costs of the multitude of courses available in the FE system. The funding methodology established by the FEFC is complex and involves the conversion of student numbers to student units (see FEFC, 1993c). The new formula has been established as a response to the previous funding methods in both further and higher education, whereby students had been grouped for funding purposes into various modes of attendance. The FEFC considered that this method of calculation was becoming irrelevant as students began to seek more flexible forms of education and training and as institutions started to seek more efficient ways of providing it.

The benchmark for tariff funding purposes is that a current one-year full-time equivalent student is 'broadly equivalent to 100 tariff units' (FEFC, 1993d, para. 9) and is made up of a standard value, entry element and on-programme elements representing 'the standard relative volume of on-programme activities deemed to be necessary to bring students to the point where they can achieve the intended qualification aims or other objectives of their programmes' (ibid., para. 20). This clearly does not include all provision for students with learning difficulties and disabilities for whom the Council has decided that additional support should be made available. Neither does it include those students who require additional tutoring in numeracy, literacy or English and are pursuing a primary learning goal which is not itself a qualification in basic literacy. Arrangements for establishing and claiming the additional units of support have now been officially defined and recognized by the Council. It is proposed that the costs of providing additional support to students on their learning programmes should be defined and assigned to one of six bands (see Table 9.1).

Table 9.1 *Additional support units per student per year for 1995–96*

	Band 0	Band 1	Band 2	Band 3	Band 4	Band 5
Additional cost	£170–£500	£501–£1,000	£1,001–£2,000	£2,001–£4,000	£4,001–£5,600	£5,600–£8,800
Units per student per year	19.0	42.0	83.0	166.0	266.0	400.0

Source: FEFC (1994b)

Additional support has been defined as any support that is provided over and above the programme activities included in a standard learning programme which aims to help an individual student to complete their learning programme.

This funding methodology is based on the notion of individual student tariff units. They can be claimed as a result of identifying student need and calculating the additional support costs on a standard pro-forma. These may include such things as the extra costs of specialist assessments at the point of entry to college, extra staffing, or specialist teaching arrangements. This demand for accountability strengthens the impression both that there is a genuine commitment towards students with learning difficulties and disabilities and that funding can now more closely follow the student. However, whilst this is welcome there are a number of anomalies and complications surrounding both the interpretation and completion of the pro-forma for additional tariff units.

When the funding methodology was first introduced in 1994 there had been criticism that the lowest band – Band 0 – then based at £200 was too high to trigger minimum in-class support for a student (Oxspec, 1994). In similar fashion, the highest band – Band 5 – at £5,600 had been claimed to be too low to support a student with profound and multiple difficulties who may require significantly greater expenditure and additional resources. It is encouraging to see that some of these considerations have been tackled and clarified in the revised guidance for recurrent funding. The new upper limit of £8,800 in any single year, for example, can be re-assessed and possibly increased on application to FEFC regional office.

Whilst the FEFC has acknowledged a strong requirement for and commitment to provision for students with a range of difficulties in this sector, slight variations in tone and emphasis have begun to appear and there is a tightening in the requirements for evidence. The basis for claiming additional support units is anticipated to be a result of an initial assessment process with three main elements:

- initial identification of the students who will need learning support;
- detailed assessment of their learning support needs;
- development of a plan to provide additional support.

> Institutions will use a range of assessment instruments and strategies throughout the learning programme to identify students' additional support needs ... There is no 'standard' assessment method which all institutions should use and institutions will make their own judgememts as to the most relevant assessment methods and materials to use with particular students.
>
> (FEFC, 1994b)

The shifts and slight differences of language that have characterized the emergence of new funding provision have been worrying to some. The Oxspec paper (Oxspec, 1994) had pointed out the increasing concerns of further education managers that the wording of FEFC circulars was gradually becoming less strong than the statement in Circular 93/05, which stated the following when addressing the issue of recurrent funding allocations for 1993–94:

> The Council is likely to make it a condition of funding that colleges continue to make at least the same level of provision for students with learning difficulties and/or disabilities.
>
> (FEFC, 1993b, p. 8)

Similar nuances of difference had also been identified in the *Funding Council News* no. 14, which changed the words 'endeavour' in the Draft Guidance to 'expected':

> . . . colleges will be expected to:
> – enrol at least the same number of students with learning difficulties and/or disabilities as in 1993–94 . . .
>
> (Oxspec, 1994, p. 2)

The more recent circulars from the FEFC have been more reassuring in their confirmation that some students will need additional support 'in order to reach their primary learning goal'. This overall affirmation of commitment to the development of learning support from the colleges and the FEFC is evidence that the Tomlinson Committee is beginning to play an effective advisory role in ensuring educational opportunity. At the same time, it is notable that access to further and higher education had originally been excluded from the Disability (Discrimination) Bill. This is presently passing through Parliament and there is room for concern that the language of the FEFC definitions may become part of what Dee and Corbett (1994) have referred to as a 'backlash' that may begin to reduce, rather than increase, opportunities for those with physical and learning disabilities. If there is a reluctance on the part of learning support staff to wholeheartedly embrace the notion of total learning support within a new climate of integration it may be due to a scepticism about the basic purposes of the exercise:

> the enthusiasm with which some senior management teams greet the notion of abandoning discrete provision may be more related to cutting costs than reflecting a philosophical stance and fundamental belief. . .
>
> (Dee and Corbett, 1994, p. 323)

SUMMARY

The influence of management attitudes to the teaching of students with learning difficulties and disabilities is crucial to the development of effective services in a climate that places importance on the cost-effectiveness of further education. We see how a managerial style and mentality imposes itself on the ethos of provision for all students and particularly those with learning difficulties and disabilities. The funding of learning support through the calculation of additional support units has become an important consideration in the development of effective college provision. This places a premium on those students with disabilities who can be considered capable of making academic or vocational progress on a college course. Additional support for equipment, or aids to learning, can be achieved for such students via additional 'units'. Nevertheless, the funding for students who are unlikely to be able to demonstrate their capacity for 'progression' is less clear-cut. This search for quality and effectiveness, in terms of vocational outcomes, is a relatively recent feature of post-compulsory education in the United Kingdom. The comparison with vocational training in other countries forms the basis for the next chapter.

10

Cross-cultural perspectives on further education and vocational training

This chapter addresses some cultural comparisons between the different approaches to further education and training for students with learning difficulties and disabilities in the United Kingdom and some of the countries of the European Union. It also makes reference to the impact of civil rights legislation for disabled people in North America. However, it is worth remembering from the outset that vocational development and further education of young people with learning difficulties and disabilities can also be viewed in a wider cultural context. Hindsight makes us consider that life in earlier society was substantially simpler than in the rapidly changing circumstances of the present. Those societies typically supported fewer vocations and most young adults were already likely to be familiar with many of the jobs available, through either observation or apprenticeship. In our present multi-faceted society the cultural difference between an urban and rural or small-town upbringing also has its own impact. Young people from a rural and perhaps less stressful background are far more likely to have observed adults pursuing the occupations they are considering entering. They are more likely to have had opportunities for informal or occasional early apprenticeships such as summer or after-school work. Such observations are in marked contrast with the experiences of young people raised in a city culture, who may have only a vague conception of the work of their own parents and those of their friends.

Cross-cultural comparisons in relation to minority groups have also been exacerbated by ethnocentricism, subjective judgements and the assumptions of social scientists conducting ethnographic studies. They retain a belief that beyond home shores and in different social strata there are either 'simpler' or alternatively 'better' or more sophisticated societies against which cultural habits are judged. By way of example, and for the moment taking us beyond the boundaries of students with learning difficulties and disabilities, we can take the behaviour of a still extant tribe of North American Indians. The aggressive emphasis in most 'advanced' societies, of winning at all costs, of being no. 1, would have been considered most unseemly if not bizarre amongst 'primitive' cultures such as the Zuni Indians (Benedict, 1934). In Zuni culture, considerable effort has traditionally been made to avoid any appearance of individual superiority or the exercise of power over others. Moreover, positions of leadership have been accepted reluctantly, and then only temporarily. For the Zuni, a rational and rewarding existence, in work as well as in all other areas of life and interpersonal relationships, is built around co-operation, rather than competition. The race may 'go to the swift', but the traditional Zuni would prefer not to win the race! Benedict recounts the failure to organize competitive foot-races amongst Zuni youth as one after another each discreetly attempted to avoid being the winner. Such interpretations fail to acknowledge the subtle status differentials that still tend to exploit the politically weak to the benefit of the politically strong in all societies.

THE QUALITY OF LIFE IN EUROPEAN COUNTRIES

Within a European context Daunt (1991, 1993) traces the emergence of equal opportunities and citizenship within the European Union and its impact on students with disabilities. He has usefully identified how the essentially political interventions to develop European policy for the improvement of quality of life and employment for disabled people across the European Union have been patchy:

> here the record has been disappointing. Far less has been attempted than was at one time hoped and little indeed has been achieved. The Commission's first proposal, on employment, was adopted in 1986; it took the form of a Recommendation rather than the much stronger Directive which the Commission's own legal service preferred.
>
> (Daunt, 1993, p. 4)

Daunt also draws attention to some of the differences between the original twelve member states of the European Union:

> the fact that the British approach to industrial relations is so vastly different from that of all other eleven countries of the Community, has no doubt something to do with the difference

between the Conservative Party and Christian Democratic parties on the continent; perhaps however it has also a deeper cultural base, witness our predilection for the adversarial mode also in the law courts and in Parliament. Anyway, here again we have a contextual factor that will not go away.

(ibid., p. 6)

The British government's ideological commitment to the maintenance of market forces is a recurring barrier to the expansion of opportunities for disabled people. It has recently been reaffirmed by the spat between the European Commission and the Eurosceptical Department of Employment (*Guardian* leader, 13 August 1994, p. 20). This arose over the strict British interpretation of a European Union directive that proposes alterations in competitive tendering for public purchasing contracts, e.g. work in sheltered workshops. The Department's interpretation of the ruling threatens the long-standing Priority Suppliers Scheme for disabled people's workshops. Its demise would make the task of winning government contracts much more difficult, and thus threaten the future of sheltered workshops for disabled people.

This element of pessimism fails to acknowledge the potential of Europe for collaborative community activities designed to promote equal opportunities in education and employment for disabled people. The enthusiasm with which colleges are collaborating and networking with training providers across Europe suggests that individuals are more enthusiastic about Europe than governments. European funding such as the HELIOS programme can be used for the funding of European links for groups of disabled people, their organizations and the staff who work with them. It is through such initiatives that the development of further opportunities for disabled people will be shaped on a European stage.

THE QUALITY OF LIFE FOR DISABLED STUDENTS IN THE EUROPEAN UNION

It is important to remember that the concept of transferring from school to college, as many young people do in the United Kingdom, is neither universally understood nor practised in the rest of Europe. There is considerable variation in the education system in each European country and in the way that special education is related to the main educational systems. Whereas theoretically all countries offer the same range of educational opportunities to disabled and non-disabled students alike, in line with their individual academic and cognitive capacity, the reality of actual opportunity for participation tends to be influenced by resources.

All the countries in the European Union except the United Kingdom and Denmark have separate secondary schools for young people following academic rather than vocational courses. There is also a fairly complex hierarchy of division in the range of subject or vocational choices in most countries. In the United Kingdom the comprehensive school system has usually established internal divisions that have separated the 'academic' from the 'vocational' student and this has tended to be replicated within the further education system. The Skill survey of European students with disabilities suggested that in all the countries surveyed:

> education for those with learning difficulties is likely to be in most ways separate or offered as the least likely stream of the school... The majority of young people with learning difficulties in all countries will have been through a system of education in which they have constantly been at the bottom of the academic achievement levels.
>
> (Stowell and Cooper, 1986, p. 18)

In the United Kingdom we have a point of division at the age of 16 (19 in the case of most young people with more severe learning difficulties) when compulsory schooling ends and a college career can begin. The following list shows the minimum age at which pupils may leave school in some other European countries. Only in Greece is there a compulsory difference between leaving ages of disabled and non-disabled pupils:

Belgium	18
Denmark	16
France	16
Germany	15*
Greece	14.5–15 (17 for disabled school-leavers)
Ireland	15
Italy	15
Luxembourg	15
Netherlands	16*
Portugal	15
Spain	16
United Kingdom	16

* there is a part-time compulsory schooling after this age

(Table compiled before the expansion of the EU in 1995)

The age of school leaving differs considerably and varies by up to three years. Therefore, when one is comparing post-compulsory education there are inevitable differences in philosophy and expectation. Not only will levels of educational attainment be different between countries, but there will also be variations in levels of maturity and social independence.

It is interesting to note that in Germany and the Netherlands part-time further education and training that is job-specific is compulsory after full-time education. It is normal for young people to continue in school until the age of 18 or beyond in schools established specifically for this purpose. Also, whilst the age at which pupils *may* leave school is of interest, the age at which most pupils actually do leave school is of equal, or more importance. This varies between countries, but in general youngsters with handicaps and disabilities tend to stay at school longer than others (who leave either for employment or for specific vocational or higher education). There is also a trend towards staying on at school as unemployment has risen inexorably across Europe.

Generally speaking, disabled young people have achieved the same rights in law to education beyond compulsory school-leaving age as all other young people. However, this 'right' varies from a guarantee to educational entitlement in Denmark, to a system of provision that is non-statutory in most other countries, based either on tradition or on a vague commitment.

In some countries there are special measures that guarantee disabled students extra time in school: for example in Belgium and Luxembourg children can stay at school until 21 or beyond. In Denmark and most other countries there are arrangements for additional support for disabled youngsters who wish to continue in some form of further education or go on to higher education. As has been pointed out in relation to provision in England and Wales, there is now a statutory requirement to 'have regard' for students with learning difficulties and disabilities up until the age of 25. But, as in the United Kingdom, the laws in the rest of Europe relating to disabled young people are relatively recent. As a result the various attempts to co-ordinate and pull together the vested interests and different services that have previously operated under separate pieces of legislation are proving both problematic and difficult to fulfil. The problems of developing effective legislation for the co-ordination of a continuum of services from childhood and school to adulthood still defeats most countries within the European Union. Only Denmark and latterly the United Kingdom have established the beginnings of effective liaison between services.

In most European countries there is some relationship between the body that assesses a young person's needs and the organization that subsequently develops provision. The Skill survey (Stowell and Cooper, 1986) found that information and advice on adult services for people with disabilities is offered by both government and voluntary organizations at either local or national level in all countries. The depth and quality of advice tends to vary. Thus, in Denmark, where provision appears to be the most advanced, advice and information is provided by the social services departments of the local communes, or by the educational/training establishment that the young person attends. Students in what would pass as the Danish further education system each have their own nominated adviser. In other countries, help and advice will be provided mostly, if at all, by voluntary groups. The amount and quality of information available may depend as much on the category and severity of disability as on the skills of individual advisers. By way of example, the amount of information and advice for the development of provision for students with sensory disabilities is far better and more extensive throughout Europe than that available to people with moderate learning difficulties. This distinction may be even more typical of countries where voluntary organizations have developed as the primary source of help and advice.

Ironically it is the very success of voluntary organizations which may have led to the lack of central government responsibility for the co-ordination of provision. Where a plethora of non-government organizations has emerged, there is no consistency of knowledge either to better inform policy-makers or to advise students. In the United Kingdom, Skill operates as a national organization concerned exclusively with the education and training issues of students and trainees with learning difficulties and disabilities. This intensity of focus can be diluted in the other countries. In the Netherlands, for example, organizations covering the interests of specific handicaps may provide advice on education and training, yet with little relevant expertise. As a result information tends to circulate in the offices of policy-makers and administrators, but often has little impact on the lives of disabled people themselves. The Handicap and Studie organization in the Netherlands is beginning to address this need for co-ordination, but there are few initiatives to develop a European perspective.

The OECD research on transition conducted throughout the 1980s and the 1986 Skill survey suggested that no country has tackled the transition from school to adulthood for young people with learning difficulties or disabilities with either total success, or a single piece of legislation. Instead there are a number of separate, smaller measures, operating in different countries, that serve as adjuncts, or markers for suggested change, scattered amongst other bits of legislation.

Information and advice are clearly of importance to students with learning difficulties and disabilities across Europe, but they are also of importance to lecturers and training staff. Staff can frequently feel isolated and out of touch with current developments. In some parts of Europe impressive attempts at staff development have been initiated in order to address this. Organizations such as Handicap and Studie and Skill help to bring together teaching staff. The broader umbrella of EASE (the European Association of Special Education) has begun to create further opportunities for staff to exchange experiences and yet the whole area of staff development in teaching students with disabilities across Europe remains an underdeveloped area.

The transition years for young people with disabilities in the United Kingdom have generally been acknowledged and perceived as a time of uncertainty; a period of clumsy transfer from child to more adult services. It appears to be a less traumatic and exclusive affair in other parts of Europe. Whether this impression is true or not, the more adult-oriented service referred to as Further Education in the United Kingdom is not readily understood in the rest of Europe. In Europe the transition is more easily understood as a period for concentration on vocational education and training.

Discussion about differences between education and training are at the heart of this tension and incomprehension. At the same time a rhetoric of supposed commonality between education and training has masked the real dilemma, which is that of elitism and class differentials in both the UK education system and Europe as a whole. These status differentials in society have bedevilled the future planning of coherent transition from school to post-school for all school-leavers across Europe, and crossed all political parties, for at least a quarter of a century. While the concern for the economic prosperity of different nations has resulted in a good deal of comparative research relating education and training to economic performance, relatively little attention has been drawn to the status of students with disabilities and/or learning difficulties as they progress from school to adulthood. O'Hanlon (1993) has outlined and examined the practical and political response to special education at school level in the twelve European countries which at that time made up the European Union, but there are little data at post-school level.

There are a number of 'commonsense' perspectives for analysing policies for moving from school to post-school provision. These suggest that the different approaches to further education and vocational training across Europe arise as a consequence of school experiences, individual preferences and the levels of ability/disability experienced by any particular individual. A more sophisticated analysis might suggest that the aims of training are to provide a more skilled workforce funded within the limits of centrally directed resources, while taking into account the expectations of the future market-place. Such an analysis would suggest marked differences across different countries in direct relation to national economic prosperity. However, Vianello and Monige (1993a) in their research of the literature, indicate that despite differences of legislation in different member states of the European Union, there is a common thread of financial investment in vocational and technical training for disabled young people. Normally, young people with moderate or more severe learning difficulties are trained apart from those whose main handicap is physical or sensory. The financial investment of countries like Belgium, Germany and the Netherlands in special, but mainly separate, vocational training centres is particularly impressive. The expenditure is considered to be an appropriate investment and preparation for possible future employment, but is also linked to the wider consideration of rights and entitlements and ultimately to a quality of life for disabled people.

In confirmation of this the European Community has made a commitment to the development of collaboration on the fullest possible integration of disabled children and young people; the predominant terminology in European documentation is 'the handicapped'. (For a fuller account of these developments see Daunt, 1991; O'Hanlon, 1993.) The central policy thrust throughout Europe has been towards the wider integration and inclusion of people who at school would have been described as having special educational needs. There is an extensive literature on the subject and a generally established commitment to the principles and rhetoric of integration. However, this consensus is maintained only at the very broadest levels of policy. As soon as practicalities are discussed it is evident that there are differences of educational and social philosophy which expose a variety of approaches.

THE EMERGENCE OF INTEGRATED PRACTICE IN EDUCATION AND TRAINING

The differences of approach might be considered as a continuum, at one end of which come those who believe that all ordinary opportunities should be made fully accessible to all disabled students and young people. Such an extreme approach would logically include a belief in the need to radically reappraise all post-compulsory education and training. This reappraisal of the curriculum would be in the interests of all young people, including those with learning difficulties and disabilities. With the barriers removed, there would be no need for any specialist forms of discrete provision for students categorized as having special needs, learning difficulties or disabilities. This, for some, is the only true expression of integration; all other forms and approaches amount to segregation.

At the other end of the continuum the view is held that, while it is almost certainly desirable that as many disabled young people as possible should take part in ordinary further education and training opportunities, the reality is that most are effectively better served by separate provision. By adopting this educational approach the opportunities for curriculum support, assessment and certification may be better met for students who would otherwise not be able to cope. Supporters of separate provision suggest that it allows for greater flexibility and more focused investment of resources. It is argued that a degree of segregated education and training provides better prospects for eventual, successful integration in adult life.

There are obvious dangers in generalizing about any country's approach to the development of integrated services. There may not be a united approach, particularly in countries that are able to turn to a range of either voluntary or statutory providers, each of whom will have developed differences in management style and educational philosophy.

In Sweden, for example, a country that has long been associated with an integration philosophy, compulsory education begins at the age of 7 and lasts until 17. Young people with disabilities have the opportunity to undertake vocational training while still at secondary school as well as afterwards in further vocational education.

There are also considerable variations in local employment outlets in different parts of Sweden, and in some places the options for vocational choice are minimal. However, employment choices can range between shop and office work, carpentry, stock working, cleaning and local options in forestry and farming. Rosenqvist (1993) has suggested that another problem for disabled adolescents in Sweden is that some districts only offer vocational training, so that a student may have to move to another district or another city to get any real vocational education. There are problems here for students who do not want to leave home and yet who wish to achieve their academic and vocational potential. Some parts of Sweden also offer an alternative form of education that combines the learning of vocational skills on an employer's premises for four days of the week with attending a school or college for one day a week to study Swedish, maths and civics.

An overriding policy initiative in Sweden is the concept that everybody has the right to employment as an adult person, under the motto: 'Work for All'. However, as Rosenqvist (1993) points out, reality produces a rather different picture. An underlying and hidden unemployment exists that belies the official level of Swedish unemployment of 6–7 per cent. Among the hidden cases are the population of disabled school-leavers, only 40–50 per cent of whom can find employment in the so-called open labour market. According to Rosenqvist, this figure is probably unrealistic because it does not take into account employment that has been subsidized in some way to compensate employers for taking on someone with a disability.

Within the Swedish training network some limitations are placed upon individual choice of courses, depending upon the level of disability. Nearly all disabled school-leavers continue their education in some form of vocational training schools. Fewer than 10 per cent of disabled and handicapped children stop their education altogether at 17. Some 25 per cent begin training in a vocational school for a particular occupation, while 65 per cent receive more general occupational and activity training. People with learning difficulties are able to participate in vocational training, although less than 50 per cent of those classified as mentally handicapped are accepted into the vocational schools; the majority are occupied in sheltered workshops or relief work.

It would be unrealistic to suggest that the Swedish approach to further education and training is not connected to the over-arching Swedish social policy of integration. Swedish society has led the way in promoting non-segregation for all groups of people. However, there are clearly some exceptions to the rule and among these are found many of the disabled adult population. Schools in Sweden today are almost totally integrated in the 'functional' sense: the classrooms for disabled students are embedded in ordinary school buildings and increasing numbers are being individually integrated into ordinary classroom settings. To a large extent Swedish schools 'succeed in integrating their students, but society fails to integrate its adult persons. The latter especially applies to the labour market, but to some extent also to housing, leisure time activities and social relations' (Rosenqvist, 1993).

Soder (1980), writing at around the same time as the Warnock (1978) recommendations and with similar ideas, has provided operational definitions of integration that divide it up into four main groups:

(1)   Physical integration, i.e the physical (or geographical) dis-
      tance between the handicapped and non-handicapped is
      reduced. This is the most common form of integration of
      handicapped young people in Sweden, which means pro-
      vision in ordinary schools and college buildings, but not
      necessarily integrated classrooms;
(2)   Functional integration, i.e. the functional distance is reduced.
      This means that handicapped and non-handicapped students
      are using the same educational equipment and resources.
      In turn the functional integration can be divided into two
      branches, where co-utilization (which can be simultaneous
      or non-simultaneous) means that students only share material
      and co-operation means planned common activities;
(3)   Social integration, i.e the social distance is reduced. This
      means that the handicapped person forms part of a com-
      munity with non-handicapped persons and comes into regular
      and spontaneous contact with these;
(4)   Societal integration, i.e. the adult handicapped person has
      the same access to resources and opportunity to influence his
      own situation as others; he has a productive working role and
      forms part of a social community with others.

                                          (Soder, 1980, pp. 10–11)

This hierarchy of form has been expanded by others such as Nirje
(1980), who has added three further levels rather than radically
altered Sodor's original four steps. Nirje's fourth level is termed
'personal integration' and is given the following definition:

> Personal integration is related to the developing and changing
> needs for personal interaction with significant persons. It includes
> the opportunities to have a satisfactory private life with meaningful
> relationships, for example for the child: parents, siblings, relatives
> and friends; and for the adult: relatives, friends, marriage partner
> and children.
>
>   (Nirje, 1980, p. 48)

The fifth and sixth steps of Nirje's hierarchy refer to societal integration which: 'relates to the expressive functioning as a citizen
regarding legal rights and opportunities for growth, maturity and
self-determination' (ibid.). The final sixth stage is concerned with
organizational integration and builds on the first five steps by
deepening 'organisational forms and administrative structures
that assist and support the furthering of the above (five) facets
of integration' (ibid., p. 49).

Some problems with this concept of integration have already
been alluded to, but they have been subject to a good deal of
critical scrutiny. Nirje's definitions of integration fit well with his
widely developed construct of 'normalization' and clearly have
links with the debate about 'quality of life'. But it is interesting to

note that the most common forms of integration in educational settings remain at the lower end of the hierarchy. This raises a number of questions about the appropriateness of applying levels to a concept that is in a proper sense indivisible. As Rosenqvist (1993) has pointed out, in a wholeness no exclusions are possible, since everybody is needed in forming this wholeness: 'if someone is taken away the wholeness has lost some of its contributions and is thus spoiled'.

Implementation of integration reforms in educational settings has shown that social goals are not always realized. Various Swedish studies have indicated that young people with disabilities establish very few relationships with non-handicapped young people and that those students who have been encouraged to integrate socially often appear to become excluded even in the integrated setting (e.g. Soder, 1980; Walton *et al.*, 1990). Some of the possible reasons for this tension between the ideals of full inclusion and the reality of only partial success have been attributed to the lack of social networks that are available to people with disabilities. Thus, as has been noted in the United Kingdom, the ideology of integration in Sweden has not been removed very far from its historical roots in the isolation felt by people with disabilities.

Soder (1980) has criticized the expectations that people with disabilities, and especially those with more severe learning difficulties, will begin to establish social relations with non-handicapped people. This optimistic expectation assumes that society is ready to accept the integration of disabled and non-disabled people as unproblematic. In fact, the reality is that in Sweden integration has come to mean only that disabled and non-disabled children belong in the same school system, or the same building. The integration of the classroom is not translated into the fuller realization of social integration in employment, particularly for those people with learning difficulties.

VOCATIONAL TRAINING IN DIFFERENT COUNTRIES

In Greece, legislation has been used to encourage further education of disabled young people in the form of vocational training. All young people have the right to attend school until the age of 18, although vocational training can begin between the ages of 14 and 20. Although the number of school-leavers with disabilities in Greece is unknown, their further education and vocational training is funded centrally by, and is the responsibility of, the Ministry of National Education. Legislation passed in 1979

(Law 963) and 1983 (Law 137), concerning the occupational rehabilitation of disabled people and those who display reduced abilities, has encouraged the establishment of vocational training centres and employment facilities for the disabled. Collaboration between pre-vocational training centres and the school system is co-ordinated by the Greek Manpower Employment Organization. The Greek programmes for further education and training are partially funded by the European Union and partially by the Greek government.

The European Association for Special Education (Vianello and Monige, 1993a) reports that there are some 677 disabled young people attending vocational training programmes in Greece. This development is comparatively recent as there is no long-established pattern of post-school education and training establishments.

Across Europe there is a range of provision, depending upon the characteristics of the individuals considered to be disabled, the internal organization of the different countries and the relationship between further education and training and the world of work. In some member states where integration is the norm, vocational schools have been set up that are attended by both disabled and non-disabled young people. However, in the majority of European countries some form of segregation tends to perpetuate itself.

In Italy, legislation has also influenced the form and structure of further and vocational education. Vianello and Monige (1993a, 1993b) indicate that the further training of non-academic young people is followed in vocational schools that are generally organized to provide programmes of vocational training of some 600 hours each. After three or four programmes, it is compulsory for students to be provided with some suitable job experience. People with disabilities can be placed in ordinary classes with non-disabled students or can follow parallel activities, arranged according to their abilities and needs. At the completion of a programme of study and training, students are awarded a certificate that can help in the choice of open or semi-sheltered employment. Generally, these training opportunities are designed more for people with mild and moderate disabilities; for example, they could include someone with Down's syndrome. For those with more severe disabilities, other possibilities are made available in sheltered workshops, which are now almost exclusively reserved for the more severely handicapped. These workshops are managed either by the local health department or by private associations. Many have been created and continue to be organized by parents of people with severe disabilities, or by groups of volunteers.

In the Netherlands nearly 6 per cent of the working population or some 660,000 people either cannot or do not want to work because of a handicap or disability (Vianello and Monige, 1993a). In the education system, the majority of students with severe learning difficulties attend segregated secondary special schools for moderately and severely retarded children. The more severely mentally and learning disabled usually attend school until they are 20, receiving both basic social instruction and vocational training, prior to transferring to a regional sheltered workshop. These workshops cater for a maximum number of 80,000 and are funded by the government. In order to address the costs of running sheltered placements, an admittance policy has been introduced based on the production performance of the employees. If an employee does not achieve or sustain a work-rate at one-third the work performance of an 'average' worker he/she cannot be employed in the sheltered workshop. Even when people reach that level of performance they have to be put on a waiting list. This new spirit of competition has forced workshop managers to develop training and education programmes within the sheltered workplace in order to encourage more people to leave for a job in the open labour market. There are nevertheless a number of reasons why this aspiration may not be achieved. If sheltered workshops lose their most productive workers the production targets set for the workshop will become more difficult to reach for those who remain. It may also be in the interests of employees to remain in sheltered employment, thereby protecting their right to state benefits and pensions.

The development of further education and training of the less severely disabled has benefited as a result of a research project on labour orientation started in 1990 by the Ministry of Education. Teachers in secondary schools have developed contacts with industrial and commercial companies in order to facilitate appropriate work placements for disabled school-leavers. Employers can also take advantage of employment legislation that awards grants and subsidies to companies that employ disabled students within the overall framework of the labour orientation project.

The link between training and eventual employment is forged by legislation in the Netherlands. In 1986 the Employment of Handicapped Workers Act came into force. The main purpose of this Act was to reintroduce people with disabilities to working life and to reduce the large numbers of people receiving state subsidies from the Disablement Insurance Act. This law tried to oblige employers to take on and integrate disabled people into the workforce through an 'obligation of effort' on the part of employers, employers' organizations and the trade unions. Companies unable to achieve a target norm of 5 per cent registered disabled employees within the workforce will be fined. The possibility of financially rewarding companies that employ above the 5 per cent norm is currently under discussion (Stowell and Cooper, 1986; O'Hanlon, 1993).

In Germany a variety of provision has been established for disabled young people beyond the age of 16. Legislation has ensured that some type of education or training is available until the age of 18 for all pupils and this is extended to age 25 for some categories of disablement. Three forms of training provision are available in either training workshops or vocational schools. The heavy emphasis is upon the development of practical skills and the curricular activities available stress skill training that develops a degree of pride in purpose and achievement. The net result of the German commitment to training means that 90 per cent of all young people under the age of 20 are entitled to full-time education or are on training courses. The commitment to vocational rehabilitation of disabled young people means that they too are entitled to benefit from an extended period of education and training.

Harris (1992), visiting a number of vocational schools in Germany, for people with learning difficulties (mentally handicapped) between the ages of 16 and 25, found the central focus to be upon functional independence. A range of theoretical and practical programmes had been developed concerned with recreation, daily living and the development of craft skills. Integration involved drawing students from a fairly wide catchment area and attempting to link with the local community through social activities such as gardening, shopping and simple repair work. Interestingly, although the goal of the educational process whilst children are still at school is integration, the teaching provision remains specialist and segregated:

> The location is school-like with conventional classrooms as well as workshops. It has the appearance of a small further education college and indeed operates on a similar basis. The major significant difference is that all students are mentally handicapped (a mix of moderate and severe learning difficulties). Thus, the provision remains specialist in terms of teaching although its focus is on integration. (By contrast such parallel provision in the UK would be likely to be seen in a unit in a further education college with its students integrated into 'normal' classes wherever possible.)
> (Harris, 1992, p. 6)

Vocational training is also available in residential provision in

Germany. Students attending are usually slow learners or have moderate learning difficulties and are selected for entry to the school on the basis of their case histories and evidence from psychologists, social workers and vocational placement officers. Students are provided with a mixed curriculum of vocational training and social and life studies, with the target of achieving a vocational qualification at the end of three or four years of study. There is a heavy emphasis on the practical development of skills across a wide range of vocational areas (e.g. hairdressing and metalwork). The system is carried out and often enhanced by a residential environment that attempts to provide a model of social living which is often at odds with a student's previous unstructured and frequently disadvantaged background.

This 'village' community approach to training is expensive. Although it can provide a framework within which students can operate, it requires the resources of house parents, instructors and teachers as well as workshops, classrooms and residential facilities. The closest equivalent in the United Kingdom would be the residential communities such as Botton Village, established on the values and philosophy of Rudolph Steiner.

SUMMARY

The search for employment opportunities and rights for disabled people is better protected by European legislation than in much domestic policy. The Social Chapter (from which the UK government has opted out), for example, has proposed that the fullest possible integration into working life be made available to disabled people. Specific reference is made in European Union legislation to vocational training, professional 're-insertion' and re-adaptation, improvement in both mobility and adaptive means of transport and housing protection within a European perspective.

The potential for the development of more extensive disability anti-discrimination legislation at the European level is, nevertheless, limited by the need, in many instances, for such proposals to be agreed unanimously by member states. Unfortunately, for disabled citizens of the United Kingdom, it is the government's policy generally to reject legislative solutions to the development of civil rights, particularly if they are emerging from Brussels or Luxembourg. Ironically, whilst a lead is coming from continental Europe in terms of the co-ordination of employment rights and vocational training initiatives for disabled people, educational initiatives for students with disabilities are possibly at their most innovative in the United Kingdom. The umbrella organization of Skill, the National Bureau for Students with Disabilities, has guided and researched the promotion of post-compulsory education for students with disabilities since 1974. It has served as a model of good practice for other emerging organizations of a similar nature on the continent of Europe, such as Handicap and Studie and the European Association of Special Education.

11

Emerging issues and future directions across the spectrum of further and higher education

The shape of further education for students with learning difficulties and/or disabilities is inexorably being set by the messages from the Funding Councils. For the last twenty years schools have been the targets for radical reform and now attention is turning towards colleges. This final chapter returns to a re-examination of the market philosophy of competition that is marking out educational thinking in both schools and colleges in the United Kingdom. A National Curriculum in schools, followed by GNVQs and 'NVQs for all', appears to be considered the appropriate vehicle for raising educational and training standards. However, as has recently been bluntly pointed out with reference to changes in the National Curriculum, 'it won't, despite the considerable costs of the reforms in terms of money and teacher energy since 1988. Performance will probably improve to some degree, but it's too little too late' (Hargreaves, 1994b).

Hargreaves relates his call for a radical reshaping to the need for developing an education system for the next century. To this end, he makes a markedly different claim from the Prime Minister, John Major, in the foreword to the White Paper *Education and Training for the 21st Century*. Hargreaves suggests that as they presently exist, most of our educational institutions are fossilized relics of nineteenth-century ideology, based essentially on notions of custodial child-minding and keeping adolescents out of mischief. Colleges, like schools, are insulated institutions and thus, remarkably resistant to change. Despite the famed entrepreneurial initiative and flexible response to local need that has been the distinct contribution of further education, it still tends to be shaped by a social tradition that perceives life and advancement 'in the monocultural unitary and largely segregated institutions of family, education, work, leisure and religion, and life courses take the form of single, life-long careers between the end of schooling and the beginning of retirement' (Hargreaves, 1994b).

Incorporation and the demands for greater accountability have presented new challenges for all college staff who come into contact with students with learning difficulties and disabilities. Fifteen years ago it was considered enough for students with disabilities, and particularly those with learning difficulties, simply to attend college, as the 'college experience' in itself was valuable socially and educationally. This rationale is no longer enough and there are new expectations that both staff and courses must demonstrate measures both of effectiveness and efficiency. This is work that needed to be done if the further education system was to become the context for taking forward the new ideology of entitlement. Incorporation has acted as a catalyst for change that was already in the process of evolution.

The 20 per cent of children that formed the Warnock (1978) population of children with special educational needs have now progressed to further education and brought with them new funding structures for learning support, within which extra personal support can be located. Further education has always had the tradition of providing 'second chance' opportunities and the new systems and structures that have accompanied incorporation have given rise to new opportunities for innovative development work, for example the establishment of foundation programmes for students with learning difficulties and disabilities, which has provided a structure for learning support.

However, when these initiatives are placed against some of the more easily visible and mechanistic demands for accountability that is measured in terms of progression as qualification, it is easy to see how this falls in line with the populist accountancy demands that are being made of the Funding Councils. There is less opportunity, it seems, to move ahead in areas that are less easily quantifiable and often impressionistic. The notion of 'distance travelled' is part of the consideration of educational progress for all students but particularly those with learning difficulties and disabilities. 'Progression' can take many forms, but its measurement is not well understood. Research into the implications of Schedule 2 for students with learning difficulties and disabilities is required here. Such investigation should explore a number of confusions:

(1) the links that can be built between LEA provision and those courses funded by the FEFC;
(2) some consideration of the means of assessment of those students who are likely to be able to benefit from courses identified in Schedule 2 and the identification of those students who have to operate outside this funding;

(3) the reappraisal and consultation of the tariff funding for students with learning difficulties and disabilities, especially at the top end of the scale, where it appears there is some need for additional resources, in recognition of high levels of support for some students, e.g. a deaf student requiring a signer.

There are virtually no attempts in any form of education, but particularly further education, to identify successful teaching methods and the reasons for their effectiveness. Teaching methods and courses tend to be based upon teachers' subjective judgements and preferences, not evidence about effectiveness. It may be that the strengthened role given to TECs for the monitoring and reporting of progression within college programmes can address some of these issues.

It is to be hoped that the Tomlinson Committee of Inquiry can cast some light upon these areas of concern. This inquiry is a key consideration in the development of a successful educational future for all young people moving from school to adulthood. Some research is needed into the transforming nature of further education. The funding mechanisms that underpin the educational opportunities for all students may currently offer the potential for developing courses that recognize the special status and extra costs of students with learning difficulties and disabilities. But this too needs to be protected. There is a danger that further education will become ossified by a new bureaucracy and return to the assumptions of the nineteenth century. Far from developing opportunities and entitlements for students from marginalized groups, the spectre of restricted educational opportunity appears. This would lead to a form of further education that conformed to the class divisions and prejudices inherent in market forces and would also tacitly legitimize the separation of the intellectually inefficient from the more academically able.

In order to challenge this, it is possible that some colleges, while retaining the essential quality of responsiveness to the local community, will choose to become highly differentiated and distinctive through specialization and 'niche marketing'. By this it is not meant that segregated provision should re-emerge, or that colleges should develop courses specifically for students with disabilities. Instead there should be specialization in terms of subject choice or vocational training. This will offer more choice to students, parents, employers and lecturers. In similar fashion the savings that can be made by investing in the new interactive technologies and specialist equipment will provide improved opportunities for students of varying ability levels to participate in the negotiation of their own pace and style of learning. The emphasis on equality of opportunity and the development of student choices is central to this approach.

INFORMATION TECHNOLOGY

It is evident from the rapid growth in technological aids in every phase of education that here is one of the major influences for improvement in access both to the curriculum and to wider participation in community involvement for people with disabilities. Vincent (1993) has actively promoted the use of information technology for helping to overcome the handicapping effects of physical and sensory disabilities. The opportunities for the development of physical mobility are also enhanced by advances in microelectronic technology through, for example, remote control devices for opening and shutting doors and improvements in overall standards of access to buildings and teaching spaces.

Just as advances in communication technology have begun to make it easier for pupils with sensory disabilities to attend ordinary schools and to interact with their non-disabled peers, so have colleges of further education been able to make some dramatic advances in developing computer-assisted access and aids to student independence and environmental control. Visual display units attached to voice-sensitive switches have begun to revolutionize communication for those who are physically disabled or deaf. Optical scanning devices such as the Arkenstone Scanner or the Kurtzweil Reader, linked to Braille printers and voice synthesizers, benefit students who are blind. Moreover, where once such equipment was considered prohibitively expensive, it has now fallen to a price that makes the purchase not only viable but an important dimension of a college's marketing and student support strategy.

Hegarty (1993) and Wolff (1986) have made the important point that information technology is also instrumental in raising student expectations. Where the lack of such aids to communication had prevented students from participating in a more independent style of learning, students (and staff) worked within these limitations. The past decade has shown that students with disabilities now expect to develop access to the curriculum and subsequently to new employment opportunities as a result of advances in microelectronics and information technology. Difficulties in note-taking, personal record-keeping and drafting written work can now be surmounted through the use of new technology. These advances have played their part in the development of access to equality of educational opportunities in post-16 settings.

Nevertheless, although many students have benefited from information technology, these benefits are neither universal nor fully realized. Vincent (1993) suggests that this is due to the lack of appropriate support beyond the mere provision of equipment and devices. The first line of development for appropriate support is assessment of individual needs in relation to the technology available. Simply having access to a computer does not guarantee the development of independent learning or of educational opportunity. Other frustrations with the use of microcomputers have emerged in some of the limitations in available software. Where the hardware, speed of loading and amounts of memory have improved dramatically, 'much of the available software is, for all its quantity, educationally inadequate' (Hegarty, 1993). Nevertheless, many available programs seem to offer little that could not be achieved as well by other means and without the accompanying frustration for learner and lecturer alike. In other words, much of the available resource material is packaged in a fashion that anticipates teaching and learning styles akin to pen and paper exercises. These fail to exploit the potential of the microcomputer or take into account theories of learning or the needs of young adult learners.

The FEFC has set great store on the development of appropriate assessment strategies of individual learner needs. In the area of applying information technology to the support of students, the requirements for specialist advice and ongoing assessment are essential. The value of the National Federation of Access Centres cannot be underestimated. To the inexperienced eye, it may be considered impressive that a severely disabled student can learn to operate a switch with the blink of an eyelid and as a result communicate through a computer. But it requires the sensitive involvement of specialist assessors to determine if this is all that is required to sustain or improve the quality of the student's education. It may be that the interface with a keyboard could be improved by using another part of the body to operate a switch, or that a speech synthesizer could improve communication, or even that the position of the equipment could be determined in a more ergonomically efficient fashion. 'The difference between non-assessment and assessment can be the difference between frustration and the benefits of an enabling technology that opens up new opportunities' (Vincent, 1993, p. 2).

Some of the more exciting possibilities of developing the use of computers relate to the development of electronic mail and tutorial links via telephone modems. Such facilities have been developed for the use of disabled students studying with the Open University and only recently have begun to be considered as possibilities for students working in FE. The possibilities of using the immense storage and interactive power of CD-ROM technology and the portability of computers suggests that it is only a matter of time before they can be used by students who wish to study part-time and yet remain in regular touch with a 'home base'. Electronic tutorials, arranged with a personal tutor working from a modem-linked computer terminal some distance away at a college or university, may offer further opportunities for the development of responsive learning.

Interesting examples of the use of computer technology in further education are cited in Hawkridge and Vincent (1992) and Vincent (1990). These studies indicate the value of developing expertise and experience in conjunction with research organizations such as the National Federation of Access Centres, in order to develop both wider networks and staff self-confidence. They indicate how, through the use of appropriate programs, colleges have facilitated the mastery of social and life skills for young adults with learning difficulties. This collaboration with regional and national resource centres for the development of both software and hardware (e.g. tracker balls and adapted keyboards) has enabled students to engage in activities which they consider to be not only appropriate for their age, but also on a par with activities they see being done by 'mainstream' students. The study by Hawkridge and Vincent (1992) reporting their research within the OECD programme 'Supporting active life for young people with disabilities' has pointed to some important reminders on the strengths and limitations of computers for staff and students alike:

(i) The new technology can give students with disabilities and special educational needs a wider choice of courses and enhanced educational and employment opportunities. This is broadly true for all aspects of disability and special educational needs, but the new technology cannot provide enablement, access or opportunities without proper assessment and re-assessment of individuals' needs, training for students and their teachers and carers, information, advice and technical services.

(ii) Because providing the technology, assessing and training students and others, and using the technology are complex activities, further education colleges need 'facilitators' with access to advice, experience and good practice. Students will then have opportunities that, in turn, can increase their independence.

(iii) The new technology can enable students to acquire skills that match current and future requirements in employment. Many employers are still unaware of this.

(iv) Staff training must be continued, particularly in how the technology can meet individual needs. Students' expertise and experience should be recognised because they have made significant contributions to staff development.

(Hawkridge and Vincent, 1992, pp. 219–20)

LINKS BETWEEN FURTHER AND HIGHER EDUCATION FOR STUDENTS WITH LEARNING DIFFICULTIES AND DISABILITIES: THE NEED TO MOVE ON

Statistical returns indicate that the number of students with disabilities in higher education in this country is increasing as a percentage of the total student population. Nevertheless, this growth has built from a low base. The survey conducted by Skill indicated that in the mid-1980s the number of disabled students in higher education was extremely low, at less than 2 per cent of the total student population (Stowell, 1987). There are still very few studies that have critically examined the reasons why the total number is so disproportionately low in relation to the numbers of disabled students with access to non-advanced further education. Even so, this situation is improving and the issue of widening access and further opportunity is both the subject of reports and an integral aspect of the Further and Higher Education Act 1992.

This issue of disproportionate representation in higher education circles has long been shared by disabled people with other marginalized groups in society. However, in comparison with other minorities, it is interesting to note the comparative invisibility of the rights of disabled people, even in publications that are intended to highlight the need for structural change in higher education. The low levels have been noted in a number of publications in the last five years. The Royal Society of Arts' *More Means Different* (Ball, 1990) mentions disabled people, somewhat in passing, while drawing the distinction between widening participation and increasing participation in higher education: 'widening participation in higher education will mean attracting and providing for both men and women, mature and young students, all the socio-economic groupings, the disabled as well as the able, every ethnic group' (p. 35). There is also a mention of disabled people in relation to Access courses and some general platitudes concerning people with disabilities in paragraph 5.34 (p. 38):

institutions still make inadequate provision for potential students with disabilities. The development of technologies with more distance-learning could materially improve conditions for study for disabled students (as well as enhancing the work of all students). Alongside physical provision, there needs to be training for staff to enable them to work effectively with students with physical or sensory disabilities.

The report *Widening Participation in Higher Education* (PCFC, 1992) demonstrated further awareness of the entitlement of disabled people to participation in higher education. It also usefully summarized some of the barriers which operate as obstacles to widening participation:

(1) *Market and policy limitations*: the mission, shape and geographical location of the institution influenced both the extent to which it was proactive in widening participation and the type of groups it could target positively.
(2) *Physical environment*: the nature of the institution's site could restrict its ability to expand the number of students with physical disabilities.
(3) *Student support*: as a result of changes in the system of student support, many potential students from under-represented groups were said to be put off by the perceived costs of embarking upon higher education.
(4) *Funding*: providing for students from under-represented groups was seen to be expensive by many institutions. To enable an institution to provide appropriate programmes with sufficient support and the necessary academic infrastructure, additional resources were said to be required.

The relatively enlightened stance taken towards students with disabilities by the Polytechnics and Colleges Funding Council (PCFC) during its short life-span has been continued by the new funding body that succeeded it. The Higher Education Funding Council (HEFC) emerged from the amalgamation of the former Universities Funding Council (UFC) and the PCFC; its major role is the allocation of funds. Under the direction of Professor Graeme Davies it has continued to place widening access to higher education for disabled students as a key feature of its work. The Council has recognized that the provision of a service of some quality to disabled students does not come cheaply. During the academic year 1993–94 some £3 million was made available from the HEFC to colleges and universities for the purposes of widening participation in higher education for students with disabilities. This exercise, currently being repeated for a second and final year in 1994–95, has helped to focus the attention of Britain's burgeoning university sector.

The financing of individual students in higher education has long been acknowledged as proportionately more expensive than for the average student. The expenses incurred by disabled students can be considered under four headings:

- *everyday living costs as a student* financed by an LEA mandatory award that is means tested as it is for all other students;
- *tuition costs* paid by mandatory award in the same fashion as for all other students;
- *additional living costs* resulting from a disability, including personal care, travel, etc.;
- *additional tuition costs*, including costs of equipment, photocopying, examination supervision, field trips, etc.

In recognition of these additional costs and following effective consultation with a group of disability organizations, the government has introduced a series of financial changes in relation to disabled students. The long-standing one-off disabled student award was raised to a more realistic sum (£1,185 in 1994–95) and two additional allowances were introduced. First, an annual award to pay towards the costs of non-medical personal care such as note-takers or signers (£4,730 in 1994–95). There is also an award as a single payment to go towards the purchasing of specialist equipment such as a lap-top computer (£3,560 in 1994–95). These allowances recognize additional cost but have done little to widen access. There are still additional groups of students who are unable to benefit from the disabled student allowances. The most numerous of these are part-time students, some of whom may deliberately wish to study part-time as a result of their disability. As part-time students they are excluded from the mandatory award. The success of the Open University is testimony to the success of part-time study, particularly for disabled people. It shows there is a demand for wider participation, yet the extension of financial support to part-time students has been denied.

If more students with disabilities are to be attracted to further and higher education, it has to be acknowledged that some (but not all) disabilities will prolong the time required to attain certain goals. As a society we have long been prepared to accept the educational evaluation of children and students differentially, especially where pupils and students with disabilities are concerned. For example different regulations in examinations may need to allow different modes of assessment due to the nature of a particular handicap, or interrupted study as a result of medical treatment or hospitalization. However, these considerations should not set up red-tape or spurious administrative reasons for reducing the curriculum entitlement available to a person with a disability who wishes to study for a degree in a higher education setting.

I have already suggested that we cannot be surprised if disabled children take on the sick role in young adulthood. It is no surprise to find high-ability disabled youngsters emerging from the special education system at 18 or 19 seeing themselves as somehow even more 'different'. As a number of researchers have pointed out (Oliver, 1987; Hurst, 1992), these students can be even more demanding of higher education institutions because they have 'broken the mould' of dependent victim. Teachers on the whole have subscribed to this view and higher education was not seriously considered as a valid option, until comparatively recently.

What should now be determined is whether the expectations of students with disabilities are simply to remain within the boundaries of non-advanced further education. It is fairly apparent that the somewhat elitist division between further and higher education is already beginning to disappear of its own accord and it is clear that students are not perceiving the distinctions between the two. The new elitism, if it exists, is between the old and the newly established universities. For students with disabilities the perpetuation of barriers is both patronizing and discriminatory. It continues to focus on the limitations of the individual rather than the restrictions imposed by a badly designed campus, or the limited conceptions of tutors and staff in the world of higher education. If higher education is to be offered as an attractive and acceptable alternative in the post-school sector, more attention needs to be paid to the provision of equipment that is effective and more recognition given to the autonomous voice of people who are seeking to break the chain of dependency through access to higher education.

In the same way, students in schools must not be discouraged, on the grounds of disability alone, from considering the move to further education, including sixth-form colleges and higher education. Higher education institutions themselves have a duty to become more proactive if these ideals are to be achieved. Expectations have to be raised and the opportunities for access increased. Higher education institutions must be prepared to accept and assist students with disabilities on equal terms to their able-bodied counterparts. This may involve making arrangements for extra assistance and support that enables rather than disables. Policy-makers must look at their services to seek to identify ways in which they are perpetuating images of disability, whether because of poor physical access, negative attitudes among staff or an inappropriate or inaccessible curriculum. Some would urge that even this is not going far enough and advocate instead discrimination in favour of disabled applicants.

To promote awareness of what higher education has to offer people with disabilities, active marketing strategies putting the case for higher education as an acceptable ambition must also be developed. There is a duty, too, to mature students with disabilities. For many reasons, a number of people have missed out or failed to achieve within the conventional educational system. Some may never have been in it! The mature student is, of course, not a new creation. However, the declining numbers of 18- to 25-year-olds in the population has meant that the active courting of mature students for courses in higher education is a new growth area. Many potential mature students are from disadvantaged groups; or rather groups for whom the expectation of higher education was never encouraged. People with disabilities form a large segment of this population.

The other major source of mature students is from those who are 're-starters': people who are changing the course of their lives, from either choice or necessity. Disablement in adulthood is often a necessary reason for new or re-education. For such potential students the chance to gain credit for prior learning offers exciting possibilities. In this third area, the higher education institutions are not necessarily alone, but they have been lagging behind. Many mature students go into further education and training, their special needs arising from a combination of altered personal circumstances and damaged egos. They may suffer from a lack of self-confidence in their ability to learn, so may set their sights no higher than a leisure course in a college of further education, even though they may have the intellectual capacity to profit from a course of study to diploma or degree level.

This raises the requirement for the development of positive links between institutions that in the past have remained too separate and isolated. In a time of competitive recruiting, this may be an over-ambitious ideal. Up to now the development of school/college links has been encouraged and promoted in this direction. Now higher education must join in too.

WHAT IS THE FUTURE OF FURTHER EDUCATION FOR STUDENTS WITH LEARNING DIFFICULTIES AND/OR DISABILITIES?

It is important to stress that the further education student with learning difficulties and/or disabilities is not simply a disabled schoolchild who has grown up. The successful development of further education relies to a great extent upon its remaining distinct from the type of education that has been experienced in school. Many of the general features of both sectors remain the same but further education is about further opportunity and entitlement to choice, not simply more of the same. At present colleges of further education are redefining themselves in relation to a range of new student groups, including those with learning difficulties and disabilities. They have been forced to examine their principles and values through the development of mission statements and strategic planning and by so doing they have had to take account of the parameters within which they work. These are in part defined by funding and legislation, in part by curriculum theory and delivery and in part by 'consumer' pressure, however voiced. (For an interesting discussion of these 'value conflicts' see Wolfensberger, 1994.)

The drive towards a more inclusive form of further education is still being shaped by the rhetoric and values of two distinct camps at either end of the integration continuum. But the future of inclusion is about more than rhetoric; it involves the reordering of resource provision, as much as breaking old models of practice. It is about moving away from the individualistic notions of disability and about enabling the further education *system* to reconsider issues of access. The future is about opportunities for all students to take control of their educational entitlement, and this does not deny the possibility of separation on grounds that are relevant. Indeed, if taken forward effectively, the new GNVQ qualifications, and foundation GNVQs framed within the context of competences, may actually reinforce the exercise of students' control over their own learning. The concept of competence can, in effect, help to remove the historical conventions of time limits on learning and places the responsibility for both pace and extent of learning back in the control of the student learner him- or herself.

It is exciting to consider the possibilities for further education. Ideally it should provide the opportunity for working towards qualifications that combine a sense of purpose and progression towards employment. At the same time they should attempt to retain the sense of a 'customer' perspective for the student. The latter consideration is even more important for students with learning difficulties and disabilities. The future for further education will need to alter and move this emphasis: away from *disability*, towards *ability* and the commonality of goals between all learners.

References

Adams, J. and Whittaker, C. (1994) The meaning of special education: a cross-cultural perspective. *Bridges* **1** (1), 23.

Ainley, P. (1988) *From School to YTS: Education and Training in England and Wales 1944–1987*. Milton Keynes: Open University Press.

Ainley, P. (1990a) *Training Turns to Enterprise: Vocational Education in the Market Place*. London: Hillcole Group.

Ainley, P. (1990b) *Vocational Education and Training*. London: Cassell.

Ainscow, M. (1994) *Creating the Conditions for School Improvement*. London: Fulton.

Ainscow, M. and Tweddle, D. (1979) *Preventing Classroom Failure*. Chichester: Wiley.

Ainscow, M. and Tweddle, D. (1988) *Encouraging Classroom Success*. London: Fulton.

Ainsworth, S. (1959) *An Exploratory Study of Educational, Social, and Emotional Factors in the Education of Mentally Retarded Children in Georgia Public Schools*. Athens, GA: University of Georgia.

Anderson, E. and Clarke, L. (1982) *Disability in Adolescence*. London: Methuen.

Aspis, S. (1991) My special school experience. *Educare* **40**, 15–17.

Baginsky, M. and Bradley, J. (1992) *The Transition to FE: LEA Support for Students with Special Needs*. Windsor: NFER.

Ball, C. (1990) *More Means Different: Widening Access to Higher Education*. London: Royal Society of Arts.

Barton, L. and Tomlinson, S. (1984) *Special Education and Social Interests*. London: Croom Helm.

Bayles, T. (1966) *Pragmatism in Education*. New York: Harper & Row.

Benedict, R. (1934) *Patterns of Culture*. Boston: Houghton Mifflin.

Berrington, E. and Johnstone, D. (1994) *The People Factor Interim Report 2: Health Care Concerns of Disabled People in West Lancashire*. Ormskirk: Edge Hill College.

Bleakley, C. (1993) Piloting inclusive education in a college of further education through drama. *Educare* **46**, 20–2.

Booth, T. (1983) Integration and participation in comprehensive schools. *FORUM* **25** (2), 40–6.

Booth, T. (1992) *Making Connections*. Milton Keynes: Open University Press.

Bradley, J. (1989) Multiprofessional support for young adults with special needs. *The Vocational Aspect of Education* **40** (107), 97–100.

Bradley, J., Chesson, R. and Silverleaf, J. (1983) *Inside Staff Development*. Windsor: NFER.

Bradley, J. and Hegarty, S. (1981) *Students with Special Needs in FE*. London: FEU.

Brechin, A. and Walmsley, J. (1989) *Making Connections*. London: Hodder & Stoughton.

Brimblecombe, F. and Russell, P. (1988) *Honeylands: Developing a Support Service for Families with Handicapped Children*. London: National Children's Bureau.

Brindley, A. (1977) 'The physically handicapped school leaver and further education'. Unpublished MEd thesis, University of Birmingham.

Brisenden, A. (1986) Independent living and the medical model of disability. *Disability, Handicap and Society* **1** (2), 173–8.

Brown, C. (1990) *My Left Foot*. London: Mandarin.

Brown, S. (1991) The influence on policy and practice of research on assessment. *Cambridge Journal of Education* **21** (2), 231–43.

Browne, G. (1978) What type of further education? *Special Education Forward Trends* **5** (4), 8–9.

Browne, G. (1981) The factory is our blackboard. *Youth in Society* (February), 18–20.

Bruner, J. (1975) Poverty and childhood. *Oxford Review of Education* **1** (1), 31–50.

Bryans, T. (1993) 'The 1981 Education Act: a critical review of assessment principles and practice'. In Wolfendale, S. (ed.) *Assessing Special Educational Needs*. London: Cassell.

Burton, P. (1993) In NATFHE, op. cit.

Bynoe, I., Oliver, M. and Barnes, D. (1991) *Equal Rights for Disabled People*. London: IPPR.

Callaghan, J. (1976) What the Prime Minister said. *Times Educational Supplement* (22 October), 6.

Campbell, B. (1993) *Goliath*. London: Methuen.

CBI (1989) *Towards a Skills Revolution: A Youth Charter*. London: Confederation for British Industry.

Cheseldine, S. and Jefree, D. (1982) Mentally handicapped adolescents: a survey of abilities. *Special Education Forward Trends* **9**, 19–23.

Child, D. (1987) *Psychology and the Teacher*. London: Holt, Rinehart and Winston.

Christensen, C. and Dorn, S. (1994) 'Competing notions of social justice and contradictions in special education reforms. Unpublished paper. University of Queensland, Graduate School of Education.

Christensen, C., Gerber, M. and Everhart, R. (1986) Toward a sociological perspective on learning disabilities. *Educational Theory* **36**, 317–31.

Cicirelli, V., Kitsuse, A. and Grainger, H. (1969) *The Impact of Headstart: An Evaluation of the Effects of Headstart on Children's Cognitive and Affective Development*, Vols 1 and 2. Springfield, VA: Office of Economic Opportunity, US Department of Commerce.

Clair, M. (1990) *Developing Self-advocacy Skills*. London: FEU.

Cooper, D. (1993) Further education: starting afresh. *British Journal of Special Education* **20** (2), 55–7.

Cooper, D. (1994a) Multi-agency collaboration and further education for students with learning difficulties and disabilities: the legislative background in England. *Educare* **48**, 3–7.

Cooper, D. (1994b) *Further and Higher Education Acts 1992*. London: Skill.

Corbett, J. (1991) Moving on: training for community living. *Educare* **39**, 16–18.

Corbett, J. (1992a) *Further and Higher*. Milton Keynes: Open University Press.

Corbett, J. (1992b) *No Longer Enough*. London: Skill.

Corbett, J. (1993) 'Entitlement and ownership: assessment in further and higher education and training'. In Wolfendale, S. (ed.) *Assessing Special Educational Needs*. London: Cassell.

Corbett, J. and Barton, L. (1992) *A Struggle for Choice: Students with Special Needs in Transition to Adulthood*. London: Routledge.

Corbett, J. and Myers, L. (1993) Support for learning in further education. *Support for Learning* **8** (4), 151–6.

Corlett, S. and Dumbleton, P. (1992) The implications of the Further and Higher Education Act 1992 for students with disabilities and learning difficulties in England, Wales and Scotland. *Educare* **43**, 5–8.

Cruickshank, W., Bentzen, F., Ratzeburg, F. and Tannhauser, M. (1961) *A Teaching Method for Brain-injured and Hyperactive Children*. Syracuse: Syracuse University Press.

Daunt, P. (1991) *Meeting Disability: A European Response*. London: Cassell.

Daunt, P. (1993) Changes abroad – a European overview. *Educare* **45**, 3–7.

Davis, G. (1983) *Educational Psychology, Theory and Practice*. Reading, MA: Addison-Wesley.

Dee, L. (1993) 'What happens after school?' In Visser, J. and Upton, G. (eds) *Special Education in Britain after Warnock*. London: David Fulton.

Dee, L. and Corbett, J. (1994) Individual rights in further education: lost, stolen or strayed? *British Educational Research Journal* **20** (3), 319–26.

Department of Employment (1991) *Employment and Training of People with Disabilities: A Consultative Document*. London: Department of Employment.

DES (Department of Education and Science) (1977) 'Further education colleges and the young handicapped adult'. Unpublished HMI Report No. 83. London: Froebel Institute (July).

DES (1987) *A Special Professionalism*. London: HMSO.

DES (1991a) *Education and Training for the 21st Century*. London: HMSO.

DES (1991b) *Transition from School to Further Education for Students with Learning Difficulties*. HMI Ref 24/91/NS. London: HMSO.

DES/FEU/NFER (1985) *From Coping to Confidence*. London: DES.

DfE (Department for Education) (1992a) *Managing Further Education 1990–91: A Review from HMI*. London: HMSO.

DfE (1992b) *Choice and Diversity: A New Framework for Schools*. London: HMSO.

DfE (1993a) *The Charter for Further Education*. London: DfE.

DfE (1993b) Statistics of further education college students in England 1970/71–1990/91. *Statistical Bulletin* 14/93.

DfE (1994a) *Code of Practice: On the Identification and Assessment of Special Educational Needs*. London: HMSO.

DfE (1994b) *Enrolments on Further Education Courses at Colleges in the Further and Higher Education Sectors 1993/94*. Circular 196/94. London: DfE.

Disability Now (1994) Directors oppose Civil Rights Bill. (May), 1–2.

Dunn, L. (1968) Special education for the mildly retarded – is much of it justifiable? *Exceptional Children* **35**, 5–22.

Dyson, A. (1991) Rethinking roles, rethinking concepts: special needs teachers in mainstream schools. *Support for Learning* **6** (2), 51–60.

Dyson, A., Millward, A. and Skidmore, D. (1994) Beyond the whole school approach: an emerging model of special needs practice and provision in mainstream secondary schools. *British Educational Research Journal* **20** (3), 301–17.

Edinburgh Review (1865) Idiot asylums. **122**, 37–72.

Enable (1994) *Consultation on Government Measures to Tackle Discrimination against Disabled People*. Bristol: Enable.

Faraday, S. and Harris, R. (1989) *Learning Support*. London: FEU/DES/Skill.

FEFC (Further Education Funding Council) (1992a) Circular 92/01. London: FEFC.

FEFC (1992b) *Funding Learning*. Coventry: FEFC.

FEFC (1992c) *Letter of Guidance*. Circular 92/08. London: DfE.

FEFC (1992d) *Students with Learning Difficulties and Disabilities*. Circular 92/14. Coventry: FEFC.

FEFC (1993a) Circular 93/01. Coventry: FEFC.

FEFC (1993b) *Students with Learning Difficulties and Disabilities*. Circular 93/05. Coventry: FEFC.

FEFC (1993c) Circular 93/32. Coventry: FEFC.

FEFC (1993d) Circular 93/34. Coventry: FEFC.

FEFC (1994a) *Students with Learning Difficulties and Disabilities*. Circular 94/03. Coventry: FEFC.

FEFC (1994b) *How to Apply For Recurrent Funding Formula 1995–1996* (issued 23 December 1994). Coventry: FEFC.

FEU (Further Education Unit) (1978) *A Basis for Choice*. London: FEU.

FEU (1980) *Developing Social and Life Skills*. London: FEU.

FEU (1981) *Experience, Reflection, Learning*. London: FEU.

FEU (1986) *Strategy and Processes*. London: FEU.

FEU (1989) *Towards a Framework of Curriculum Entitlement*. London: FEU.

FEU (1990) *Planning FE: Equal Opportunities for People with Disabilities or Special Educational Needs*. London: FEU.

FEU (1992) *Supporting Learning: Promoting Equity and Participation*, Part 1. London: FEU.

FEU (1993) *Supporting Learning*, Part 2. London: FEU.

Finn, D. (1987) *Training without Jobs: New Deals and Broken Promises*. London: Macmillan.

Fish, J. (Chair) (1985) *Educational Opportunities for All?* London: ILEA.

Fish, J. (1988) *Descriptions, Definitions and Directions*. London: FEU.

Fish, J. (1990) 'Collaboration and cooperation: the road to adulthood'. The First Walter Lessing Memorial Lecture. *Educare* **37**, 3–6.

Fulcher, G. (1989) *Disabling Policies? A Comparative Approach to Education Policy and Disability*. Lewes: Falmer Press.

Gleeson, D. (ed.) (1990) *Training and Its Alternatives*. Milton Keynes: Open University Press.

Glendinning, C. (1983) *Unshared Care*. London: Routledge & Kegan Paul.

Griffiths, I. (1994) Diagnosis and assessment of children with special educational needs. *Bridges* **1**, 20–1.

Griffiths, M. (1990) 'Enabled to work'. In *Working Together*. London: FEU.

Halsey, A., Heath, A. and Ridge, J. (1980) *Origins and Destinations: Family, Class and Education in Modern Britain*. Oxford: Oxford University Press.

Hargreaves, D. (1994a) *The Mosaic of Learning*. London: Demos.

Hargreaves, D. (1994b) Ten new rules for schools, *The Guardian* (17 June), 24.

Harris, K. (1994) *Teachers: Constructing the Future*. London: Falmer Press.

Harris, R. (1992) *Report of EEC Study Visit to the Federal Republic of Germany: Innovation in the Field of Education of Young Disabled Persons*. Bolton: Institute of HE.

Harris, R. and Clift, J. (1988) Into the subculture of FE: some observations on the role of staff development in the evolution of special needs provision. *The Vocational Aspect of Education* **40** (107), 105–10.

Harrison, R. (1993) Speech to the Second National Conference 'Special Needs: Access to NVQs' (22–23 February), pp. 31–5. London: Department of Employment.

Hatton, S. (1994) Students with profound and multiple learning difficulties coming to a college of further education – not really possible is it, let's be honest? *Educare* **48**, 37.

Hawkridge, D. and Vincent, T. (1992) *Learning Difficulties and Computers: Access to the Curriculum*. London: Jessica Kingsley.

Hegarty, I. (1990) 'Can further education for students with disabilities be justified?' Unpublished MEd paper, Manchester University.

Hegarty, S. (1993) *Meeting Special Needs in Ordinary Schools*. London: Cassell.

Henstock, S. (1989) 'Training in systematic instruction'. Unpublished paper. Tameside Health Authority.

Hevey, D. (1992) *The Creatures Time Forgot*. Basingstoke: Macmillan.

Hirst, M. (1987) Careers of young people with disabilities between ages 15–21 years. *Disability, Handicap and Society* **3**, 3–26.

Hirst, M. and Baldwin, S. (1994) *Unequal Opportunities*. London: HMSO for SPRU.

Hirst, M., and Parker, G. (1993) 'Disabled young people'. In Oliver, M. (ed.) *Social Work: Disabled People and Disabling Environments*. London: Jessica Kingsley.

HMI (1977) 'Further education colleges and the young handicapped adult'. Unpublished paper for HMI Course N83. Froebel Institute, London, July 1977.

HMI (1989) *Students with Special Needs in Further Education*. Education Observed 9. London: DES.

HMI (1991) *Transition from School to Further Education for Students with Learning Difficulties*. 24/91/NS. London: HMSO.

Horobin, G. and May, D. (eds) (1988) *Living with Handicap: Transitions in the Lives of People with Mental Handicaps*. London: Jessica Kingsley.

Hurst, A. (1992) Widening participation in higher education and people with disabilities. *Personnel Review* **21** (6), 19–36.

Hutchinson, D. (1992a) 'Students with special needs'. In Bees, M. and Swords, M. (eds) *National Vocational Qualifications and Further Education*. London: Kogan Page/NCVQ.

Hutchinson, D. (ed.) (1992b) *Supporting Transition to Adulthood*. London: FEU.

Hutchinson, D. and Tennyson, C. (1986) *Transition to Adulthood*. London: FEU.

Huxley, M. (1993a) Changes at home. The Walter Lessing Memorial Lecture Part 2. *Educare* **46**, 3–8.

Huxley, M. (1993b) 'Ensuring quality'. In Hewitson, C. (ed.) *Meeting the Needs of Students with Learning Difficulties and Disabilities in Specialist Colleges*. London: Skill.

Huxley, M. (1994) 'Quality of provision in England'. In Hewitson, C. (ed.) *Further and Higher Education Act 1992: Funding Quality in Further Education*. London: Skill.

Jerrold, M. and Fox, R. (1979) The ESN school leaver. *Education and Training* **13**, 192–8.

Jessup, G. (1991) *Outcomes: NVQs and the Emerging Model of Education and Training*. Lewes: Falmer Press.

Jessup, G. (1993) *Special Needs: Access to National Vocational Qualifications*. London: Department of Employment.

Johnson, G. (1950) A study of the social position of mentally handicapped children in the regular grades. *American Journal of Mental Deficiency* **55**, 60–89.

Johnson, G. (1962) Special education for the mentally handicapped – a paradox? *Exceptional Children* **29**, 62–9.

Johnstone, D. (1986) Post-school life-styles of adults with severe learning difficulties: is there life after 16? *Educare* **25**, 18–23.

Johnstone, D. (1987) Home thoughts: two views of transition in the 1980s. *Educare* **29**, 43–6.

Johnstone, D. (1992) 'Developing employment opportunities for young people with severe learning difficulties'. Paper to EASE symposium, 2–5 July, Waldkirch, Germany.

Johnstone, D. (1994a) 'The assessment of students with learning difficulties in the United Kingdom: dilemmas in purpose and understanding'. Paper to EASE symposium, 20–24 April, Lisbon.

Johnstone, D. (1994b) 'Der Volksfacter'. Paper to International Congress of Special Education, People with Disabilities: Living and Learning, 11–12 November 1994, Aachen.

Johnstone, D. and O'Hanlon, C. (1988) *Critical Reflections on Special Education*. Ormskirk: Edge Hill College.

Kedney, R. and Parkes, D. (eds) (1988) 'From ERA to new epoch: summary and conclusions'. In *Planning the FE Curriculum*. London: FEU.

Keller, F. (1968) *Learning Reinforcement Theory*. New York: Random House.

Kent, A. (1986) Residential further education for students with special needs: the other option. *Educare* **26**, 3–6.

Keogh, B. and Becker, L. (1973) Detection of learning problems: questions, cautions and guidelines. *Exceptional Children* **40**, 5–11.

Kirschenbaum, H. and Henderson, V. (eds) (1990) *The Carl Rogers Reader*. London: Constable.

Lancashire LEA (1991) 'Assessment of students with learning difficulties and disabilities'. In *Implementing Learning Support*. Working party report. Preston: Lancashire LEA.

Lane, D. (1980) *The Work Needs of Mentally Handicapped Adults*. London: Disability Alliance.

Leithwood, K., Jantzi, D. and Dart, B. (1991) 'Toward a multi-level conception of policy implementation processes based on commitment strategies'. Paper to 4th International Congress on School Effectiveness, Cardiff.

Lillystone, C. and Summerson, L. (1987) *Compendium of Post 16 Education and Training in Residential Establishments for Handicapped Young People*. Trowbridge, Wilts.

Lillystone, C. and Summerson, L. (1994) *COPE Directory*. Trowbridge: Wiltshire Careers Service.

McGinty, J. (1993) 'The contribution of the national specialist colleges'. In

Hewitson, C. (ed.) *Meeting the Needs of Students with Learning Difficulties and Disabilities in Specialist Colleges*. London: Skill.

Maddison, E. (1993) Speech at NATFHE conference 20 April. Published as *Learning Difficulties and Disabilities*. London: NATFHE.

Maslow, A. H. (1970) *Motivation and Personality*. 2nd edn. New York: Harper & Row.

Ministry of Education, Central Advisory Council for Education (1959) *15–18* (The Crowther Report). London: HMSO.

Ministry of Labour and National Service (1945) *Recruitment and Training of Juveniles for Industry* (The Ince Report). London: HMSO.

Mittler, P. and McConachie, H. (1983) *Parents, Professionals and Mentally Handicapped People*. London: Croom Helm.

Morrissey, P. (1991) *A Primer for Corporate America on Civil Rights for the Disabled*. Horsham, PA: LRP Publicatons.

Muir, P. (1993) *Special Needs: Access to National Vocational Qualifications*. Annual conference proceedings (Ref: STN2). London: Department of Employment.

NATFHE (1993) *Survey and Conference Report: Learning Difficulties and Disabilities*. London: NATFHE.

The Nation (1994) Brown at 40. *The Nation* **258** (20) (23 May) 688.

National Development Group for the Mentally Handicapped (1977) *The Handicapped School-leaver*. Pamphlet No. 5. London: DHSS.

Neill, A. (1960) *Summerhill*. Harmondsworth: Penguin.

Neill, A. (1967) *Talking of Summerhill*. London: Gollancz.

Nirje, B. (1980) 'The normalisation principle'. In Flynn, R. and Nitsch, K. (eds) *Normalisation, Social Integration and Community Services*. Baltimore, MD: University Park Press.

Nolan, C. (1987) *Under the Eye of the Clock*. London: Pan.

OECD (Organisation for Economic Co-operation and Development) (1992) *High Quality Education and Training for All*. Paris: OECD.

OECD/CERI (1988) *Disabled Youth – the Right to Adult Status*. Paris: OECD/CERI.

OECD/CERI (1985) *Handicapped Youth at Work*. Paris: OECD/CERI.

OECD/CERI (1986) *Young People with Handicaps: the Road to Adulthood*. Paris: OECD/CERI.

OFSTED (1992) *Unfinished Business: Full-time Educational Courses for 16–19 Year Olds*. London: Audit Commission.

O'Hanlon, C. (1988) 'The perceptions of teachers in special education'. In Johnstone, D. and O'Hanlon, C. (eds) *Critical Reflections on Special Education*. Ormskirk: Edge Hill College.

O'Hanlon, C. (1992) An overview of influences and changes for post-16 students with special educational needs. *Support for Learning* **7** (2), 67–73.

O'Hanlon, C. (1993) *Special Education Integration in Europe*. London: David Fulton.

Oliver, M. (1986) Social policy and disability: some theoretical issues. *Disability, Handicap and Society* **1** (1).

Oliver, M. (1987) From strength to strength. *Community Care* **19** (February).

Oliver, M. (1990) *The Politics of Disablement*. London: Macmillan.

Oliver, M. (1992) Education for citizenship: issues for further education. *Educare* **42**, 3–7.

Oxspec (1994) *Planning for Students with Learning Difficulties and Disabilities in Colleges of FE* **12** (June). Oxfordshire County Council and Oxford Brookes University.

Panckhurst, J. and McAllister, A. (1980) *An Approach to the Education of the Physically Handicapped*. Windsor: NFER.

PCFC (Polytechnics and Colleges Funding Council) (1992) *Widening Participation in Higher Education*. Bristol: PCFC.

Rea, S. and Corbett, J. (1992) The changing role of the special needs co-ordinator: shared partnership. *Educare* **42**, 25–27.

Richardson, A. and Ritchie, J. (1989) *Letting Go: Dilemmas for Parents Whose Son or Daughter Has a Mental Handicap*. Milton Keynes: Open University Press.

Richler, D. (1991) 'Inclusive education as social policy'. In Porter, G. and Richler, D. (eds) *Changing Canadian Schools: Perspectives on Disability and Inclusion*. North York: Toronto Roeher Institute.

Roberts, K. (1984) *School Leavers and Their Prospects*. Milton Keynes: Open University Press.

Rogers, C. (1965) *Client Centred Therapy: Its Current Practice, Implications and Theory*. London: Constable.

Rogers, C. (1990) *The Carl Rogers Reader*. London: Constable.

Rosenqvist, J. (1993) 'The concept of integration in schools and society in connection with adult quality of life'. Paper to EASE symposium, 4–6 March, Waldkirch, Germany.

Rowan, B. (1990) Commitment and control: alternative strategies for the organisational design of schools. *Review of Research on Education* **19**, 353–92.

Russell, P. (1991) 'Children with physical disabilities and their families'. In Oliver, M. (ed.) *Social Work: Disabled People and Disabling Environments*. London: Jessica Kingsley.

Shilling, C. (1989) *Schooling for Work in Capitalist Britain*. Lewes: Falmer Press.

Shipman, M. (1985) *The Management of Learning in the Classroom*. London: Hodder & Stoughton.

Short, A. (1992) 'Self-advocacy work with adults with learning difficulties: the parents' and carers' perspective'. Unpublished MA thesis, University of Lancaster/Edge Hill College.

Simnett, M. (1991) Voices from the pupil's corner. *Educare* **40**, 18–20.

Skilbeck, M. (1990) *Curriculum Reform: An Overview of Trends*. Paris: OECD/CERI.

Skill (1995) *Disability Discrimination Bill at Commons Report Stage: Comments from Skill*. London: Skill.

Skinner, B. (1968) *Beyond Freedom and Dignity*. London: Cape.

Slavin, R. (1991) *Educational Psychology: Theory into Practice*. New York: Prentice-Hall.

Smith, M. and O'Day, J. (1990) 'Systemic school reform'. Unpublished paper. New York: Stanford University.

Smithers, A. (1993) 'All our futures: Britain's education revolution'. *Dispatches*, Channel 4 Report.

Smithers, A. (1994) Smithers still not convinced. *The Lecturer* (June/July), 2.

Soder, M. (1980) 'School integration of the mentally retarded – analysis of concepts, research and research needs'. In *Research and Development concerning the Integration of Handicapped Pupils into the Ordinary School System*. Stockholm: Skoloverstyrelsen.

Soder, M. (1984) 'The mentally retarded: ideologies of care and surplus population'. In Barton, L. and Tomlinson, S., *Special Education and Social Interests*. London: Croom Helm.

Stoney, M. and Lines, E. (1987) *YTS: The Impact on FE*. Windsor: NFER.

Stowell, R. (1987) *Catching Up?* London: National Bureau for Students with Disabilities/Skill.

Stowell, R. (1988) The student population in further education. *The Vocational Aspect of Education* 40 (107), 101–4.

Stowell, R. and Cooper, D. (1986) *European Students with Disabilities*, Vols 1 and 2. London: Skill.

Stubbs, W. (1992) 'Implementing the FHE Act for students with learning difficulties and disabilities'. Paper to John Baillie memorial conference, 4 December. London: Skill.

Sutcliffe, J. (1992) *Integration of Adults with Learning Difficulties: Contexts and Debates*. Leicester: NIACE.

Tomlinson, R. (1982) *Education for Adult Life?* Milton Keynes: Open University Press.

Tomlinson, S. (1985) The expansion of special education. *Oxford Review of Education* 2, 157–65.

Tomlinson, S. (1994) 'The political economy of special educational needs'. Paper to conference: Learning Support: The Challenge of Change for Schools and Colleges. University of East London (17 March).

Tuckey, L., Parfit, J. and Tuckey, R. (1973) *Handicapped School Leavers*. Windsor: NFER.

Tyne, A. (1993) The great integration debate (part 3). *Mental Handicap* 21 (4), 150–2.

United Nations (1983) *World Programme of Action Concerning Disabled People*. Res: 37/52. New York: United Nations.

Vianello, R. and Monige, S. (eds) (1993a) *Job Possibilities and Quality of Life for Disabled and Handicapped People in Europe.* EASE No. 3. Karlsruhe: European Association of Special Education.

Vianello, R. and Monige, S. (1993b) *Vocational Education and Training: A European Overview.* Workshop Proceedings. Waldkirch: EASE.

Vincent, T. (ed.) (1990) *New Technology, Disability and Special Educational Needs: Some Case Studies in Further Education.* Coventry: Empathy Ltd/Hereward College of Further Education.

Vincent, T. (1993) 'Foreword'. In Broadbent, S. and Curran, S., *The Assessment, Disability and Technology Handbook.* Oldham: North West Access Centre.

Wade, B. and Moore, M. (1993) *Experiencing Special Education: What Young People with Special Needs Can Tell Us.* Milton Keynes: Open University Press.

Walton, W., Emmanuelson, I. and Rosenqvist, J. (1990) Normalisation and integration of handicapped students into the regular education system: contrasts between Sweden and the United States of America. *European Journal of Special Needs Education* 5 (2), 111–26.

Warnock, M. (Chair) (1978) *Special Educational Needs: Report of the Committee of Enquiry into the Education of Handicapped Children and Young People* (The Warnock Report). London: HMSO.

Warnock, M. (1991) Equality fifteen years on. *Oxford Review of Education* 17 (2), 143–54.

Warnock, M. (1993) 'Foreword'. In Visser, J. and Upton, G. (eds) *Special Education in Britain after Warnock.* London: David Fulton.

Weinstock, A. (1993) 'Preface'. In *Special Needs: Access to National Vocational Qualifications.* London: Employment Department.

Wertheimer, C. (1986) *Living for the Present: Older Parents with a Mentally Handicapped Person Living at Home.* London: CMH.

Whelan, E. and Speake, B. (1977) *Adult Training Centres in England and Wales.* Manchester: University of Manchester Press.

Whittaker, J. (1988) The special needs co-ordinator in further education – the key to effective provision. *The Vocational Aspect of Education* 40 (107), 123–8.

Whittaker, J. (1991) Inclusive education for a more creative and effective further education sector. *Educare* 39, 24–7.

Whittaker, J. (1993) Colleges have the disabilities. *Times Educational Supplement* (8 October), 20.

Williams, F. and Schoultz, B. (1982) *We Can Speak for Ourselves.* London: Souvenir Press.

Wolfensberger, W. (1972) *Normalisation.* Downview, Ontario: National Institute on Mental Retardation.

Wolfensberger, W. (1994) The growing threat to the lives of handicapped people in the context of modernistic values. *Disability and Society* 9 (3), 395–413.

Wolff, H. (1986) The disabled student in 2001 – deserted or liberated by new technology? *Educare* **24**, 3–9.

Name Index

Adams, J. 95
Ainley, P. 12, 13, 14, 15, 51
Ainscow, M. 77, 88
Ainsworth, S. 107
Anderson, E. 131
Aspis, S. 36, 37

Baginsky, M. 33, 35, 39, 40, 42–3
Baldwin, S. 33, 34
Ball, C. 175
Barnes, D. 7
Barton, L. 6, 9, 51, 52, 96
Bayles, T. 78
Becker, L. 96
Benedict, R. 155
Berrington, E. 34
Bleakley, C. 111
Booth, T. 6, 144
Bradley, J. xviii, 8, 33, 35, 39, 40, 42, 43, 116, 118, 124
Brechin, A. 134
Brimblecombe, F. 133
Brindley, A. 14
Brisenden, A. 3, 4
Brown, S. 101
Browne, G. 11, 14

Bruner, J. 96
Bryans, T. 95, 97
Burton, P. 147
Bynoe, I. 7

Callaghan, J. 14
Campbell, B. 48
CBI 146
Chesson, R. 118
Child, D. 90
Christensen, C. xiv, 42
Cicirelli, V. 96
Clair, M. 134, 136, 138
Clarke, L. 131
Clift, J. 39, 40
Cooper, D. 17, 38, 127, 128, 129, 155, 157, 165, 166
Corbett, J. x, 6, 9, 19, 41, 43, 51, 52, 83, 101, 102, 104, 145, 150
Corlett, S. 102
Crowther Report xiii
Cruickshank, W. 96

Daunt, P. 153, 159

Subject Index